DELIBERATE DISCOMFORT

HOW **U.S. SPECIAL OPERATIONS FORCES**
OVERCOME FEAR AND **DARE TO WIN**
BY **GETTING COMFORTABLE**
BEING UNCOMFORTABLE

JASON B. A. VAN CAMP
WITH ANDY SYMONDS

Contributing Authors:

The Mission Six Zero Team:

Matt Chaney, *US Army Special Forces*

Nate Boyer, *US Army Special Forces*

Leróy Petry, *US Army Ranger*

Florent Groberg, *US Army Infantry*

Brian Petit, *US Army Special Forces*

Dan Quinn, *US Army Special Forces*

Joey Jones, *US Marine Corps*

Rusty Whitt, *US Army Special Forces*

Joseph Serna, *US Army Special Forces*

Jeff Adams, *US Army Special Forces*

Steve Mueller, *US Army Special Forces,*
   US Army Ranger, US Navy SEAL

With Scientists

Andy Riise, *Contributing Editor*

Casey Van Camp

Sarah Spradlin

Shelley Smith

Michael Gerson

Sean Swallen

Nate Last

Tyler Christiansen

Jason Mitchler

Petra Kowalski

Rebecca Cañate

John Roman

Jay Long

Ballast Books, LLC
Washington, DC
www.ballastbooks.com

ISBN 978-1-7334280-1-9

Library of Congress Control Number has been applied for

Printed in Canada

Published by Ballast Books
www.ballastbooks.com

For more information, bulk orders, appearances or speaking requests,
please email info@ballastbooks.com

Dedicated to Tony Sparano

A great friend and supporter of Mission Six Zero.
We miss you, pal.

TABLE OF CONTENTS

NOTE FROM THE AUTHOR

This book is about getting comfortable being uncomfortable.
When you make the courageous decision to deliberately choose dis-comfort, you prove to yourself that you are no longer satisfied with the way things are and you won't tolerate it any longer. You're ready for change, for growth. You are ready to accept and embrace suffering because you want a better life for yourself, your family, and/or your business.

What's stopping you? Fear. Fear kills more dreams than failure ever will.

What are you afraid of, then? You've heard of fear of the unknown, but that's not entirely accurate. Fear *is* the unknown. You're only afraid of what you don't know. What you don't see or understand. Once you truly know something, you're no longer afraid of it. It's not the obstacle you fear; it's the unknown result of attempting to overcome that obstacle. You must have the courage to willingly choose to confront that unknown, whatever it may be, head on.

Speaking in public, playing in the big game, and starting a business are all challenges with unknown results. You don't fear the activities themselves. It's the ambiguity of what happens next that keeps you up at night.

Your unknown could be taking a sales position at a start-up company. You aren't afraid of *taking* the job or even *doing* the job. You're afraid of the unknown that comes with leaving the stability of a safe company with a regular salary and 401(k) for the uncertainty of a start-up. The comfortable thing to do would be to stay where you are and cash the paycheck. But with the proper tools, you can learn to embrace the discomfort and succeed in the unknown.

You must deliberately choose to place yourself in the uncomfortable position of facing your fears. *Deliberate Discomfort* is how strong people are made. Unfortunately, that is not what society is teaching right now. Society is cultivating indignation and victimhood. We are encouraged to place ourselves in an environment where we will not be exposed to criticism, opposing opinions, or emotional harm.

It's detrimental to progress. That's not how we learn and grow. We learn by voluntarily choosing to face our fears, not by avoiding them. Our willingness to confront fear is more powerful than fear itself. You don't grow by hiding or avoiding. You grow by being bold, confronting, and overcoming.

By implementing this *Deliberate Discomfort* mind-set, you will find that your life will change in a profoundly positive way. Instead of questioning why bad things seem to happen to you, you will look at them as blessings. Instead of moaning about the pain you are enduring, you'll recognize and appreciate it as a strength builder. You'll appreciate these events as opportunities to grow, improve, and become the best you can be. You'll laugh at how hysterically uncomfortable an experience was rather than complaining and feeling sorry for yourself. Those embarrassing moments? Your regrets? You will look at them as nothing more than learning experiences. You can't truly win until you learn how to lose.

This book will serve as your roadmap to getting what you want in life by deliberately, carefully, and methodically choosing to be uncomfortable.

Your humble servant,

Jason B. A. Van Camp
Major (Ret.), US Army Special Forces

INTRODUCTION

During my military career, I served with some incredibly powerful and inspirational leaders. After my service, I asked them to join me in creating a company, which we call Mission Six Zero. Here is the genesis of that name:

Mission: A clearly defined statement that aligns individuals and/or teams with a sense of purpose, direction, and motivation toward common goals. We believe in Mission First, People Always. While the mission always comes first, investing in people is at the core of accomplishing the team's mission.

Six: The term "Got your 6" references the face of a clock, where the number 12 is to your front and the number 6 is at the rear. In combat, the rear-facing direction is often the most vulnerable, and saying you have someone's six means you have their back no matter what. This term has come to define the vital trust, loyalty, respect, and commitment that all teammates expect of one another on a mission. Six is also the numerical call sign or designator for the unit leader or commander.

Zero: True north on a magnetic compass. Zero represents a baseline, or a means of measuring progress during a mission. In the whole person concept, zero symbolizes balance and striving for equilibrium in all facets of life.

M60: In short, it's the weapon that Green Beret John Rambo is famous for.

Mission Six Zero was built by high performers determined to empower our clients to live life to its fullest. We identify, assess, and develop human behaviors to help our corporate and professional sports clients achieve optimal performance results. This book is a blueprint for how we do that.

We'll outline our company's curriculum, the Total Warrior Model, in the pages within. Our model focuses on consistent, sustainable improvement in six areas: *mental, physical, spiritual, social, emotional,* and *professional.* This model was derived from the training that made us Green Berets, Navy SEALs, Army Rangers, etc. It focuses on the "Whole Person" concept and is used to transform door kickers into warrior diplomats capable of high-stakes negotiating, rapport building, and unconventional warfare in the most stressful environments imaginable.

Lessons we learned on the battlefield have major relevance in the business world. Let me be clear: signing a new client is not life or death. A mistake in the boardroom does not have foreign-policy implications. But that doesn't mean those life-or-death experiences can't teach us how to be better salespeople or insurance agents or leaders. Better parents, spouses, friends, coaches, or members of society.

The good news is, the people of Mission Six Zero—those who have "been there, done that"—are going to show you how. We're going to take those critical scenarios we've been through and explain how to apply what we learned on the battlefield to the business world. We're going to use science and psychology to relate our challenges to yours so you can make better decisions in your business and personal life.

As a Green Beret, I pride myself on being a "quiet professional." However, we cannot be *silent* professionals. We need to stand up and speak out and share the truth with those who are searching for it. That's what this book does. It does so by capturing actual stories from the members of elite military units (all of whom are members of the Mission Six Zero family) and applying those experiences in a teaching platform. Our team will expose their hearts, get uncomfortable, become vulnerable, and answer the question, What was it really like?

Prepare yourself. These stories are real. They capture the authenticity of war. At times, the book is dark and cold. Other times humorous and inappropriate. Above everything else, it all happened. **If at any point you find yourself uncomfortable reading this book, then we have accomplished our objective.** That is the greater mission of writing this book—we want to inspire you to think and explore conversations.

We will show you how to get comfortable with the uncomfortable—to embrace the suck—and how to turn those pain points into a competitive advantage. For those with no military background, that's OK—at its core, this is a business book. However, we do have a brief explanation of how US Special Operations Forces work in the back of the book, as well as terms and acronyms explained throughout.

Mission Six Zero is our business, and this book contains our training curriculum. There is no political agenda, and this isn't a review of foreign policy. The book isn't intended to coddle anyone nor to hurt feelings. It is to simply share our experiences with those who see value in the lessons learned under intense stress, when life-or-death decisions are part of your daily routine. This is also a work of nonfiction, meaning everything in this book actually happened (more or less). It is very important for us to be authentic. However, due to the sensitivity of our operations, **certain names, units, locations, and timelines are adjusted or omitted to protect national security and personal privacy.** Conversations in the book all took place, albeit to the best of our recollection. Lastly, the chronology of the book does not always accurately reflect what happened in reality. It was difficult to meet these concerns and still call our book a work of nonfiction, but I believe we achieved that.

Each chapter will focus on a different component of the Total Warrior Model. We encourage you to take Bruce Lee's advice: "Absorb what is useful. Discard what is not. Add what is uniquely your own." In each chapter, you will learn how to get comfortable with the uncomfortable through the first-person perspective of a different elite military operator. Following each chapter, one of our highly decorated cadre of scientists/experts/researchers/PhDs will explain how to incorporate the lessons learned to your personal and professional lives. Following that, we provide examples of how our clients implemented those lessons with their teams and businesses. Ultimately, we are teaching you *how* to think, not *what* to think. This *Deliberate Discomfort* mind-set will help you make better choices. Success or failure depends on making the right decision in the right moment.

As evolved creatures, we crave certainty and predictability. The world makes more sense to us when we're comfortable. The problem with that is simple: the world doesn't always make sense. The only way we can really make sense of the world is to embrace the chaos and get used to accepting dissonance. If you can get used to this discomfort, you will excel.

My hope is that you find value in this material not because it took place on a battlefield, but because it took place inside each of us. The Green Beret motto is De Oppresso Liber, a Latin phrase that roughly translates "To Liberate the Oppressed." The men and women of Mission Six Zero believe that this book can empower everyone struggling personally or professionally to liberate themselves from their internal oppression.

DOL
—Jason Van Camp

NOTE FROM THE PUBLISHER

Over the past year, I've had the pleasure of working closely on this book with the author. Jason Van Camp is one of those powerhouses whom we encounter every so often and are so much better for the experience. Jason has "it."

His book is aptly titled *Deliberate Discomfort*, and it takes the stories of twelve highly decorated combat veterans and applies the lessons they learned as Army Rangers, Green Berets, Marines, and Navy SEALs to everyday life. If they could slow their heart rate, see through the fog of war, keep their emotions in check, and make life-saving decisions on the battlefield, they can certainly help us excel in our quarterly review or improve our marriage.

The biggest thrill for me was getting to work with the quality men and women who make up Mission Six Zero and provided the content for the book. Jason isn't the only one who has "it." *Deliberate Discomfort* has contributions from everyone from two Medal of Honor recipients to Super Bowl–winning NFL players. All touting the same theme: They never took the easy path, the comfortable way. They made tough choices and excelled by embracing discomfort. And they can teach you how to do it. They taught me.

Somewhere along the way, Jason's message did more than just resonate with me. It started to seep into me. It became a part of how I operated. I found myself applying these lessons in my business and personal life. What I learned gave me the courage to step out of my comfort zone and make some hard—but correct—decisions.

One phrase in the book that really jumped out at me was "Fear kills more dreams than failure ever will." The statement isn't new, and I certainly had heard iterations of it before. But within the context of this book, as explained by the caliber of people who share their stories in

Deliberate Discomfort, the statement shook me to my core. Was I missing out on opportunities because I was scared?

I could continue doing what I was doing. I was happy, making a good living. I was comfortable. But I knew I could do more, even though doing more scared the shit out of me. But after working so closely on this book, I realized I had developed the tools to overcome that fear and make the best decision for me and my family. So that's what I did.

I chose to leave my stable job in publishing and start my own publishing company. I chose to get uncomfortable because I knew the effort and sacrifice would be worth it. Ballast Books is the result of that bold decision.

And I learned how to do it from this book.

"Who dares, wins."

—Andy Symonds,

President and publisher, Ballast Books, author of *My Father's Son* and *Enemy in the Wire*

1 The Commander

with **Jason Van Camp**

Jason is a retired US Army Special Forces (Green Beret) officer. He earned the Bronze Star with "V" device for Valor as well as two additional Bronze Stars during three combat rotations in the Middle East and Africa. He attended the United States Military Academy at West Point and earned his MBA from Brigham Young University.

I was uncomfortable.

There was no denying it. Unnerved, stressed, under pressure, whatever you wanted to call it. That was, of course, by design.

I was at the crossroads of "how the hell did I get here?" and "what will happen next?" One of those pivotal moments in life when you take a step back and realize that you have no idea how you got where you are. What I did know was that this meeting would be the start of a journey that would define my life for years to come. Mine and those of the men I would someday lead into battle.

I thought back to where this path began: my graduation from West Point six years earlier, followed by an officer's commission into the United States Army. It had taken me through Ranger School and countless other leadership, marksmanship, and physical training courses, culminating with three years at the Special Forces Qualification Course at Fort Bragg, North Carolina. I had passed that final test just two weeks earlier, officially becoming a Green Beret and the new commander of an A-Team full of experienced, capable Special Forces operators who would be looking to me to lead them. A daunting task, to be sure.

How did it all go so fast? I had never stopped to appreciate the journey. And now here I was, in Fort Carson, Colorado, waiting to meet my new boss, the company commander, Major Brian Petit, a legend in the Special Forces community.

I was fifteen minutes early. I had to make a good first impression. My uniform looked good. Well, better than usual. I considered myself a "muddy boots" soldier. I had heard the term when I was a young cadet at West Point and decided it applied to me for no other reason than I simply hated shining my boots.

Clutched with white knuckles was my professional binder, an "I love me" book full of embellished bullet points in the muted and straightforward way of the military, blade running the line between truth and fantasy. In our world, where a poorly written evaluation report could mean the difference between getting promoted and getting blacklisted, it was a necessary evil.

I sat with my "I love me" book and waited.

Around me, a flurry of activity went on undisturbed by the anxious officer perched on one butt cheek in the midst of soldiers preparing for war. The B-team[1] guys were hauling in Pelican and Contico boxes, pallets and equipment of who knows what, alternating between complaining loudly and masterfully talking trash to each other. I thought for sure the banter would end in a fight, but it never did. They didn't seem to notice me or even care that I was there. For that I was glad. I was uncomfortable enough as it was.

"Captain Van Camp?"

I jumped up and came face to face with Major Brian Petit. At first glance he seemed normal enough, but after looking closer, I recognized a certain quality, a presence about him that seemed profound and uncomplicated. I wasn't surprised; I had heard the stories. I saluted crisply, looked him in the eye, and stated loudly, "Yes, sir!"

A few of the NCOs (non-commissioned officers) looked at me, smirking, and shook their heads disapprovingly.

I noticed.

---

1 A Special Forces B-Team, otherwise known as operational detachment bravo, acts as the headquarters element of a Special Forces company.

"Better get used to it," the major commented as he ushered me into his office.

"Get used to what, sir?"

"Being uncomfortable," he said matter-of-factly.

I said nothing.

"Come in. Have a seat."

We stepped into a modest office with a drop ceiling and glaring fluorescent lights. It was much smaller than I would have thought. I began to scan the room for diplomas, plaques, pictures—anything I could use to build rapport. Nothing but the back of a computer screen and a stack of papers on his desk. I got the feeling that he didn't care much for fluff, that he was a minimalist who focused on the bottom line.

"Good to finally meet you in person," he said, taking my resume and offering me a seat. "I'm Major Brian Petit. Welcome to the team."

"Thank you, sir. I'm ecstatic to be here."

Instead of sitting behind his desk like I'd expected, Major Petit grabbed a chair and pulled it next to me. He straightened his back and looked me in the eye.

"Let me start by telling you, Captain, that anybody who steps through that door and is a qualified Green Beret, I value. I want you to know that you are valuable, and I value you. You've gone to hell and back to get here, and you deserve a measure of respect for what it took to do that. I understand that I'm not dealing with an amateur. I am dealing with a professional. I don't know you yet, but I know where you've been."

I was a little taken aback by the introduction. I certainly hadn't expected to be welcomed so enthusiastically to the company, especially as a new guy. My guard remained up, but I felt cautiously optimistic.

He continued. "The first lesson that I need you to understand is that the difference between a good Green Beret and a great Green Beret is their ability to listen. When you talk, you are only repeating what you already know. But if you listen, you may learn something new.

"The first thing I want to do is listen to you. Tell me about yourself. You see, this is going to be a long-term relationship. I want to understand you, I want to know who you are. What makes you tick?"

Damn. There was that pang of uneasiness again. I hated talking about myself. It always felt so awkward and braggadocious. But he asked, so I began to talk. I started telling him about my hometown, about playing football at West Point, about my family. I felt incredibly long-winded. As the verbal diarrhea spewed from my mouth, I noticed that Major Petit was meticulously reviewing my file.

I looked down in self-defeat. "I'm sorry, sir. I tend to be very thorough to the point of boredom."

He examined me. "Jason, you told me about what you have done, but who are you?"

"I'm not sure I follow, sir."

"Let me put it to you this way—when you have nothing to think about, what do you think about?" he asked.

The major could tell I was still having a hard time answering his question. "OK. I'll try to explain my intent through a story," he said. "There was a young man who wanted to be a physicist. His father was a physicist, and he figured that he would follow in his footsteps. As the young man was studying for an important exam, he kept going back to his father to ask him questions.

"One day, the father finally said, 'Son, we've been over this several times. You just aren't picking this up. You're incredibly intelligent, and this should make sense to you by now. Haven't you been working on it?'

"The words cut the way only a respected parent's can. The boy shook his head in shame. Then his father asked, 'When you walk down the street, when you're in the shower, when you don't have to be thinking about anything else, is physics what you're thinking about?'

"The son said no.

"The father paused and said, 'Then you shouldn't be studying physics. You ought to find something you love so much that when you don't have to think about anything, that's what you think about' (Lund, 1995).

"When I first heard that story," Major Petit finished, "it hit me hard. Who am I?" The major's voice grew louder and deeper. "I dug deep and realized that I'm passionate about serving my country. I knew that was my calling and who I was."

Now I understood what he was asking me. I couldn't contain my excitement, exclaiming, "Sir, I think that must be one of the most profound questions anyone has ever asked me." I paused to ensure my answer was heartfelt. "What do I think about? I think about my family. I worry about them. I think about my hometown sports teams. I think about my former soldiers, wondering about their quality of life. Our time together in combat and training. That's a deep question, and I appreciate that."

Major Petit smiled. "The key is knowing who you are. First and foremost, the foundation to success is knowing and understanding yourself. It's self-awareness. Jason, who you are right now is a Special Forces captain. You are coming into an organization that has a history of Special Operators doing epic things. Make no mistake, we need you. We need you on that A-team.

"You see, senior NCOs want a strong officer. They are better when they have a good, solid captain. On their best day, your A-Team might be a 10-2 ball club, but if you are a good captain, you will make them 12-0. Officer leadership is *commanding* the team, not *leading* the team. A-Teams work best with strong captains who command their teams."

Something he said had struck me. "Sir, what did you mean by, 'Officers don't lead the team, they command the team'?" I asked.

The major adjusted his seat before answering. "Jason, what I mean is that wherever you go, no one should have to ask, Who is in charge here? Your presence, your attitude, your body language, should leave no question as to who is in charge. If you ever have to remind your soldiers that you are in charge, you aren't. Being a commander means stepping up and out front, taking accountability, and providing a clear vision of where you want to go. It's not about forcing others to do what you want because of your rank. Make no mistake—in order to be a commander, you must first be a leader. As a leader, you must love those you lead before you can be effective. Once you have earned the trust of your soldiers and you know they would follow you anywhere, then you need to channel that energy and commitment and push your foot down on the accelerator. Once you are operating at that level, you are truly commanding.

"You set the culture and the vision. You are the enforcer of standards. If you let the standard slip, you'll find that that becomes the new standard. I know you are going to be brand new to the team. You might feel like the FNG (Fucking New Guy). You may feel uncomfortable, but if you begin to let things go that are illegal, unethical, or immoral, guess what? You bought them. You are the owner. Having courage on the battlefield is one thing. Having moral courage to stand up to your team is another, oftentimes harder, challenge. Right off the bat, I need you to establish credibility and trust with your team. If you see something wrong, I don't care how uncomfortable you might feel, I need you to have the courage to say something. Tell your team what you value. 'Hey, this might have been acceptable with the last team leader, but it's not going to work for me because of these reasons.' This is what is important to me."

I nodded my head in approval and did my best to process what he was saying. It was clear he was passionate about this, and the information would be important to me as I took command of my A-Team.

The major saw his message had resonated, and he was ready to move on to his next point. "You graduated from West Point. What did West Point teach you about leading and commanding men?"

I smirked and laughed low, not knowing whether an honest (or smart-ass) answer was appropriate. "Well, sir, where do I even begin..."

Major Petit was not in the mood for humor and clarified himself. "OK, let me put it another way: What advice would you give to a recently graduated cadet commissioned as a second lieutenant about leadership?"

Immediately, I responded, "Three things come to mind: First, officers eat last. I've noticed that in order for you to get anything accomplished, your soldiers need to know that you care about them. Once they know that, they'll do anything for you. The thing is, you can't fake it. You either care for your guys or you don't. One of the easiest ways to display that is to make sure that your soldiers all eat before you feed yourself. It shows them that you place their needs above your own."

"Second?" the major asked.

"Second, and probably most importantly, is that anything your team does or fails to do is your responsibility. I'm talking about accountability. Placing blame or pointing fingers is the quickest way to lose the trust of your men. Sometimes that's a tough pill to swallow. I had to take responsibility for one of my soldiers who lost ammunition on an overnight bivouac. Unfortunately, I was injured and in the hospital when the ammunition was unaccounted for. Although I was not there, I was accountable for his actions. I should have created better systems and processes to prevent the loss of the ammunition."

The major quickly asked, "What's your third leadership lesson?"

"I suppose, trust your NCOs. When I graduated from West Point, I asked every officer I could find the same question: What advice do you have for this second lieutenant who is going to lead troops for the first time? To a man, like a knee-jerk reaction and without hesitation, they all responded, trust your NCOs."

The major dipped his head and calmly asked, "How has that worked out for you?"

I thought for a moment. "Not as well as I'd hoped."

He nodded knowingly. "Jason, there are good NCOs and bad NCOs in the army, just like there are good officers and bad officers. Unfortunately, you are going to find the same is true in the Special Forces. There are good NCOs and bad NCOs. My advice is this: don't trust your NCOs."

I was shocked.

"Sir, I think I am going to need some clarification on that. You recommend that I do *not* trust my NCOs?"

"That's correct. Trust but verify. Trust that your NCOs are going to do the right thing, but verify that they are. Trust is earned and given with *belief.*"

I thought about that.

"Jason, why would you blindly follow someone just because they have three chevrons and a couple of rockers on their rank insignia?

That's ludicrous. Don't trust someone just because they have a 'Sergeant' in front of their name. Your NCOs need to earn your trust, just as you need to earn theirs. At some point, you are going to trust Mike Daniels because you know him as a person, he has proven himself to you, and has earned that trust. And vice versa. Only after you trust him as a person can you begin to truly trust Mike as Sergeant Daniels. But in order to begin the process of trust, you need to take a risk. You need to believe in that person; you need to believe that you *can* trust them. Does that make sense?"

I was starting to feel confident. I liked where this conversation was going. I felt comfortable enough to ask my own question. "Sir, what is most important to you as a commander?"

He leaned back before responding, but it was clear he had an answer. "Most captains come into my office and try to impress me. They talk about their resumes, deployments, and awards. The ones that actually *do* impress me are the ones who realize that I have to prove myself to them just as much as they have to prove themselves to me. I appreciate it when a captain asks me questions.

"What is most important to me as a commander is communication. This is not 'I give you an order, and you go away to do it.' Everything here is a dialogue. We talk through problems and solutions together. We ideate together. Do you understand?"

"I think so, sir."

"Jason, your job is to provide me the information that I need to make the best decisions. Decision-making requires trust, communication, and clarity. And communication goes both ways."

"I follow you, sir."

"We are going to be operating in the gray, in uncomfortable, nebulous spaces. The only way we can be effective is if we trust one another. We need to earn one another's trust if we hope to succeed.

"There needs to be a constant feedback loop. If you know when to push the mic, give me updates, report things, give me situational awareness, and if you can give that communication to me with clarity, then that is going to be the difference between winning and losing. Clarity of communication allows me to know what you are contending with. Therefore, I can enable you, resource you, and advocate for you. I need you to enable me to see through your eyes so I can pull levers for you that will make you successful. I only know what you are telling me. I want to hear from you. Regularly. Jason, I need to hear from you, and I expect to hear from you."

"Lima Charlie (loud and clear), sir."

"Guess what? Between now and the next twelve months, you are going to make mistakes. I promise you that. Mistakes are OK if they are aggressive mistakes. In fact, sometimes mistakes show you are willing to take risks. It will impress me more if you are willing to stretch out. You can't run an organization that doesn't allow mistakes. I will be lenient with you, and I expect you to be lenient with your men. All mistakes are not equal, however. Your actions and intentions will not only be judged by your men, they will be judged by me. I need you to avoid mistakes like being unprepared, focusing on personal gain, or anything with malintent behind it. I will not tolerate sloppy mistakes—being negligent, lazy, or stupid. I *will* let mistakes lapse if you are focusing on three things—fighting, surviving, and winning in this environment."

The major's passion hit me hard. I finally realized just how real this was. His guidance directly impacted not only my ability to stay alive, but my team's as well.

"One of the great things about combat is that it provides a clarifying vision of the seriousness of our profession. Under the compression of combat, unimportant things will fade to gray. If the actions that you take are technically and tactically competent, I will always have your back. I'll take the heat for everything else—don't worry about the minutiae.

"We don't want to be staring at one another on game day only to realize that we spent too much time focusing on unimportant things. We have a responsibility to prepare men for combat. We can only be liberated on game day knowing that we did everything we could to win the moment. After all, the Green Beret motto means 'to free the oppressed.'

"I want you to succeed, Jason. I will give you the opportunity, the resources, and the mentoring to succeed. If you don't succeed, it's our failure. If you don't succeed, there was a breakdown somewhere. Either you didn't get mentored, supported, informed, or empowered. If you succeed, it's because I helped you get there. If you fail, the failure is mine and yours together.

"Jason, we have a short window until we deploy to Iraq. For now, I am going to sit back and let you settle in, get your footing, and allow your value to show through. You might be thinking, 'Am I up for this? Do I have the skills?' I believe you do. I believe in you."

I was pumped. That was all I needed to hear. I knew that I performed at my absolute best when I had a leader, commander, or coach who believed in me. I knew I had that in Major Brian Petit. I was motivated and ready to get to work—to prove to the major he was right for believing in me. But he wasn't done. "I want you to show me that you understand the mind-set that is required to be a great Special Forces commander. Are you ready?"

"I am, sir."

"Good. There are a handful of people that I want you to talk to before I assign you a team. Jason, I need you to understand how serious I am. You are going to lead men in combat. The enemy is smart, and they are doing their best to kill you and your men. I need you to pay attention, listen, and ask intelligent questions of the people I want you to meet with. Do your best to understand how they think. Once you feel ready, I want you to report what you learned about their mind-set because I need you to adopt a similar one if you are going to succeed in our company. Remember what we talked about, and if you ever feel the need to speak with me, my door is always open."

I saluted Major Petit, he handed me back my "I Love Me" book, and I followed him out the door and down the hallway.

This was how my whole Special Forces experience began, and the things that were to come are too fantastic not to tell.

SOF to Science with **Andy Riise**, Chief Learning Officer

Andy is a US Army lieutenant colonel with over twenty years of experience leading soldiers into combat, including two assignments with US Special Forces units. Andy attended the United States Military Academy at West Point and earned his master of arts degree in sport and performance psychology.

Trust is the essential currency for all high-performing individuals and teams. Getting comfortable with the process of earning and giving trust is a skill that is developed through intentional practice over time.

The interaction between Major Petit and Captain Van Camp highlights the importance of trust in establishing and developing a high-performing team culture. During their first conversation, note that Petit told Jason, "I believe in you." In Petit's mind, Jason had met every certification and qualification to be in his current position according to both the army and the Special Forces regiment. However, Petit did not yet know Jason on a personal or professional level. In other words, there were no artifacts or evidence to suggest that Jason was worthy of Petit's trust. In the end, Petit made a conscious choice to both trust himself and the institution of which he was a product, and simultaneously believe in his new subordinate leader. This is a choice that we make every day when it comes to interacting with others. In that moment, Petit chose to grow trust in his company by believing in Jason. In doing so, he not only gave Jason the opportunity to earn his trust but to reciprocate with trust on his own team, the right way.

So What?

1. Trust begins with self

Trust begins by investing in oneself through an inner belief in your abilities. This is the cornerstone of self-confidence. There are two complementary mind-sets, or patterns of thinking, known as the **training** and **trusting** mind-sets, that allow individuals and teams to be at their best when the pressure is on and it matters the most (Rotella, 1995).

Training and trusting mind-sets

The **training** mind-set allows individuals to bring skill in. It is related to higher levels of effort, analysis, reflection, and judgment. It is the traditional means by which you get better at something. In Western cultures, especially the United States, we are really good at the training mind-set because we believe that through hard work, anything is possible. By itself, the training mind-set has limitations in the form of diminishing returns, especially when we don't see the immediate results of our efforts (Rotella, 1995).

The complementary **trusting** mind-set allows performers to let skill out through freedom, focus, and fun in the moment. The trusting mind-set is present in our most cherished memories, stories, and vivid experiences. But trusting alone without planning, preparation, and competency is also limited. Too much trust without ability can lead to complacency.

Optimal performances, or moments when you're great in the most extreme situations, require a blend of both the training and trusting mind-sets before, during, and after a performance. Facilitating playmaking, flow states, or individual zones of optimal function, also known as "the zone," requires the ability to harness both mind-sets at the right times and situations.

2. Trust sets you free to be at your best

On a cellular level within the brain, the trusting mind-set appears on a functional MRI with lower levels of neural activity. Training mind-sets are characterized by higher levels of neural activity. Through the trusting mind-set, a quieter brain allows for a looser body and quicker reactions, and thus it increases the likelihood for higher levels of confidence and better decision-making in the moment. Before you can truly trust others on your team, you must first learn to trust yourself (Csikszentmihalyi, 2008).

3. Leaders are the banks of trust

To use a metaphor that demonstrates trust beyond self, think of effective leaders as banks of trust. One of the leader's primary responsibilities is to lend and secure trust to their subordinates. Unlike a financial loan, lending trust is an interpersonal process and not transactional. Because trust is interpersonal in nature, there are both cognitive (thinking) and affective (emotion) components (Bandura, 1977). This means that humans are constantly determining, often subconsciously, whether someone is trustworthy using a combination of their hearts and their heads. There is no right or wrong answer because trust is often situational, and it's an ever-changing process that requires deliberate attention and energy to develop and sustain.

4. Humans are more important that hardware

The interpersonal nature of trust creates a tendency for human beings to invest or buy into other humans rather than institutions or systems. Pioneering research by Dr. Paul Zak determined that when human beings received or transmitted evidence of trust or trustworthiness, an otherwise insignificant neurotransmitter called oxytocin was released in the brain. Through hundreds of experiments replicated in various cultures around the world, he found that teams with higher levels of oxytocin—thereby trust—had increased job performance, productivity, and overall job satisfaction (Zak, 2018).

5. Trust is a contract with terms

Like a loan, trust becomes an unwritten contract between leaders and the led. These loans come with terms in the form of expectations and standards to include payments, penalties, and interest. As an agreement between people, trust is the means by which the loan is paid and repaid over time. These agreements must be effectively communicated and clearly understood by all parties involved. In the military, this is facilitated through the philosophy of mission command and the counseling process (Department of the Army, 2012).

6. Trust requires accountability, the right way

A common refrain for military leaders is "trust but verify." What this means is that leaders can best hold their subordinates accountable to these terms or expectations and standards by checking on them and their work periodically. This does not equate to micromanagement where leaders tell their subordinates what to do and how to do it. When, where, and how to verify is both an art and science.

7. When trust is broken

When leaders or subordinates default on their loans of trust, it can become very difficult to apply for new loans and gain trust back. In some instances, a breach of contract and violation of trust can be irreparable. For example, breaking the law, intentionally lying, cheating, or gaining an unfair advantage are examples of "red lines." It's important for both leaders and their subordinates to know what this sliding scale of trust looks like in terms of acceptable mistakes, causes for concern, and unacceptable behavior. Since human beings are flawed and make mistakes, leaders and followers must learn when and how to forgive and find the path toward rebuilding trust.

8. Trust is earned and given with belief

Contrary to conventional wisdom, successful leaders must be both trust givers and earners. If all things are equal, leaders must take the leap of faith by believing in an individual first. This is difficult for some people because it requires becoming vulnerable and taking a risk. Leaders who are willing and able to believe in a person are twice as likely to have their subordinates' faith and confidence. Leaders can get comfortable being uncomfortable by willingly believing in a person while knowing they may not get that same belief or trust reciprocated by their subordinates.

Now What?

1. Think of a time when you were performing at your very best. Imagine there was a video camera there filming that masterful moment and could capture you both on the inside and outside. Write down all the words that describe what that performance looked and felt like.

2. Was the moment described above more aligned with the training or trusting mind-set? Assign a percentage to both (while not exceeding 100 percent). How did you bring skills in before and after the event? How did you let your skills out in the moment(s) during the event?

3. Like Major Petit did for Jason, think of a relationship or team you were on that was good at cultivating trust among its leaders and teammates. Write down the common attitudes and behaviors that helped develop and grow trust.

4. Think of a time when your trust was eroded by someone you know or someone on your team. If that trust was eventually repaired between you, what did you or that person do to regain the trust that was lost? If that trust was never repaired again or was not quite the same again, what did you do or not do?

5. What can you do as both a leader and/or a subordinate to intentionally build trust with your teammates?

Practical Application with Jason Van Camp

Special Forces is a climate where adapting to unconventional circumstances is mandatory. Asking questions, seeking truth, and being creative are all encouraged. Leaders in this climate must have the highest level of trust in their people, and in turn those people must have the highest level of trust in their leaders.

The biggest difference between elite military units and businesses is shared culture. That culture is built on trust. No one in corporate America talks about trust.

Trust begins by effectively welcoming a valuable new employee to your team, clearly setting expectations, and establishing effective, open communication. Most importantly, letting this new employee know that they are valued and believed in. Trust is established through time, cultivated through patience, and strengthened by leveraging the following six foundational pillars:

Communication: Trust is achieved through honest and clear communication. A leader's ability to listen and communicate effectively has, arguably, the strongest effect on an employee's commitment and loyalty. Take the time to understand your employees' different communication styles and find the pulse of your team.

Relationship: A leader that builds an organization of trust ultimately creates a tribe. Your employees will connect with you and with one another. Your employees will put their faith in you because you will have shown them that you care beyond yourself. People who have close friends at work rarely voluntarily leave the organization.

Integrity: People notice your actions. They pay attention to your stories and conversations. People trust leaders with integrity and character.

Persistence: Trust is achieved through determination and persistence. Leaders are going to go through trials and errors while attempting to develop trust. They must maintain action regardless of negative feelings and doubt. Press forward. Overcome adversity.

Accountability: Actions speak louder than words. Leaders who hold themselves accountable for producing results earn the trust of their teams. Your employees will respond to results.

Consistency: A leader creates routines, manages expectations, and builds momentum. Consistency is the foundation for habit-forming behaviors and reputation. Predictability leads to trust. If you are consistent, you will keep the trust you've earned.

At Mission Six Zero, we work with both Fortune 500 companies and professional sports teams. Our very first client, the NFL's New York Jets, will always be special. At the time, the head coach of the New York Jets was Rex Ryan. Among other things, Rex was known as a bold, brash, and fearless coach. I came to recognize how much his players and coaches loved him. Rex was able to inspire such love and devotion from his men because he truly believed in them. But that belief needed the proper attention and cultivation to turn into trust.

When Rex hired us, we sat down in his office and talked about what he wanted to accomplish. "Jason," he said, "I thought that I had my finger on the pulse of the team, of the locker room. After last year's final game, I'm not sure I do anymore."

In the previous season, Santonio Holmes, a former Super Bowl MVP, had been named captain of the Jets by Ryan. But during the last game of the season, Holmes was banned from the huddle by the entire offensive line. Earlier in the game, he had made some comments about the offensive line not giving quarterback Mark Sanchez enough time to throw. Those comments led to an argument with right tackle Wayne Hunter. Hunter yelled at Holmes, "If you don't fucking want to play, get your ass the fuck out!"

The offensive line then banned Holmes from the huddle. On the field. In the middle of an NFL game.

Holmes didn't want to escalate the situation, so he sat on the bench, ending up with zero catches in the game. He had made similar comments in the past, which the offensive linemen described as "having a fracturing effect in the locker room" and "not something a captain does." Quarterback Greg McElroy said the locker room had a "corrupt mind-set" with "extremely selfish individuals." Teammate and Hall of Fame running back LaDainian Tomlinson said about the situation, "It's tough for guys to follow a captain that behaves in that manner. You've got to play your tail off until the last play" (Wine, 2012).

As the leader of the organization, Rex had to question the pulse of the team, the commitment from his players, and the trust he placed in them.

The issue we discussed with Rex was that he didn't know how to make the proper evolution from belief to trust. He trusted individuals when they did not merit his trust. He assumed that belief would translate into trust over time without further investment. He trusted without verifying. He trusted all his coaches and players to enforce and articulate his standards; however, some of his coaches and players weren't trained properly on how to effectively articulate and enforce those standards on their own. He mistakenly trusted some of his people who hadn't done anything to actually earn his trust.

The solution was accountability and follow-through. After you have established belief with an individual, you need to take the time to develop that belief through actionable trust-building opportunities. Build that belief into trust through quantifiable and measurable tasks. This goes both ways, for both the leader and the subordinate—identify an opportunity, follow through with it, and prove yourselves to each other.

During our time together, I admired Rex for his willingness to be vulnerable. Rex was willing to take the uncomfortable leap of faith by believing in every single one of his coaches and players. Rex told the truth. He established his trust through truth. No matter how uncomfortable or harsh the truth was, his coaches and players respected and even loved him for it. He was unapologetically himself, and that is the foundation of a quality leader.

In the business world, employees are looking for a supervisor to have their back and lead, but often supervisors don't prepare their people to do so. At best, new employees get a brief walk-through of their new responsibilities and are never truly groomed or prepared to lead unless they have prior leadership experience. This is a missed opportunity to empower someone to lead. This unfortunate approach often leads to a failure in culture and, ultimately, a failure in business.

Rex was a very confident coach, and he instilled that confidence in his players. He'd tell them they were the baddest men who ever walked the earth, and he wanted them to act as such. That was great, but he had players who hadn't earned anything buying into that bravado. Guys who just assumed they were leaders because Rex told them they were. But when you take a guy who's never really been a leader before and make him a captain, it sends the wrong message to the team. It tells them it's a political decision. And that's when you lose the team.

We helped Rex understand that he was setting Holmes up for failure by assuming that he would be a leader because he was a talented player.

When we concluded our last training event with the Jets, everyone was emotionally exhausted. We had exposed our hearts. We did everything we possibly could to ensure our training was not only memorable, but that it provided a real return on investment. It was our first event, and I was unsure how the Jets players and coaches had responded. When you are in charge, you notice all the mistakes and all the dropped balls. It was time for honest feedback.

It felt similar to watching game tape after each football game in college. You had a feeling about how well you played, but you never knew what your position coach was going to say after watching film. Sometimes you felt as if you dominated the game, but when you reviewed the tape, your coach would let you have it while pointing out all the mistakes you made. Other times, you would dread going to watch film because you felt you played poorly and then were surprised to receive positive feedback. I remember a coach saying, "You never played as bad as you thought you did, nor did you play as well as you thought you did."

At the Jets compound in Florham Park, Rex spotted me and began walking toward me. I knew this was the moment of truth. He would be blunt and let us know exactly what he thought of our training.

Rex told me, "Jason, we knew after your initial presentation that you would bring it, but you completely blew it out of the water." He said he wanted to bring us back every year for what he dubbed "Jets Basic Training." I remember thinking, "Rex believes in me." I felt appreciated and valued. I want to follow a leader who believes in the best version of me. I thought, "I would follow Rex into battle."

Many of our corporate clients come to us with the same question: How do I get buy-in from my employees? They want to know how to get their people to buy into the company with the same level of commitment and passion that they have.

Why does someone buy in? People don't buy into an idea or a vision. They buy into a person. When you are fighting side by side in real combat, you aren't thinking about the flag or the Constitution or freedom. You are thinking about the person to your left and to your right. You don't want to let them down. You don't go in to battle because you think the plan is solid and the motivating politics behind the operation fit your values. You follow your leader. You believe in him or her.

In order to *get* buy-in, you must *give* buy-in. If you want trust, loyalty, and commitment, you must put yourself in the uncomfortable position of trusting, displaying loyalty, and committing. This deliberately uncomfortable process of trust starts with believing.

Trust begins with believing, but the process takes follow-through. Don't make the same mistake that Rex did—don't assume. You need a plan to turn that belief into actual trust. Major Petit inspired belief and established a foundation of trust. He showed how to effectively welcome a new employee to a professional organization by clearly articulating how much he valued me and how much value he believed I could bring to the organization. When a leader who wants you on the team expresses belief in you, your loyalty and commitment to both the leader and the business is multiplied exponentially. When you know that someone believes in you, you don't ever want to disappoint that person. Your performance and motivation are optimized.

Major Petit focused attention on me and placed an emphasis on my ability to listen, going so far as to say that the difference between a good Green Beret and a great Green Beret hinges on that one defining characteristic. Not only did Major Petit say that, he actually *did* it. He asked me questions and then attentively listened to my answers. Major Petit wanted me to buy into his company. In order to inspire my buy-in, he did it first.

Finally, Major Petit followed up on that foundation by preparing me to lead with an actionable task. He asked me to speak to several officers and NCOs associated with his company. At the end of the day, I knew my commander, Brian Petit, wanted me to succeed. He immediately made me feel like I had a purpose and community.

Rex Ryan and Brian Petit both displayed exceptional leadership abilities by building an organization established in belief and value. The difference is that Brian Petit actively followed through with his belief by giving me an actionable task that would further my leadership development and build on the foundation of trust that was established.

Remember:

- Immediately let your people know they are both valuable *and* valued in your organization.
- Trust is earned *and* given with belief.
- Place an emphasis on the ability to **listen.**
- Be a commander. A commander is a leader who has scars, is experienced, and is trusted by his people.
- If you don't succeed, failure is shared.

2 The Team

with **Steve Mueller**

Steve is a retired US Army Special Forces (Green Beret) officer. He also served as an Army Ranger in the 75th Ranger Regiment and prior to that was a Navy SEAL. He attended the University of Illinois with a major in kinesiology.

I was behind my computer on the second floor of the team room when the doors opened and Major Petit walked in, a young and uncomfortable-looking officer in tow. I couldn't help but smile. So this was the new team leader, Van Camp. Fresh from Q Course and now about to take command of his own team. I hoped he had thick skin.

A minute earlier I had been bullshitting on the second floor with Pat, our team sergeant, while he did paperwork. He had been giving me a hard time because my Dallas Cowboys had just lost in the playoffs again, but I was used to the aggressive, familial backdrop of Special Operations. I'd been on a lot of Special Operations teams in my career, as well as growing up with older brothers who had teased me and made me self-conscious about everything I did. Those proddings are what ultimately allowed me to succeed in the military.

I looked the new captain over as Major Petit introduced him to my team. Uncomfortable, but who could blame him for that? He didn't look like much of a runner, but it was clear that he had spent time in the gym. Good. Everybody brings a unique skill set to the team. Where would we be if we had five hundred guys who could all run sub-five-minute miles but couldn't bench press more than ninety pounds? Diversity breeds success.

My gaze moved around the room, and I noticed the guys acting hard to impress the new captain. The first test. My team had done it to me when I was a new captain. Cocky bastards. I couldn't help but love them all.

Max and Jonah, our weapons sergeants (18 Bravos), were dipping mint-cut Copenhagen into plastic Mountain Dew bottles while watching Fox News. They paused from an intense debate about preworkout powders to give the new captain a glance, then went back to their argument. It appeared Max was losing his claim that No-Xplode was impossible to beat. Jonah, frankly, didn't give a shit. He just loved demonstrating his superior arguing abilities and mastery of the English language.

Our three comms guys (18 Echos), Nate, Pedro, and Jack, had been cramped underneath the stairs checking the radios and equipment in the dark when Captain Van Camp was ushered in. Nate was the senior Echo and actually seemed to be paying attention to the new captain.

Next to him, Pedro leaned coolly against his locker. Our resident cholo gangster, Pedro, was 5'6", solid as a rock, and lived for someone stepping up to him to fight. When he first got to the team, he would get pissed at everything. So we made sure he got acclimated to every derogatory Hispanic term we knew, which eventually blossomed into a relationship where we would relentlessly talk trash to him until he mumbled something unintelligible back in a beautiful mix of Spanglish and bad grammar. He once told me, "People only hear what they want to hear. If you mumble everything and people can't understand you, they assume you're saying something profound." At least I'm pretty sure that's what he said.

Jack was…interesting. A bit of an odd duck, he possessed an off-the-charts IQ and knew everything about communications. Ultimately, he wanted to travel the world—"walk the earth," he called it. Some of the things he intended to do transcended common sense, but we just accepted it and let him dream. When we first told him what we thought of his idea to walk the earth, he called us, and I quote, "A clueless mishmash of infantile philosophers and heathens that actually think you are providing something of significance." That's just too beautiful to be offended by.

The engineers (18 Charlies) were spread across the room. The senior engineer, Tyrell, sat stoically on the staircase. His dominant presence felt like the center of the room. He was a get-it-done type of guy from the backwoods of Georgia, known for his prowess with the ladies. Whenever the team went out, everyone went to him to hook them up with the friend of whichever girl he happened to be chatting up at the bar. He generally refused, but enjoyed the attention nonetheless. His stories after a long weekend were legendary.

Where the hell was Bob? Boston Bob, we called him, as much because of his thick Boston accent as because he hated the nickname. Boston Bob was fairly new to the team but had already proved himself absolutely hilarious, a welcome skill in a tight-knit Special Forces team. Just because his practical jokes didn't always play out the way he intended them to didn't mean he didn't continually subject us to them. But he was a solid operator, even if we couldn't understand him half the time. On our last deployment in Iraq, Bob was on the radio as we took indirect fire (mortars) from the enemy. His job was to coordinate return fire from our 81 mm mortars. He kept reporting, "They're shooting houses at us!" We had no idea what he was talking about until we returned to the team house.

I asked him, "Bob, what were you saying on the radio?"

"What do you mean?" Bob asked without the slightest clue of what I was talking about.

"You kept saying, 'They're shooting houses.'"

Without skipping a beat, Bob responded, "Yeah, that's right. They were."

I laughed and looked around. Everybody was standing behind me. "Bro, what the hell are you talking about?"

Bob scanned the room and stated loudly, "Captain. THEY. WERE. SHOOTING. HOUSES. AT. US. What don't you understand?"

We couldn't catch our breath, we were laughing so hard. The team sergeant finally spoke up. "I think he means howitzers."

The senior medic (18 Delta), Dave, sat at a table with a water bottle.

Dave was unquestionably the toughest guy on the team, and that's not just my opinion. Dave had been the combatives (mixed martial arts) instructor for the entire group before he asked to go back to the team. Full of fire and inspiration, he could get you excited about any mission. He had this calming voice…what do they call that for doctors, bedside manners? I'm pretty sure that's it. For us, battlefield manners. Dave had that and then some.

Then of course there was our previously mentioned team sergeant (18 Zulu), Pat. Pat was sort of a world-weary, been-there-done-that type of dude, exhausted with not only the world but everything in it. He rarely let the guys see his sharp sense of humor, but he had one, and despite his demons, Pat was as loyal as the day was long. God help any of his men who weren't.

His credo was "You'll go far in life if you walk around looking pissed off all the time." He lived that motto.

Major Petit slapped Captain Van Camp on the back and finished his introduction. "Jason, I suggest you have at it." He promptly left without looking back.

A moment of what I would call deafening silence followed. I wondered what the new captain's next move would be. We all did. Finally, he summoned his deep voice and bellowed, "How y'all doing?"

Nobody responded.

I laughed a little, knowing that the team was finding this introduction absolutely comical. Captain Van Camp recovered and walked over to Max and Jonah.

Max spoke first. "Hey, sir. Have you ever been in a hucklebuck?"

The new captain clearly had no idea what Max was talking about. He paused and smiled cautiously. "Maybe…" he answered with a sort of optimistic dread.

I had heard enough. Time to stop the pain. I walked down the stairs and held my hand out to the new captain. "Hey, it's great to have you in the company, Jason. I'm Captain Steve Mueller. I'll be working with you as one of your sister detachment commanders."

We shook hands, and Jason leaned in. "I'm glad you interrupted that conversation," he whispered. "I felt like we were about to launch into an ad hoc MMA fight right on the floor of the team room."

"That would be an accurate assessment," I said, taking inventory of the room. Everyone was already back at what they had been doing before Jason arrived except Jack, who walked over to the captain to shake his hand.

"Never mind Max," he said. "Just the delusional rantings of a testosterone-addicted thug."

I agreed and opened the door to the team room. "Jason, let me show you around a little bit. C'mon, let's take a walk."

He nodded and followed. A healthy mix of fear and pride in what he'd seen of my team flashed across his face. I smiled and led him through the company area. We went outside through the loading bay, which we used to stage our gear when heading out to train or deploy. Outside under the sky and sun felt far away from the pressure of the team room.

"I know this is exciting, but it can be a little overwhelming," I told him. "I've been in your shoes. Mind if I offer some candid advice?" We stopped at a bench on the edge of a blacktop basketball court and sat down.

"Oh, absolutely. I could use all the help I can get," Jason answered sincerely.

"Good. Because I'm here to help you. I exist for my team and will do everything in my power to help my team be successful. I ask you to use me as much as possible. I'm not one to beat my chest or talk a lot about what I've done, but I have been around and have a ton of experience and knowledge about the team, our mission sets, our relationships, and really, life itself."

"I appreciate that more than you know," Jason said, then looked down at my uniform to review my badges. I watched as he took in the expected Special Forces and Rangers tabs on my sleeve. His gaze turned to the front of my uniform and saw the typical Airborne and Combat Infantryman's Badge. He stopped at my Trident. I could tell he knew what it was, but his brain wasn't processing what he was seeing. I waited for him to ask.

"Wait. Steve, is that a Navy SEAL Trident on your uniform?"

"It is."

"Hold on a second. You were a Navy SEAL? And a Ranger, and now a Green Beret?"

"What can I say? I have a PhD in 'embracing the suck.'"

"How is that even possible? I find that incredibly hard to believe."

"Let me tell you, I'm approached all over and consistently vetted for stolen valor. It gets old real fast."

We both laughed. Jason told me I had to tell him the story. I declined. He asked again.

"I don't like talking about myself," I explained. "It makes me uncomfortable."

Jason laughed. I didn't get the joke. "The major just told me I better get used to it," he explained.

"To being uncomfortable?" I asked.

"Yeah."

"I suppose he has a point," I said. "Here's the deal—I believe in authentic humility. I don't want to come across the wrong way. I don't want to appear arrogant, especially meeting you for the first time."

"I appreciate your honesty," Jason said. "But I feel like this is an opportunity to really get to know each other. The major said the difference between a good Green Beret and a great Green Beret is his ability to listen. I am ready to listen, if you are ready to talk. After all, we'll be going into combat together. I'd like to know who the guys are to my left and right. Why would I fight for you if I don't even know you? I've found that you really get to know someone when they have the courage to be vulnerable, to open up, and expose their heart."

He had a point. "OK. I see you are determined to hear this…and are a smooth talker. I'll share some of my experiences, but first I want to listen to you."

"Sure thing," Jason replied. "What do you want to know?"

"I have three questions. First—and I'm asking this in all sincerity—is, Why are you here? Why did you choose to be a Special Forces officer?"

I could tell that I had caught him off guard. Uncomfortable, he shuffled back and forth, kicking gravel at his feet while trying to organize his thoughts. Looking up, he answered, "I guess my why changes as I progress in life."

"How so?"

"When I was young, I remember my uncles sitting around the table at Christmas telling stories. Some were talking about their experiences in the military, some about traveling the world, and others were just talking about chasing women or making money in business. But they all were laughing and having a great time telling these stories. As a young man, I wanted to join in, but I couldn't. I didn't have any stories to tell. Not yet. So I resolved then and there to have more stories than all of them one day. That mind-set started me on the path that I'm on now. That was my motivation.

"As I went through life and started to collect accolades, I realized life isn't about trophies, it's about people. It's about the journey that you take with those people.

"Eventually, I tried out for the Special Forces. I tried out only because one of my closest friends convinced me that we should try out together. Ultimately, I ended up making it, and he didn't. But I stayed on my Special Forces journey because of the people I met along the way. Because of the relationships and the value that I brought to other people. I enjoyed serving others. As I served, I began to forget about myself, my problems, my misery. In a way, I became *selfish* about being *selfless*.

"Ultimately, I want to be on a team that wins. I want to be on a team that cares about one another. I want to be a part of that. That's why I'm here, Steve."

I told Jason, "I appreciate that answer. I asked that question first because it is absolutely paramount for the team's sake that you have your priorities straight. I personally believe that the highest priority should be our team's mission."

Jason enthusiastically interrupted, saying, "The mission comes first."

"Exactly. Your conviction to adhere to and place the mission first during training, even when it's tough and unpopular, will help determine your team's destiny. You are the standard bearer. We need you to always maintain that mission-first mind-set," I said.

"This mind-set is in conflict with the way the world thinks. The world teaches us to look after number one. We are wired for self-preservation. To think it's all about 'me.' I need you to ask, What's in it for the people on my team? As foreign and uncomfortable as it is to accept that it's not about ourselves, that's how you can keep your priorities straight. It may be counterintuitive, but the more you focus on others, the more comfortable you will be. Because individuals will never accomplish what a team can accomplish. I realized this for the first time when I was going through Basic Underwater Demolition/SEAL school (BUD/S)."

"I knew you were going to crack and tell me some BUD/S stories," Jason said with a grin.

"Well, you seem genuinely interested, and besides, I'm on a roll. I was sitting in the surf during BUD/S. I was exhausted, freezing, and convinced that I was going to die of hypothermia. As the waves crashed on my back, I had my head down. I was lost in my own mind, trying to find my mental toughness, trying to survive just a little longer. It seemed like seconds were minutes and minutes were hours.

"Suddenly and unprompted, I stopped what I was doing and lifted my head. I don't know why I did it. I just did. I looked around. I saw my teammates going through the same pain and suffering that I was. I realized I wasn't alone. That realization gave me courage. I noticed that some of my teammates were struggling even more than I was. I felt terrible. I wanted to help them. That's the moment I learned empathy. I started to shift my focus from me to them. I shouted words of encouragement. I got others involved. We no longer were suffering as individuals; we were suffering as a team. The exercise finally ended, and when we returned to the barracks, I realized that in helping others, I had forgotten my pain."

Jason said, "That makes perfect sense. Thanks for that, Steve. Seriously, I'm glad that you are in the company."

Jason seemed like he got it, or at least was open minded enough to get it. I could honestly say that I was glad Jason was here. I continued.

"This brings me to the team. The second highest priority is the team. The team is subordinate to the mission itself. That means as a commander, you will have to make tough decisions that may place the mission above your men's lives. Prepare yourself now for those types of decisions. Your decisions will result in mission success or failure as well as the life or death of your teammates.

"Having this perspective, this mind-set, is not normal. No one wants to lose one of their men. Prioritizing the mission over the team is uncomfortable, but growth and improvement are uncomfortable things. Winning can be uncomfortable."

I looked Jason over. It seemed to be sinking in.

"Deep down, you're probably expecting that. Being uncomfortable in combat or training is one thing, but being uncomfortable in a social environment is something completely different. It's oftentimes more challenging and more uncomfortable than combat. At least it is for me."

"How so?" Jason asked.

"Inherently, you are going to want to be liked by everybody on the team. That's human nature, and that's OK. But as the commander, you are going to have to tell your guys no. A lot. When you tell your guys no, they are not going to be happy. Sometimes they won't be cool about being told no. It's going to be tough. It's going to be uncomfortable.

"Here's the thing: it's more important to be respected. If you are respected, if the team knows that you care more about them than your popularity, if you forget yourself and focus on making your teammates successful, then everything will work out. You will be promoted faster than your peers. You will be given opportunities to shine. You will get the best missions. You won't get there by yourself; your team will get you there. You can get anything you want in this life if you help other people get what they want. That's the greatest lesson that I've ever learned," I said.

We sat in silence and contemplation before I spoke again.

"Knowing who *you* are and why *you* are here, while also under-standing who *we* are as a company and why *we* are here, will be vital to our success," I summarized. "Collectively we will achieve according to who we are, not what we want."

Jason nodded. "Steve, I am absolutely on board. I agree with everything you just said. No one has ever put it in a way that made so much sense to me."

"Few organizations, teams, and individuals figure that out. Only the elite understand that it is not about any one specific individual. It's about the mission, then the team, then the teammate, and finally you—the individual. Many teams fail because the individuals are not willing to sacrifice their personal agendas for the mission's sake," I cautioned him.

"You could have been a preacher," Jason responded.

I stifled a smile and kept going. "Now for my second question: Where are we going? You're going to be a team leader. When we walk back through those doors, the guys on your team are going to want to know where they're going. Those are the guys busting their asses for you, trusting you with their lives. That's your why. That's why you exist. It's for them. If it's not for your men, people are going to see right through you. So, what's your vision?" I was getting so carried away I inadvertently poked him in the chest. He didn't mind, and he didn't hesitate with his answer.

"I want to speak to the team about *our* vision. I don't think it should be entirely *my* vision. The major told me that this isn't about me 'giving orders and going away.' It's about dialogue. We come up with a vision together, we ideate together, we solve problems together. That way, the team will buy in, because it's our vision, not solely *my* vision or *their* vision."

He was right. "Nicely said. As the commander, it's important for you to simplify and articulate the vision. We need you to constantly reiterate and remind your team who they are and why they are here, and to tie that into the major's intent. The foundation for your vision must be clear and attractive, yet motivating enough to demand maximum effort. If there is any ambiguity, teammates might not understand the vision and inadvertently go off in a different direction with a different destination in mind."

"What if the major gives me a mission or vision that I don't believe in?" Jason asked. "How do I convince the team that we should do it?"

"Don't ever try to sell the team a turd wrapped as a Christmas gift. You must absolutely believe in the mission and the vision and that it is possible to achieve. Remember belief, trust, and loyalty. This is ever so true when it comes to the mission. You have to believe we can accomplish it as a team. If you don't believe in the mission, you need to work that out with the major. As long as you've earned his trust, I promise you he will listen.

"I guarantee you General Eisenhower didn't tell his troops before D-Day, 'Gents, I'm not sure if we are good enough to pull this mission off.' No, he told them how important their mission was and that he believed in them to succeed. If you believe the mission is possible, do not tolerate anything less than positivity from everyone. Outcome expectations are powerful because individuals tend to put forth and exert only the level of effort they expect to achieve at."

I was ready for my last question of the new captain.

"My third question is, How are you going to get there?"

"I'm not entirely sure how to answer that, Steve," Jason answered honestly.

"With all due respect, you can't do everything yourself," I stated. "I've served for a number of leaders who wanted to do everything themselves. They never asked me what I thought. These leaders did not want to give the appearance that they weren't all-powerful or all-knowing. They were embarrassed to ask. They did not want the guys to see them as incompetent or weak. And it never turned out well for them.

"Here's the thing: you will be more respected and admired by admitting that you don't have all the answers. We already know you don't. Vulnerability and honesty go a long way. If you want to do it all yourself, you're going to burn out. You need to get to know the guys on the team.

Once you do, you'll trust them. They are phenomenal. I want you to see their potential for yourself. I want you to believe in their potential and believe that they are capable of reaching it.

"In order for your team to succeed, you must rely on and believe in your brothers. We all have roles and responsibilities. If we do not give the men responsibility and hold them accountable, then we are failing our future teams by not creating leaders. I believe true leadership is the absolute foundation of every effective team.

"Commanding is going to be hard. Hell, you saw my guys in there. You are going to get frustrated. You are going to be uncomfortable. Commanding requires a willingness to try, fail, try again, fail, and try again and again. Remember that failure is fertilizer, and fertilizer is what you need to grow to your full potential.

"So, how are we going to get there? Ultimately, how we are going to get there is through a lot of training and a lot of failure. You are going to have regrets, and that's not only OK, it's expected. Regrets are a component of failure, and failure gives us the fuel and the life lessons to successfully complete the mission. If you don't have any regrets, you aren't training hard enough.

"Just remember: what we tolerate as a team is how good we will be. If we tolerate poor training, we will be a poorly trained team. If we tolerate tardiness, we will be a team that is always late for the mission."

Jason nodded. I could tell he wanted to ask me a question.

"Steve, why are you here? Why did you join the Special Forces?"

"Why am I here?" I repeated. "I am here to serve my brothers."

"But how did you arrive at this place in life?" Jason asked.

I thought about it and realized I'd have to go back to properly answer. "You were a linebacker in college, right? I was a wide receiver," I said. "My college football career started at the University of Illinois. I was a freshman starter for the Fighting Illini. First as a punt returner and then as a wide receiver. Although I was undersized, I was relentless in my work ethic. I prided myself on outworking everyone else. I earned the nickname Take 'Em Deep, because I would challenge all of the defensive backs one-on-one in practice and consistently take them deep for touchdowns. My dream was to play in the NFL.

"Unfortunately, during my junior year, my career was ended due to injury.

"When I went to the doctor to get cleared to play, he told me that I would never play football again. I was devastated. No, devastated isn't a strong enough word.

"I went to the Mayo Clinic for a second opinion. They confirmed the diagnosis. Just like that, my dreams of playing in the NFL were over. I had no idea what to do. All I knew was football. That was my identity, who I was. Without football, I had no purpose.

"I remember sitting in the doctor's office feeling sorry for myself when I started to sketch the Navy SEAL Trident on a piece of scratch paper. I knew what SEALs were from books and movies and decided that if I couldn't play in the NFL, I'd direct my focus on joining a different elite team. The doctor gave me the green light to join the navy, and I began my journey to a new purpose.

"Wow," Jason said.

"Yeah," I continued. "The problem was, I didn't know how to swim."

"You've got to be kidding me," he blurted out.

"Nope. I never learned how. So I spent the next two years teaching myself how to swim. When I graduated from college, I was twenty-three years old and in tremendous shape. I walked into BUD/S class 196 and immediately got recycled for drownproofing. I had no idea what drownproofing was or how to do it. The instructors had to pull me off the bottom of the pool when I was trying to travel with my hands and feet tied. I got rolled to BUD/S class 197, mastered drownproofing, and graduated from training. I was officially a Navy SEAL and damn proud of it.

"I still have a vivid snapshot of an event that really shaped the rest of my journey. My SEAL team was forward deployed to Africa, training the Seychelles military. We were told that even though we brought all the guns and ammo, Green Berets were going to conduct the classroom training. 'No way,' I thought. 'I'm a SEAL. I have a college degree. No way is some cigarette-smoking army soldier going to teach this class.'

"I showed up to teach this class and waited for the Green Beret instructor to arrive. Remember, this was pre-9/11, so I was dressed in standard-issue cool-guy Navy SEAL UDT shorts and tight brown T-shirt, with a whistle around my neck and floppy hat on my head. The Seychelles soldiers we were training were seated Indian style on the floor when the Green Beret walked in.

"He had spit-shined boots, a professionally starched uniform, and a velvet corrugated display with all the weapons systems mounted on the board. All the nomenclature and characteristics of each weapon were depicted on his board. He then started the class…in fluent French. I was blown away. I never forgot that lesson. That Green Beret's professionalism and humility humbled me. I never got rid of that mental snapshot.

"I served six years in the navy before getting out to pursue a civilian career. I left the SEALs because we seemed to be doing the same thing over and over. I needed a new challenge but quickly discovered that the civilian world was not for me. I regretted getting out of the navy.

"Then 9/11 happened.

"I wanted to return to the SEAL Teams, but as an officer this time. I went to three different recruiters, and they all told me I was too old to be a SEAL officer. Already having done the enlisted SEAL thing, I decided to join the army as an officer. I figured if I could be a Navy SEAL, then I could be a Green Beret.

"I went to Ranger school first. Ranger school was a breeze for me and the easiest of all the schools I've been to. You have to remember, I was thirty-three at the time and had already gone through BUD/S. The hardest thing for me at Ranger school was fitting in with the young guys and not falling asleep. To make Ranger school harder for myself, I stopped working out for an entire two months prior to going. The only physical training I did prior to Ranger school was a little rucking. I'd walk barefoot with my daughter in my rucksack on and off hot asphalt pavement, just long enough to toughen up the soles of my feet.

"I was true blue all the way through and graduated Ranger school in sixty-one days. After I graduated, I put my packet in to join the Ranger Regiment and served with the 75th Ranger Regiment. Of the SEALs, Green Berets, and Rangers, I will offer the Ranger Regiment had the best leadership and discipline. The unit I was able to serve with at the Ranger Regiment was absolutely incredible.

"I spent five years in the conventional army and Rangers just for the chance to become a Green Beret. I started Special Forces training as a thirty-nine-year-old father of three daughters. Imagine being nearly forty years old, a former Navy SEAL, and coming straight from the Ranger Regiment to start training with guys who were half my age. The course was considerably longer than BUD/S, and though physically it was hard, it was toughest for me spiritually. I had to overcome a lot to graduate from the Q Course. There was a lot of soul searching there."

"Why was that?" Jason asked.

"It started with an injury. During our small-unit tactics phase, we parachuted into a training mission, and I broke my hip."

"Well, you are an old man," Jason joked.

"I know. Old man breaks his hip. Hilarious. I was in an enormous amount of pain after that, but I refused to quit. I joined the army solely to be a Green Beret. I fought through the pain with no meds while a bone fragment ground my hip labrum to hamburger. I grinded away for over a year until I was able to find the time for surgery."

Jason had both of his hands behind his head, enthralled by the story. "OK, then I guess you're the best person to answer to this: Which unit is the best? SEALs, Rangers, or Green Berets?"

I knew that was coming. "I get that question a lot," I said, "and I answer it honestly.

"Who is the best? Well, *better* is a relative term. Better at what, exactly? I found the army most similar to the civilian world—meaning the full range of stellar, mediocre, and absolute shit people. In my SEAL experience, that spectrum was much narrower, and the bad apples were very, very few.

"When I got to the Green Berets, I loved it and loved the men and had the best team sergeants ever. I thought the world of those men, and I am so glad I stuck with it. Looking back, Green Beret training was absolutely the most painful. I remember carrying things that made my spine feel like it was going to snap. Overall, I think Green Berets are the smartest, receive the best training, and are the most cunning.

"After I became one, I was afforded the opportunity to return to the Navy SEAL community as an Army Special Forces liaison for the Naval Special Warfare Center (NSW). I realized that the passion and unity of the SEAL community is unmatched. It is just a smaller, closer-knit group of studs who are forged in a hotter, more demanding furnace. It's not that the Rangers and Green Berets don't have studs, but when I went back to NSW, I was greeted with such secure authentic humility, it made me realize which group I felt a stronger bond with. I was welcomed back and asked to be part of the community immediately as if I had never left. It just made me feel wanted as I took up more than my share of the load there.

"Bottom line: if I had to choose what to be and what community to be part of, I would choose the Navy SEALs. Going back to the NSW community after being both at the Ranger and Special Forces Regiments, I'm able to confirm that they had the most passion and best teamwork.

"But I deeply treasure the men and the relationships developed at all the units I served in. They're each filled with top-notch people who I'm proud to say I was associated with. A bunch of alpha males who would not hesitate to die for you and ask nothing in return. I learned so much from each of them. I learned to fail and get up again. I was humbled over and over at the selflessness and sacrifice exhibited from all the units.

"To answer your question, they all are the best, dammit. I love them all and would do it all over again just to say I belonged with such people."

Captain Van Camp said quietly, "I appreciate you, brother."

I looked at him sternly. This was where the rubber met the road. "We have an opportunity to make our company the best. I truly believe that. If you want to make your ODA the best, then make sure you can answer those three questions I asked you.

"We've got some work to do. You're brand new, and we'll be deploying soon. We need to get you to your team and make sure everyone is up to snuff on SOPs, mission set, and mind-set."

Jason looked confused. "Wait. When are we deploying?"

"You didn't know? Our teams are going into isolation in a few weeks. We'll be infiltrating into country quickly after that. Better tell your wife."

SOF to Science with Petra Kowalski, Social Science Officer

Petra has ten years' experience teaching, training, and coaching performance psychology and resilience for athletes, tactical populations, and civilians. Petra earned her master's in sport and exercise psychology from California State University, Chico in 2009 and her Level 4 Master Resilience Trainer Primary Instructor Certificate from the University of Pennsylvania in 2015. When not working, Petra enjoys trail running, downhill skiing, and spending time with her wife and two kids.

If you want employees who are fully and deeply committed to your organization's mission, goals, and values and you want employees who are happier, healthier, and more engaged and who perform better at work, then you'll want to learn exactly how Steve's focus on his team helped them succeed.

Motivation is an indispensable precursor to high performance. Unfortunately, motivation is often thought to be an individual personality trait that you have or you don't. However, leader motivation style and the social context of the work environment are significant influences on individual motivation, performance, and organizational commitment. If done wrong, motivation can be thwarted. If done right, leaders and organizations can have a significantly stronger influence on motivation, well-being, and job satisfaction than commonly believed.

Self-determination theory (SDT) is a broad framework for the study of human motivation with a primary position that individuals experience optimal functioning and self-motivation when the three basic psychological needs are satisfied: *autonomy* (some sense that one's behavior is freely chosen), *competence* (the feeling of mastery and growth), and *relatedness* (meaningful connections with others) (Ryan & Deci, 2000). Additionally, SDT research is clear that leaders play an important role in creating and sustaining an environment where these three basic needs are met (Slemp et al., 2018).

Steve's experience in the crashing surf at BUD/S highlights how leaders can improve individual motivation and team performance by supporting those three basic human psychological needs. In the moment he looks up and decides to engage in the task in a different way, he enables others to do the same and helps the team see that they also have some choice in their actions—*autonomy*. In focusing on his teammates and shouting words of encouragement, he helps his teammates believe that they can master and succeed at an immensely challenging task—*competence*. In recognizing that his teammates are suffering as well, some worse than he, and choosing to face and move toward their pain, he develops meaningful connection with and among his teammates through a deep sense of empathy—*relatedness*.

When leaders are able to do what Steve did and enable his teammates to feel autonomy, competence, and relatedness, the benefits can be astounding.

A few key findings from SDT research highlighted with this chapter are:

1. When the three basic psychological needs are met, individuals more fully and deeply internalize the organization's mission, goals, and values.

2. When the three needs are met, employees are happier, healthier, more engaged, and they perform better.

3. Leaders play a key role in whether needs are met (Slemp et al., 2018).

So What?

Teams of all kinds want happy, healthy employees who are invested in the mission. As Steve highlights, "Many teams fail because the individuals are not willing to sacrifice their personal agendas for the mission's sake." SDT helps us to understand that the path to full organizational commitment and employee wellness is found by focusing on your people and choosing to foster their autonomy, competence, and relatedness.

Increased organizational commitment (internalization)

The level of support for the three basic needs is critical to organizational commitment. That is, whether your employees resist, partially adopt, or deeply internalize the values, goals, and mission of your company is largely dependent on how good the leadership is at any level in the organization. Leadership must create an environment that supports autonomy and relatedness. When people feel they have some choice in their behavior and feel connected to and supported by important people, they are more likely to be fully committed to, engaged with, and attached to the organization—what SDT labels "Internalization." (Gagne, 2003; Slemp et al., 2018; SDT Overview, n.d.)

Leaders who create supportive environments also facilitate internalization of work motivation which in turn leads to healthier, happier, and more productive employees.

Improved employee health, wellness, and work performance

In addition to increased mission commitment, leader support for the three basic needs also has significant impacts on employee wellness and performance. SDT research (Gagne & Deci, 2005) shows leader autonomy support is associated with:

- Increased job satisfaction
- Higher levels of trust in corporate management
- Positive attitudes
- Higher performance evaluations
- Greater persistence (stick-to-it-ness)
- Greater acceptance of organizational change
- Increased prosocial behavior and volunteering

Now What?

1. Check your motivation beliefs

SDT and all the research supporting it is based on the belief that humans have an innate/natural tendency toward growth, mastery, motivation, and internalization. Leaders need to understand and adopt this belief in order to foster motivation instead of thwart it (SDT Theory Overview, n.d.).

What do you believe about your own/your employees' motivational tendencies? Where does this belief come from? If you don't currently believe humans have a natural tendency to be motivated, how could you work to shift that belief? If you do believe that natural human motivation simply needs to be fostered, how can you help others in your organization see that as well?

2. Check your leadership behaviors

The SDT research has identified specific leader behaviors that help create an autonomy supportive environment (Gagne, 2003; Slemp et al., 2018; SDT Overview, n.d.). They include:

- Empathy or taking the perspective of their team members and specifically acknowledging if an assignment is not interesting.
- Deliberately creating opportunities for choice and input within the work environment.
- Encouraging self-initiation.
- Supporting a sense of ownership, interest, and value.
- Providing rationale or the "why" for assignments and associated tasks.
- Avoiding use of extrinsic rewards and punishments (see more below).

Which leader behaviors from Steve and Jason can you most relate to in chapter 2? Which leader behavior do you currently use most/do best? What enables you to do that? Which leader behavior do you currently use least/struggle most to implement? What might be standing in your way and how could you address it?

3. Avoid use of rewards/punishments

Cognitive Evaluation Theory (CET), a subtheory under SDT, specifically examines the influence of external factors such as rewards, deadlines, punishments, surveillance, and evaluations on individual motivation (Gagne & Deci, 2005; SDT Theory Overview, n.d.).

While there are some ways that rewards can be used without undermining motivation, the research is clear: tangible rewards and punishments offered as an attempt to increase motivation and performance by and large undermine our most powerful source of motivation (Gagne & Deci, 2005; Deci et al., 2001).

How readily do you, or how does your organization, rely on extrinsic rewards/punishments? Why might this be? What would it take to shift away from this practice?

Practical Application with Jason Van Camp

This chapter is about social awareness and influencing others. What makes a commander successful? I'd argue it's serving your teammates and placing them above your own needs. When you take care of the team, the team takes care of you.

When I was a new captain and getting to know my team, I learned that you were on the precipice of disaster if you heard the phrase "the captain is not listening to us." In those situations, I would think, "Yeah, I heard you loud and clear. I just don't want to do what you suggested." The problem wasn't listening, it was communication. I didn't take the time to explain to the team why we weren't doing it the way they suggested—or wanted. I didn't even realize that I was failing to communicate my intent. When you are failing to communicate, the team feels unappreciated and ignored. Individuals feel unwanted, lose their faith in you, and ultimately bring the team down.

There's a reason why elite Special Operations courses always begin with intense physical training. The shock value of initial stress overload is the best discriminator while assessing an individual or group's willingness and capacity to accomplish difficult tasks. It's because after twenty minutes, when you are tired of holding a log over your head, you can't fake it any longer. When the pressure is on and the stress increases, your true personality comes out.

The vocal, motivated cheerleader types who try hard to encourage others? They suddenly shut up. The pessimists who are there because they were told to be there but don't really want to be there? They suddenly quit. The eternal optimists who are always positive and see the good in everything? They suddenly wonder if they have what it takes to make it in the first place. The playing field is now even because everyone is in survival mode and doing whatever it takes to get by. Fatigue makes cowards of us all.

Eventually, there is a moment when everybody is miserable and focused on themselves. Our heads are down, and we are contemplating when the suffering will end. As the level of stress increases, our brains narrow our focus, and our sensory attention goes inward. Our body language reflects, as the pupils dilate, heart rate increases, breathing intensifies, heads go down, shoulders slump, and our thoughts begin to race: What in the hell did I get myself into? When will it all end? How much longer can I keep this up? Is it all worth it?

During log PT on day one of selection, for whatever reason, almost counterintuitively, even though it spent energy on something that was risky, I looked up. I looked up and looked around. I deliberately chose discomfort. The guys around me were all suffering just as badly as I was, if not worse. In that moment, my friend Pat lifted his head up as well. He looked around, and we looked at each other. He shouted, "Let's go, J. You got this!" I shouted words of encouragement back at him, even though it required energy that could have been used on myself.

More guys lifted their heads and looked around. We began to focus on one another rather than on ourselves. Looking up became infectious. Strangely enough, we began to forget about our pain, the time seemed to move faster, and the log felt lighter. The reality is that nothing changed about the situation except our attitudes. The conditions still sucked, it was hot as hell, our bodies still strained, and the logs didn't get any lighter. It was our minds that had changed. We began choosing how we thought, deciding where to direct our attention and energy.

In these difficult moments, situations that make or break individuals and teams, we find our collective purpose. When the pressure is on and you're on a team, it's never about you. It's about the people to your left and right who are going through the experience and process with you. In this moment, I found purpose. My purpose was to make the team succeed.

Misery is suffering without a purpose. The guys who make it through these types of courses are the guys who experience an aha moment. When they realize that they're not alone. That they are on a team and the success of the team is more important than their own personal success. The people who *don't* make it are the guys who are self-centered, who don't risk any energy that doesn't immediately serve their own interests. The people who don't look up.

The secret to the elite mind-set of Special Operations Forces, no matter how many books you read or podcasts you listen to, **is to look up.**

The same "look up" mind-set applies to the everyday mundanity of real life. As a lot of well-intending families do, my wife and I are committed to attending church services every Sunday. As a couple with young children, parenting lessons come early and often. Our daughter is a toddler with boundless energy, which means that we spend a good majority of the service outside in the foyer. Whenever she acts up, screams, or causes a distraction during the sermon or in Sunday school, we do the polite and sensible thing and remove her from the situation.

After several months of faith in the foyer went by, my wife and I looked up at each other and asked ourselves, "What are we doing here?" We don't hear the sermon; we don't hear the Sunday school lesson. We just sit out in the foyer and distract our daughter. What's the point of getting up early and getting dressed to come to church and play with our daughter in the foyer? I thought back to my experiences during log PT. I was embarrassed that I had forgotten that critical lesson from years ago. I realized that I wasn't going to church for myself. I was going for the other members of the congregation. I asked myself, What can I do this Sunday to serve the church and church members' needs? Sitting out in the foyer with a screaming daughter, maybe all I could give was a hello or a smile. If that was all I could give, then I would give that.

For me, Sundays are sacred because they represent our commitment to spending that quality time together in fellowship to reflect and celebrate our common values and beliefs. This is the foundation of our collective purpose. Is the quality of time we invest now showing an immediate return? Certainly not immediately, but that's a limited and short-sighted way of looking at the situation. That's the same reason why people decide to quit: the log is too heavy right now, and they want to make the pain stop. It's not about the log, and it's not about the foyer. It's about the people to our left and right.

We chose a different perspective and approach to the situation. Through this choice, we realized that if we continued our routine, our daughter's behavior would eventually improve. With the help of a few trusty toys or coloring books, she will sit quietly in a pew among the congregation. She will learn how to listen to the sermon through our example, and grow through others during Sunday school. By the time she is old enough to know better, this routine as a deliberate and weekly choice will not just be something she does but an integral part of who she is. Suddenly on Sundays, chasing my daughter in the foyer doesn't seem as bad as it once did.

Remember:

- Look up.
- When you take care of the team, the team takes care of you.
- It is about the mission, then the team, then the teammate, and finally you—the individual.
- Being comfortable with who you are is the first step in navigating uncertainty and overcoming the inevitable discomfort.
- Courage on the battlefield is sometimes easier than having the courage to stand up to your team and telling them no.

---

3 The Self

with **Matt Chaney**

Matt is an active duty US Army Special Forces (Green Beret) officer. He earned the Silver Star and Purple Heart as well as two Bronze Stars during four combat rotations in the Middle East. He earned a bachelor of science in economics from the United States Military Academy at West Point and a master of public policy from the University of Chicago.

"Matt, when is this new captain showing up?" Luke, my team sergeant, growled at me, voice gravelly, deteriorated by years of tobacco and Johnny Walker. Around us, the rest of the team buzzed throughout the team room, grabbing coffee, prepping equipment, and taking out their green logbooks for notes.

Major Petit had volun-told me that I would be mentoring a new team leader for the day. I didn't mind. Experienced captains had taken me under their wing when I first arrived at the company, and I never forgot their professionalism. It was time to return the favor. Besides, I would do anything for Major Petit.

The team was preparing to go to the range for close quarters battle (CQB) training. This type of training is crucial for the asymmetric, unconventional warfare our country relies on us to conduct in the Middle East. Many of our missions over there take place on city streets and in alleys, houses, and buildings where the urban surroundings severely limit maneuverability and visibility to the point where standard methods, equipment, and tactics are no longer suitable.

We needed to develop and perfect our standard operating procedures (SOPs) to ensure everyone was playing from the same sheet of music. Each individual operator must understand how to operate as a collective team in order to have success when conducting CQB operations. Even more importantly, as we continuously train, we need to get to the point where we know each other so well that we can intuitively feel how each man on the team will react when faced with certain scenarios.

Eventually, the new captain walked through the open doors to our team room. He was fifteen minutes early. We had already been there for forty-five minutes.

I spoke loudly as soon as he entered. "Gentlemen, let me introduce you to Captain Jason Van Camp. He will be taking over one of the teams in our company. I want you to show this new captain how the best team in the battalion operates."

While I was happy to have Jason with us, I also couldn't wait for him to leave. We were getting ready to go to war. I wanted to remove distractions, and make no mistake, mentoring this new captain would be a distraction.

After quick introductions, we left for Range 67, where we would conduct our training. We arrived at the range and quickly exited our vehicles and met under the outdoor planning bay. We downloaded our equipment and converted our M4 rifles into nonlethal, simunition weapons by replacing the bolt and barrel with simunition products. Nonlethal, sure, but those blue rounds hurt like hell. Every time you got hit, it left a cigar-sized burn on your body or your face. I got shot in the groin a few years ago, and it definitely left a reminder that I had made a mistake leaving that area unprotected. A lesson I'll never forget.

We all finished loading our magazines with the aluminum-coated paintball pellets and prepared for our instructor to give us the safety brief and set the agenda for the day. Some of the guys seemed more interested in making jokes as he talked, but the team sergeant quieted them.

"Hey, sir! Why are we doing the safety brief here? Wouldn't it be better if we held it in one of the rooms in the shoot house?" one of the guys shouted at me.

"I appreciate the suggestion, but we're doing it here," I responded. Hard to please everyone. God love 'em, but these type As would complain and question everything we did, thinking they have the best solutions. Feedback was appreciated, but there was a time and place.

We'd all done CQB for years and were pros at it. Everyone knew what they were doing, which could sometimes lead to guys over articulating their level of expertise. But our level of competency didn't mean we didn't need to train on it and get better. The more you sweat in peace, the less you bleed in war. So I shut down the first round of "suggestions" and let the instructor finish his briefing.

The day's training would be scenario based, with instructors acting as our opposition. These guys were good and would provide a real challenge. That was what we wanted: to be the best, we had to train against the best.

As we walked through our first CQB rehearsal, I wanted to make sure the new captain understood the importance of operating as a team. I leaned up to Jason and said, "Listen, when we go out to train, you might ask yourself, How is this training making me a better operator? My answer to you is, it's not. It's making the guy next to you a better operator. That's the mind-set that you need to have in this company. At any time, any one of us can pipe in with a correction, regardless of rank, to make us better. Mastering this process is critical to your survival in the volatile, uncertain, complex and ambiguous environment you are deploying to."

He looked like he understood. I knew he'd been deployed before joining SF, and having just graduated from the Q course, this shouldn't be new to him.

"Look, I'm not saying any of this to beat my chest," I told him as humbly as I could. "I want to get better myself. I've been deployed to combat twice. I've been in live firefights and proved my mettle. I've been to three SFAUC (Special Forces Advanced Urban Combat) training events. I know what I'm doing, and I also know that I can get better."

"That's good to hear, Matt. I definitely need to get better too," Jason answered as we continued through the rehearsal.

Then it was time for the real thing. At least as real as it can get during training. We broke up into four-man groups. I was with Scott, Randy, and Jerome. Jason ended up in another four-man team, and we all got to work. My team flowed through the shoot house, practicing how we entered and cleared center-fed and corner-fed rooms. We moved up stairs and down hallways and addressed intersections. We worked with military dogs and battled opposition forces wearing Blauer tactical suits to protect them from the dogs. We practiced sensitive site exploitation (SSE), which meant we'd collect and analyze any intelligence left at a site. Then, after the mission was over, we'd thoroughly critique every single minuscule action we had taken. We practiced multiple rotations with every man on the team working a different position in the assault cell stack.

Nearly fifty iterations later, we were all exhausted, and it was beautiful.

On our last run-through, something happened. We were lined up shoulder to shoulder, working on moving down a hallway in a stack. My mind began to wander. I was hungry and tired and thinking about life. I let my self-discipline slip.

Self-discipline is a difficult thing to develop. You need to recognize when you are being undisciplined in the moment before you can do anything about it. I happened to be aware of this moment of weakness, and I made the decision to shake it off.

Scott was next to me, with my number-two man, Randy, immediately behind me. I took a quick peek at the guys in my stack and gave them a thumbs-up to indicate we were ready to go. They returned the gesture. Go time. Scott and I moved side by side, providing cross coverage for each other as we moved down the hall. That meant he was responsible for the area directly in front of me, and I had the space in front of him. We slowly made our way down the hallway, the words of the instructor ringing in my ears—*slow is smooth; smooth is fast*. Scott's shorty barrel was positioned where it was supposed to be, aimed down the hall, right past my face.

We approached a T-intersection. When Scott and I broke around the corner, an enemy combatant's rifle barrel was six inches from my face.

I reacted. *Poorly.*

I flinched and took a step back around the corner, bumping into my number-two man, Randy.

"What the hell!" Randy shouted in frustration and disappointment. He didn't have to say anything else. I knew what I had done, and so did everyone else.

To recover, I broke back around the corner immediately and shot the enemy role player three times at close range. We continued the exercise, flowing through the house with no further issue.

When the exercise was over, we stopped and returned to the start of the scenario. I hung my head, knowing that I had severely messed up. I had flinched. By going back behind the corner, I had exposed Scott's back to the enemy. The enemy barrel that was in my face was meant for me. It was my responsibility either to shoot or otherwise disable the threat or to take a bullet so the man next to me would be safe. Scott should have been free and clear because he had my back, and he had done his job. I hadn't.

My mistake hit home for me because there was a person on the other end of that mistake. Scott was my teammate. My friend. We had been on the team together for over a year. Had this been a real-life scenario, Scott would have died, and it would have been my fault.

That hit me hard.

I had been in combat and had conducted CQB many, many times. I knew what I was doing, yet still faltered. This failure highlighted a theme that had been drilled into me during years of training: the necessity of being focused every single time you operate.

As a commander, this incident seared in my mind the importance of creating realistic practices that got my team and me focused each and every time. Even if we had done it hundreds or thousands of times before, my role was to help them focus and orient them to the task, and vice versa.

Nowhere was this more crucial than in combat scenarios.

"Hey guys, let's run through that scenario again," I suggested. "I don't want to end on poor muscle memory…I want to ensure I get it right."

"Hey, sir, we don't practice until we get it *right*. We practice it until we can't get it *wrong*," Scott corrected.

He was right. It's like a basketball player who won't leave the court until he swishes that final three-pointer. We never want to end an exercise building wrong muscle memory. We purposefully put ourselves in those uncomfortable positions multiple times so we can retrain ourselves and build correct habits of winning. That was what we did after my mistake.

Later, we sat down for our after-action review, or AAR, where we dissected everything that happened during the exercise. The AAR is an incredible tool we use to facilitate a professional discussion of an event in order to receive maximum benefit from every real-life or training mission. The discussion enables soldiers to discover for themselves what happened, why it happened, and how to sustain strengths and improve on weaknesses. The AAR helps improve our performance by providing immediate feedback about how the training could have been done better.

I was responsible for leading the AAR.

I began by sharing my experience with the team. While humbled by my mental error, I wanted to own it, if it would help the team. If we learned from it, then it was worth it.

We all regathered under the outdoor planning bay. The lights began to flicker on as dusk settled in. Team members lounged on the picnic benches under the roof or propped themselves up on empty ammo cans and stacked pallets.

I started. "All right, gents. I want to hear sustains and improves. What did we do well, and what do we need to do better? But before we go around the horn, I want to share my own improves first. When we make mistakes, we hold ourselves and each other accountable. That's a good thing. A big improve for me is to keep my focus."

"What happened, Captain?" one of the guys asked.

"I flinched," I answered simply. "During one of our last scenarios, I turned the corner and was surprised to see an enemy barrel in my face. In that moment, I flinched and would have gotten Scott killed. Scott would have taken a bullet for my lack of focus. I must have let my mind wander momentarily as we flowed through the house. I don't know if I started thinking about dinner or my new baby on the way, but I wasn't locked in."

Jason spoke up. "The skill of compartmentalizing your life is a hard skill to master," he said. The team looked over at the new captain. I was glad he spoke out.

"No doubt," I agreed. "We have to make deliberate and purposeful decisions to focus on the here and now, again and again during operations, and the longer the operation, the harder it gets. Check our mental baggage at the door and commit to one another. Because I am counting on you to keep me alive just as you are counting on me to keep you alive. I'm not impervious to this risk, so keep an eye on me. Help me if you see me start to lose my focus."

It was well past dark by the time we concluded the AAR and loaded our equipment to head back to base. I sat in the passenger seat of our vehicle while Luke drove, with Captain Van Camp in the back.

"Jason, what did you think about training?" I asked, leaning back so I could look him in the eye. I could tell he wanted to say something but was hesitant. Finally, he spoke up.

"Well…it's just that…man, it seems like all your guys do is complain. I mean, you can't say or do anything without someone offering a critique about it. I thought it would be different," Jason said begrudgingly.

"Welcome to Special Forces!" I laughed. He was right, but it wasn't quite that simple.

"Jason, this might seem counterintuitive, but you'll find that no group complains more than a Special Forces team."

His face darkened, and I could tell he wasn't sure if I was joking or not. Next to me, Luke began to nod. I decided this would be a good learning tool for him.

"Let's talk about complainers. Why do you think people complain?" I asked.

He considered the question. "Because they are weak minded and cancerous," he stated.

Luke glanced at him in the rearview mirror. "Hey, sir, has anyone ever told you that you speak like an articulate thug?"

Jason seemed pleased with the description. "No, they haven't," he said. "But I like that. I *really* like that."

"I would disagree with your assessment," I told him. "I believe it's quite the opposite. People complain because they care. If they didn't care, they wouldn't say anything," I explained.

"Bro, that doesn't make any sense," Jason replied.

"What I'm saying is that it's OK to complain. Complaining shows that you care about the unit. You want the unit to be the best, and when it's not, it bothers you. If you truly didn't care whether the unit succeeded or failed, then you wouldn't say anything. You would just be silent and watch as the unit collapsed into mediocrity," I explained. "Does that make sense?"

"Actually, it does," he said. "I remember when I was playing football in college. My coach always told me that the only time I should be worried was if he stopped getting after me. You know, like stopped yelling at me, berating me. He said that if he did, it meant that he didn't care about me anymore. That he no longer wanted me to improve and didn't think I had a future," Jason said.

"Yes. Something like that," I replied. "You see, complaining shows that you want something to improve. Here's the thing: you can complain all day, BUT you also need to offer a solution.

"Your SF operators may bitch, but they almost always offer solutions. Classic complainers are labeled negatively because they have no follow-through. They don't provide any solutions. If your team is complaining and they don't have solutions to their gripes, then you have to explain to them that those complaints are not helpful without follow-through. Then put them in charge of planning the next training evolution to test their theory and develop their leadership. That's how you can transition classic complainers into problem solvers. And that is what we need in the company: Problem solvers.

"Most of the time, your soldiers just want their commanders to listen to them. They don't necessarily want you to do anything about it; they just want to be heard. As the commander, you need to listen to your men. Don't let your ego get in the way of success. Let them know that when our lives are on the line, we don't hold our tongues. We say exactly what we feel. All you have to do is preface anything you say with, 'With all due respect...'"

Jason chuckled. "Nice, Matt."

"At the end of the day, you've got to honestly digest all information provided and make a command decision. A committed team member will execute on that decision knowing that their thoughts have been heard, even if they disagree with the final decision. Through the process, you learn to trust in each other. At first, yeah, I was uncomfortable with it too, but I got used to it. I advise you to figure out how to get used to it as well, because as a brand-spanking-new captain, your guys are going to complain out the ass and do their best to break you. Being a commander is tough, man. It's not for everybody, but I got your back." I hoped I had relayed the message.

"Thanks, brother," Jason replied. "I really appreciate that. I do have one more question: The major told me that you were going to introduce me to the primary combatives instructor tomorrow. Jeff, I think? What's his story?"

"Jeff Adams?"

"Yeah, that's the one," Jason said.

I thought about it for a second. "I'll tell you what. Jeff has more combat experience than anyone else in group. He's a meat eater, that's for sure. Word of caution: keep your guard up, because he'll be sizing you up immediately and might feel the need to roll you up if he feels like it."

"Damn. Great to hear," Jason said sarcastically, falling back into his seat.

SOF to Science with Sean Swallen, Spiritual Science Officer

Sean Swallen is a former United States Marine Corps Infantry officer with an advanced degree in both counseling and sport/performance psychology. Sean works as a performance expert contracted with the US Army, teaching and training soldiers and their families on resilience and mental skills. He also teaches resilience and leadership at the University of Colorado–Colorado Springs.

Spirituality can be defined as a state of being completely connected to oneself and one's environment and generating strength through living out one's ultimate purpose. History and science remind us that without incisive self-reflection and understanding, we cannot grow and consistently perform at our best. Although it's oftentimes uncomfortable to look at yourself in the mirror and be honest with yourself, it is a necessity to overcome fear and achieve your life's purpose.

In this chapter, Jason and Matt emphasize the moral imperative of having self-awareness. When Matt makes a critical mistake during training, he owns that mistake. He looks inside to take an honest inventory of what occurred and then makes a conscious decision to learn from it.

Research shows us that the more self-aware and attuned we are to our innermost values, beliefs, and purpose, the more likely we are to become happy and effective. There is a profound concept in the human performance world known as being in a state of flow (Csikszentmihalyi, 1997). One researcher describes flow "as being the shortest path to [becoming] Superman" (Kotler, 2014). This summary will dive into what flow is, how it applies to Matt's ODA team, and how you can tap into and apply this optimal performance state in any environment.

Psychologist Mihaly Csikszentmihalyi first introduced the concept of flow. He defined it as "being so completely immersed in a task that nothing else matters. The ego falls away, time flies. Every action and movement seamlessly follows the previous note, like a meticulous jazz ensemble" (Csikszentmihalyi, 1997). Flow can be associated with the greatest performances ever achieved in any arena, including clutch plays to win championships, innovation and creativity, and courageous acts of bravery. In this chapter, Matt describes the end of the mission rehearsal, stating, "We were all exhausted, and it was beautiful." Folks coming out of flow states have shared similar encounters—they were so immersed, happy, thoughtless, and exhausted that it filled them with a sense of elation (Kotler, 2014).

Jason mentions how much complaining went on in the team. Yet how we perceive feedback is important. Flow research tells us that at minimum, three conditions must be met in order for us to move into flow: having clear goals, immediate and appropriate feedback, and proper balance of one's skill level with how challenging the task is (Csikszentmihalyi, 1997). The team was very passionate, provided detailed feedback, and regularly sought new and more difficult training challenges. The instructors who played the opposition in the CQB range were also very capable adversaries. In other words, the team and the training scenario met the conditions for obtaining flow states. Jason's observation was that the team was "complaining" when in fact they were relentlessly pursuing perfection through careful feedback and deconstructing the training iterations in order to be better.

This is very important, as it sets conditions for having longer periods of optimal performance. It also explains Matt's mistake that led to his teammate getting notionally "killed." Research tells us that in flow, our attention is exactly where it needs to be, and no external thoughts or distractors will impede our immediate task (Nakamura & Csikszentmihalyi, 2014). Matt admitted that by the end of the day, his mind was drifting. He was tired and thinking about going home. It is fair to assume, then, that he was not experiencing a flow state, and this exposed him to performance errors and mistakes, which put the entire team at risk.

So What?

How can strengthening our spiritual domain improve our overall well-being and performance? One of the conditions to experiencing optimal performance (or flow states) is "having an expansion of self, a sense of unity and bliss that lingers in one's consciousness and gives a sense of purpose, integration, and empathy" (Maslow, 1943). In order to better prime ourselves to get into a flow state, we must truly understand what we want in life, identify the values that shape our character, and more regularly affirm those values. Consequently, the more we reflect on and affirm our values, the greater control we have over our stress responses.

Researchers at the University of California conducted an experiment testing cortisol levels before, during, and after a stress-inducing event. They found that the group who reflected upon and affirmed their personal values daily reported lower levels of cortisol before, during, and after a stressful event. So knowing oneself and using self-affirmation can have positive physiological effects on the body and improve response times during a threat or challenge (Creswell, 2005; Sherman et al., 2009).

Furthermore, the clearer we understand what drives us, the more motivation we can sustain for implementing perfect practice and seeking new challenges. Motivation theory reminds us that the more we identify our own values within an organization or a task, the more fuel we can put into our tanks to help us persist and exceed expectations (Devloo et al., 2015). In this chapter, Matt, Jason, and the team all share the Green Beret value system and pursue perfection in their training. They embody the "quiet professional" mentality instilled in every Green Beret. In doing so, they set themselves up to more regularly achieve optimal performances, either by achieving flow, staying motivated in the process, or better regulating their stress responses.

The other exciting piece of research that Csikszentmihalyi found was that individuals experiencing flow could transfer that state into the team. He described this phenomenon as a "ballet in which the individual is subordinated to the group performance, and all involved share in the feeling of harmony and power" (Nakamura & Csikszentmihalyi, 2014). Just as attitudes and feelings are contagious to others, so too are flow states. Research tells us that Matt and his team are able to feed off one another's states of flow, which helps them move like a single organism. This, of course leads to an overall more consistent, optimal performance.

And to think this can all be achieved by simply being grounded in your own life purpose, your own value system, and knowing your own strengths and weaknesses. Of course, this spiritual practice is easier said than done.

Now What?

When was the last time you thought about the top five or ten values that you hold most dear? Go to the endnotes of this book to find a list of values. Go through the list and write down the five most meaningful values to you. Then write down a life mission statement that includes who you are (identity), what you are all about (values), and what you believe in. Try to keep this short and succinct. Begin each week by reflecting on your values and mission statement and decide how authentically you are living. In order to find flow, you must first master yourself, and that includes truly knowing what you value most and why you get up in the morning.

Secondly, determine when you or your team have been at their best. Were you experiencing flow? Remember, flow is being completely immersed in a task to the point where nothing else matters. Ask yourself what the conditions were that got you there and how you might replicate them. This might look like highly functional and efficient employees during a certain period of time, patterns of effectiveness throughout a quarter, or simply having feelings of detachment and joy throughout your day.

Some tips to identify factors that help you get into flow:
- Practice your skill or craft regularly. The more automatic, the better.
- Routinely receive and offer feedback. We cannot improve unless we sharpen. We cannot see our own blind spots and need feedback from others.
- Set your team up for success by matching the skill and challenge of the task. Create realistic goals that still push the edge of possibility.
- Become aware when you or a team member might be losing

flow states. You might be getting bogged down in environmental distractions or simply overthinking. If we can recognize when our mind wanders and reorient, we are less likely to lose a flow state and can more easily get back into flow.

Finally, being in a state of flow burns a lot of energy. We all need time to release and recharge. Identify at least three outlets that currently exist in your life to release. These outlets reset the mechanism, ideally take your mind completely off the task, and might include walking or hiking, sleeping, exercise, religious practice, or pursuing new hobbies (Kotler, 2014).

Practical Application with Jason Van Camp

One of Mission Six Zero's most successful clients is Luke Saari, president and CEO of Apex Logistics. Luke created Apex Logistics in 2008 as a multifaceted third-party logistics company based in American Fork, Utah.

Luke offers an honest self-assessment: "I want to say that the reason for my success was my authenticity. It wasn't. It was my ability to be a chameleon. I was whatever my team needed me to be. I didn't have a mentor. I did not start out as a logistics expert. I wasn't ultrapassionate about the logistics business that I started. I ended up haphazardly in the situation, but I decided to make the most of it."

Without incisive self-reflection and understanding, we cannot grow and consistently perform at our best. Although it's oftentimes uncomfortable to look at yourself in the mirror and be honest, it's necessary to overcome fear and achieve your life's purpose.

Luke goes on. "One thing that you must have is a mind-set of WIN. Not win *if*. Just win. That's it. Completely adopt that mind-set. Once you adopt that mind-set of winning, your excuses go away and behaviors change."

Luke is talking about "flow state." As we know, this can be achieved by simply being grounded in your own life purpose, your own value system, and knowing your own strengths and weaknesses. By adopting this mind-set, Luke turned a $100,000 investment into a $50 million buyout of his company in just ten years.

"When I first started out, I realized that in order to win, I needed to land a Department of Defense (DoD) contract. DoD logistics contracts paid out in seven days. That money would allow our start-up to grow. For eight months, I tried to land a DoD contract. I was told no every single day by a DoD representative. Then, on an otherwise uneventful Friday at 6:00 p.m., when everyone else had gone home for the day, I got a call from a DoD contractor. 'Luke,' he said. 'I need two trucks tomorrow at 0600 at Hill Air Force Base.'

"You got it!" I replied. I knew I would have no problem sourcing two trucks.

"Those trucks need to say Apex Logistics on the side," the DoD contractor said.

That was going to be more difficult. "Well, we don't have any trucks that say that," I replied.

"Should I find somebody else for this?" he asked.

"No. The trucks will have Apex Logistics on the side," I promised.

I didn't have any trucks, and I didn't have any signs. So I went and made four magnetized Apex Logistics signs, finishing at two o'clock in the morning. I showed up at Hill AFB the next morning and slapped the magnetized signs on the two trucks I had contracted. The signs didn't stick to the doors. That didn't stop me. I duck taped them to the trucks and paid the drivers $200 to repaint the doors.

That's the flow state mind-set. Do whatever it takes. WIN."

In the Middle East, we've come across the mind-set of "Inshallah." It's a common phrase that means "if Allah (God) allows it." For example, we could say, "We need you to attack the enemy at 0500" or "We need you to be at this meeting tomorrow at 1500." A common and immediate response is "Inshallah."

"Inshallah. If God wants me to be at the meeting tomorrow, he will. But there are so many other factors that are out of my control that might prevent me from attending the meeting. There could be a family emergency. My car might not start. There could be traffic. My alarm clock might not go off. I can't control these things. Only God can control these things, and therefore only God will decide if I will be at your meeting tomorrow."

This "disownership" mind-set takes the responsibility out of an individual's hands and places it in God's. Nothing infuriates or confounds a military man serving in the Middle East more than this mind-set of Inshallah. It confuses the Western mind-set of duty, accountability, and responsibility. It perpetuates failure, justifies blame, and stagnates growth.

For us, success means taking control. Winning is about setting flow state conditions. It is about having tough skin, being accountable for your mistakes, learning from them, and making improvements.

Luke continues: "When I adopted this WIN mind-set, my behaviors and the behaviors of the people in my company changed. We defined what winning looked and felt like to us. We stopped using words like *burnout, time away,* and *need a recharge.* We said, 'We are going to win, and we are not putting a timeline on it. If we never quit, we never fail.' We started to hold each other accountable. We started to have meetings where we were forced to get uncomfortable, check the egos, have tough skin, and go no holds barred. When we implemented this mind-set, the debating stopped."

Often, Mission Six Zero clients come to us and say, "We need to practice open and honest communication. We want to give people confidence and empower them to speak up in the moment. Too often, our leaders hold a meeting where they are the only person talking. When these leaders ask for questions or feedback, they are met with a deafening silence. Employees are unwilling to share their thoughts because they don't know how their feedback will be received. They keep silent, opening their mouths in the hallway immediately after they leave the conference room, only then sharing their unfiltered comments to anyone who will listen."

How do you create an environment where your employees feel empowered and comfortable enough to provide feedback? Remember what we learned in chapter 1:

- Make sure people understand you need to prove yourself to them just as much as they need to prove themselves to you.
- Everything is a dialogue between you and the boss— ideate together.
- Provide your boss with the best information available to empower them to make the best decisions.
- Explain that there will be a constant feedback loop between you and the boss.
- Mistakes are expected, but not every mistake is equal.
- If you don't succeed, failure is shared.

In 2014, Apex Logistics desperately needed a consistent voice and leadership. Luke made a pledge. "I will be on the floor working every single working day this year," he said. "No excuses. Is that indicative of who I am? Probably not. That's just what the business needed, so I did it."

He realized that he couldn't run the business from his office. He deliberately chose discomfort. He chose to get out of his comfortable office because he needed to sit on the floor with everyone else. His team needed real-time coaching. The only way they were going to get that was with him being close. On the floor. Leading.

Just as attitudes and feelings are contagious to others, so too are flow states. As we discussed previously, team members are able to feed off one another's states of flow, which helps them move like a single organism. This, of course, leads to more consistent, optimal performances.

By identifying not only his but the company's weaknesses, Luke created a healthy feedback loop that set conditions for a unified flow state within his team. In doing so, he muscled his way from $13 million in sales to $40 million in sales in twelve months. He was able to sustainably tap into his flow state once he deliberately chose discomfort.

Remember:

- Slow is smooth, and smooth is fast.
- Don't practice until you get it right; practice it until you can't get it wrong.
- Complaining with solutions equals problem-solving.
- A flow state is achieved by having clear goals, immediate and appropriate feedback, and properly balancing one's skills to the task.
- Take yourself out of the defensive posture and into an offensive one.

4 The Man

with **Jeff Adams**

Jeff is a retired US Army Special Forces (Green Beret) master sergeant. He has earned three Bronze Stars during four combat rotations in the Middle East, Kosovo, and Bosnia. He found his true calling in the Commander's In-Extremis Force (CIF), a no-notice rapid-reaction crisis response unit that deploys on a six-hour notice. He lives in Colorado Springs, Colorado.

Here I was, fighting yet again. Minding my own business when Chris decided to test me. Jumping me from behind, no less.

Being the barrel-chested freedom fighter I was, whose job required me to train our entire Special Forces group in hand-to-hand combat while ensuring they maintained top-notch physical condition, it was unthinkable for me to lose the fight. I was bigger, stronger, faster, and much better looking than he was.

As expected, Chris quickly tapped out after finding himself wrenched in a guillotine.

"Damn it, Jeff!" he exclaimed, gasping for air.

"You will never beat me, brother!" I mocked.

"I promise you this: I *will* be the first person to tap you out." His confidence and self-determination were impressive and warranted. I had been to war with Chris; I looked up to the guy, even if I would never tell him.

"I've lost before," I told him, "but I promise you this: if you do end up beating me, you'll be sipping your victory champagne through an IV bag. Is victory worth that much to you?"

Before he could answer, a knock rattled the door. A young captain I didn't recognize entered the gym.

"I'm looking for Master Sergeant Adams," he said. "I'm Captain Jason Van Camp. Major Petit told me to come by."

"You're in the right place, sir. That's me." I remembered that the major had asked me to meet with a new team leader to instill my brand of kicking ass between the ears. I'd seen more combat than just about anyone else at the group—not bragging, just a fact—and I had the PTSD to go with it. I examined the new captain quickly, gauging him to see if I thought he had what it took.

Chris picked himself up off the floor and addressed the captain. "Hey, sir, want some advice? Spend at least an hour a day kicking your own ass so no one has to do it for you."

"Noted," Jason shot back.

I had no interest in wasting our time, so I got right to the point. "Why are you here, sir?"

"Besides the fact that the major asked me to speak with you, I'm here to learn as much as I can, while doing so as humbly as possible," he answered.

The answer showed he had the attitude, but I wasn't sure I could give him what he was looking for. "Sir, if you're looking for the secret to success, you need to understand there is no magic pill. The only thing I can do is to help you to understand toughness. I'm not talking about being physically tough. I'm talking about mental toughness," I said. "That's kind of my specialty. Right, Chris?"

He nodded maniacally, as I knew he would, advising the captain, "If you find an obstacle in your path, you need to face it voluntarily. That's how strong people are made."

The captain nodded, like, "Yeah, no shit." I couldn't blame him. I knew he was a West Point guy and fresh from Q Course. He'd certainly been *taught* enough about leadership and mental fortitude. Doing it when each decision meant life or death was a different matter.

"We have teams right now getting ready to go back to Iraq. Chris, remember our first Iraq deployment during the initial invasion?"

"How could I forget? Worst night ever," Chris said, stretching on the mat.

"This was in 2003. Everyone knew we were about to invade Iraq, but no one knew when, or who would be sent. We just hoped it would be us. Our entire team told our families goodbye in secret, and we deployed to Jordan, hoping to get the call.

"One night our team gathered for a warning order. We were told we'd be infiltrating into country that night. It was finally going down."

Chris cut in. "Yeah, man, I remember how excited we all were."

"No shit. This was what I'd been waiting for my whole life. This was why I signed up. We were finally going to combat," I said.

"Yeah, man. You were a little too amped. I had to remind you we would be flying across SAM (surface-to-air missile) Alley while Saddam launched every missile he had at us," Chris reminded me.

As we started to tell Jason the story, I went back to that night. I could still see a different young captain standing before us in the moonlight, doing his best to prove that he belonged.

"Yo! Y'all come over here!" he called out. Our twelve-man ODA was dressed in the uniform of the Kurdish Peshmerga, which worked out well since our uniform resupply had never arrived. During isolation, we had concluded that the most effective (and decisive) course of action for mission success would be to link up with our Kurdish Peshmerga allies; hence why we were wearing their uniforms. The captain had told us that *Peshmerga* translated into "those who face death." I found that reassuring, but we'd been disappointed by indigenous forces before.

The captain began his briefing. "Check it out. The group commander basically gave us a short window to get from Jordan into Iraq. We'll be flying over SAM Alley and landing near Al Sulaymaniyah on six birds."

As he spoke, my mind began to wander. I started thinking about death. This mission could be it for me. I searched for the inspiration that would get me through the infil op. I've always enjoyed Russian literature, especially Dostoevsky. I thought about an experience that Dostoevsky had as a young man. I hadn't thought about it in years, but for some reason it popped into my mind. It's funny, the shit that just pops into my mind.

Dostoevsky had spent a year in prison. One day he was finally removed from his cell, naively thinking he was about to be released, or at the worst, given some form of light punishment. Instead, he was led to a square and lined up with his fellow prisoners. They were all sentenced to be shot. A priest gave them a cross to kiss and a chance to confess. Each prisoner had an execution hood placed over their head, and one by one the five men in front of Dostoevsky were shot. Suddenly, just as it was Dostoevsky's turn to meet his fate, a soldier's drums started rolling. The executioners lowered their rifles. A messenger from the tsar had come to pardon the prisoners. Dostoevsky and the remaining prisoners were released.

What had been going through Dostoevsky's mind? What did he think about when he knew death was imminent? That was what I wanted to know: What does a person think about when they're about to die? Dostoevsky said that whatever you think about in the moment of sure death is what is most important to you.

As we set to board the C-130s that would take us to war, I wondered what I would think about when facing certain death. The thought consumed me.

"Jeff, are you shitting me?" I looked up to find the entire team staring at me. Including our captain. Who was shouting. At me.

"Sir?" I asked casually, as though he were the one acting carelessly.

"What did I just say?" he spat, challenging me in front of the entire team.

"Sir, you said that Chris and I are going to be in lift 3, tail 31212," I answered quickly and with an air of mock disbelief that he would even question my focus.

"Damn it. At least look like you are paying attention, man."

The captain was right. I wasn't really paying attention. Time to dial it in.

"Don't forget—the enemy has a vote," the captain concluded. "Everybody has a plan until they get punched in the mouth. Let's go."

It was time. We grabbed our rucksacks and started to board our assigned planes. My mind wandered back to Dostoevsky—what I was thinking about? I couldn't pinpoint any profound thought, and I depressingly concluded that I wasn't thinking about anything.

Chris and I entered our plane from the rear and ran up the ramp with our rucksacks and rifles along with everyone else. The C-130's propellers were spinning, making it loud as hell. One of the pilots was yelling instructions at us, but no one could make out anything he said. They handed out vomit bags as we boarded. I didn't take one.

"You're fucking weak if you puke," I shouted to a pilot who was boarding us into the rear of the bird. He just stared at me like I was crazy. Kind of what I was going for. We crammed in, Chris next to me. He looked over with a mix of excitement and terror.

"This is it," he said.

"This is it," I repeated. I looked around. There were guys from six different teams. I counted thirty-three whom I knew. Then I stopped counting because it was too dark and chaotic. I took in my immediate vicinity. Where was I going to sit? Everybody else was just sitting on their rucksacks, so I did the same.

We started down the tarmac, and I realized that the next three hours were going to be the most uncomfortable I'd ever experienced. They turned the lights out, leaving us completely blacked out. No red light. No nothing. It was eerily quiet. Nobody on the plane said a word. I sort of expected somebody to give a pep talk or shout out a hell yeah, but there was nothing. Everyone just seemed focused. I hoped that I appeared the same. As the plane sped down the runway and lifted off the ground, I noticed that a lot of guys were already feeling sick. Not me. I was good to go.

Dostoevsky entered my mind yet again.

"What am I thinking about now?" I wondered. I really wanted to know, deep down, subconsciously, what I valued most in life. I was lost in thought.

BOOM!

It felt as if we got hit, but from the underbelly of the plane. I put one hand on the outboard wall of the aircraft and tried to balance myself. I found myself concerned for Chris and looked around for him in the dark.

"Chris!" I shouted. "You all right? I think we just got hit!"

"No, dude. It's sand," Chris replied, a lot calmer than I was.

"What are you..."

"Sand, dude. Just chill. We're flying so low, we hit a sand dune."

I started to think of something clever to say, but my stomach didn't have the patience for it. I was starting to feel sick, but my pride refused to let me vomit. So I just sat there listening to other dudes puke for the next thirty minutes. Some people just can't handle hitting sand dunes, I guess. I looked around for something to amuse me. Suddenly I saw a guy at the front of the plane frantically waving and shouting. "Hey! Hey, buddy!" I realized he was yelling at me.

I stood up as best I could and pointed at my chest. "Me?"

"Turn off your damn strobe light!" he exclaimed urgently.

Embarrassed, I looked down at my strobe. It wasn't on. "Shit. I must have the IR strobe on," I thought.

I quickly put on my night-vision goggles and looked down at my IR strobe. It wasn't on either. What the hell was this guy talking about?

I turned around and looked out the portal window and saw what was happening. "Hey, asshole! That's not my strobe. Those are tracers!"

We were under attack by enemy antiaircraft fire. The flashing light that the guy had mistaken for a strobe light was actually antiaircraft rounds being fired at us.

The pilot shouted over the intercom, "Missiles locked on and missiles inbound—brace for impact!"

I clutched the cargo net securing our javelin missiles. The pilot began maneuvering the aircraft so aggressively that bracing for impact was no longer an option. In a flash, I was pinned to the ceiling of the aircraft. I was stuck. In the next moment, I was slammed back down to the floor. The bird was steering and dodging up and down to avoid the enemy air-defense machine-gun fire and missiles. I was steering and dodging to avoid the puke that was flying everywhere. The pilots were doing a better job than I was. Puke splattered all over my face. Grenades got dislodged from grenade pouches and rolled onto the floor. The asshole who had yelled at me earlier had a sniper rifle, Remington 700 series, M24 with a Leupold scope. His rifle rocketed to the back of the plane, and the scope shattered right near my head.

I finally puked.

The next two hours were more uncomfortable and miserable than I could have imagined. I was scared, yeah, but more than that, I was angry and frustrated. Here I was on infil, and I wouldn't even get the chance to see the face of my enemy? What a waste if I died now. All that training, all my talent, gone to waste being helplessly killed in the back of an airplane. Without the chance to decide my own fate. It wouldn't be my decisions determining whether I lived or died. Just some random sequence of events where I had to trust a pilot to move a metal box and hope that an Iraqi missile wouldn't get lucky.

"Fuck it. Even if we get shot down, I'm going to live," I told myself. "I ain't dying." I thought back to Special Forces assessment and selection. Our instructors would tell us, "Do not self-assess!" I learned how to kill negative thoughts early in my SF career: *They won't accept me; I'm not good enough; I'm not as talented as that guy; I'm not going to make it.* I just pushed it from my mind.

I learned in training that I had a choice. At times, my choice was to convince my brain that I didn't have a choice. That quitting wasn't an option. In the same way, I convinced myself that death is a choice. No matter what happened, I knew I was going to survive this shit storm. Puke storm, whatever.

The plane eventually steadied. I felt our wheels hit pavement. If you could imagine a mongoose, a porcupine, a cobra, and a badger all thrown inside a burlap sack and beaten against a wall, then opening the sack and throwing it down, that's basically how we exited the aircraft.

I was just glad to be on the ground. To be able to shoot back. We had been helpless in the air. That was why I didn't join the air force.

The pilot ran off the bird and yelled to us, "For God's sake, be careful out there!"

84

I yelled back, "Us? You're the one who has to fly back through that shit!"

No sooner did we exit the aircraft than the captain gave us a FRAGO (a fragmentary order, which meant our mission had changed).

The captain informed Chris and me that we had been specially selected to link up with a group of one hundred Kurdish Peshmerga to destroy an Iraqi battalion of heavy artillery. If unchecked, the artillery pieces there could reach the location of other teams. Meaning, if we did not complete our mission, the other teams would be hit with heavy artillery. So before the other teams could even launch, we needed to take out this objective. Mission failure was not an option.

I started to second-guess myself. I started to worry. I was overwhelmed with all the things I could worry about: If Chris and I don't succeed in our mission, our brothers will be killed. I hope we can trust the Kurds. I hope they aren't going to shoot me in the back. Finally, I just stopped myself. "Don't self-assess." I realized I would make myself crazy worrying about things that were completely out of my control. I could only control the controllable.

I made a choice. I resolved to shift my focus to what I could control. I could control myself. I could control what I thought, said, and did. I trusted in my ability to get the job done no matter the circumstances.

It was just after midnight. Pitch black, but still as hot as hell. The team sergeant handed Chris and me a map, a compass, and the coordinates to our linkup point. Off we went, carrying 120-pound rucksacks loaded with gear, ammo, and equipment.

"One more thing. You're bringing a terp with you," the team sergeant said.

We looked across the tarmac and saw a young foreign national unathletically running toward us. He crouched over slightly and picked up his knees, which made him look as if he were running in place.

Chris looked at me and said, "He runs like Paul Giamatti."

"That's a good sign. Paul Giamatti is the greatest actor of our generation," I replied.

Out of breath, the new interpreter ran up to us and huffed, "Captain Jeff, my name is Sayid."

I wasn't a captain but decided not to correct him. "Are you an interpreter? Is that your profession?" I asked.

"No, Captain Jeff. I was in English class at the university in Jordan, and they pulled me out and said, 'You are going to work with the Americans,'" Sayid explained. "I am Kurdish, and I will fight like one," he said.

"Holy shit, bro," Chris said after a quick survey of the map. "We have to clear twenty-six miles of ridgeline tonight."

"Marathon op," I responded, feeling how exhausted I already was. My Peshmerga uniform was still covered in dry, caked puke. I could hide my physical exhaustion well enough, but I had to admit to myself that I was already running on fumes. As we walked, I just kept repeating the same phrase in my mind: One more step.

We trekked in silence. The only thing we could hear was heavy breathing interspersed with the sound of boots crunching hard sand. I started to think about Dostoevsky again, but I couldn't concentrate enough to come up with an intelligent answer to my question. I started digging deep for fuel. I remembered working at the Station 21 Fire Department in the South Bronx as a paramedic as part of my 18 Delta training. I thought about the Twin Towers going down and how the majority of the people who had mentored me at Station 21 had died. Every time I felt fatigue start to set in, I dug deep for more fuel. I made a choice to intentionally let distracting thoughts go and focus on what was at hand. I refused to let fatigue make me a coward.

After an hour, we reached a predesignated intersection linkup point and met up with a group of Peshmerga soldiers standing around smoking. We signaled them with our red flashlight. They signaled back with the appropriate signal, and soon we were in a Land Rover Defender headed to their base, where they cheerily informed us through Sayid that their captain had prepared a feast in our honor. Great, I thought. But I hadn't come to this hellhole for a feast.

We started off into the desert, our Kurdish driver flicking on the truck's headlights. Chris I quickly and violently protested.

"We cannot see in the dark. We need to turn the lights on!" the driver shouted to Sayid to translate. The rest of the Kurds in the front exclaimed their agreement.

"If you keep the lights on, you dumbasses, then the enemy can easily see us. Turn the goddamn lights off. This isn't a debate," I ordered. Finally, the light bulbs in their heads went on, and the headlights went off.

We soon arrived at the base of the mountain holding the Kurdish camp. Twenty white Toyota Hilux pickup trucks with mounted machine guns were parked around the commander's tent, which was prominently displayed and illuminated in the center of the camp.

There was quite a bit of commotion as we pulled up.

"Sayid, what's going on?" I asked.

"Sir Jeff, they are asking why our headlights are off," Sayid explained.

"Sayid, stop right there. Tell them to shut up and bring out the commander."

The Kurdish commander walked out, and I stopped him in his tracks.

"Sayid, translate this: Captain Hayman, I have heard great things about you and your men. Unfortunately, we don't have time for a feast right now. I appreciate the offer, but we have until sunrise to cover twenty-six miles of ridgeline, and we don't have a moment to spare."

Captain Hayman then walked over to me and kissed me on both cheeks. He got right in my face and said, "Captain Jeff, your safety in this mission is paramount. I will be killed if you or your friend are injured."

He was serious. The uncomfortable kiss combined with the invasion of my personal space forced me to take a step back.

"You better make sure we are not injured, then," I told him. Again, I decided against correcting his assumption that I was a captain. It was better he thought I was an officer instead of not respecting me because I was an NCO.

Captain Hayman shouted at his men, and they all started moving in formation. We left the base in a single hundred-man Ranger file and marched straight up the mountain. I was completely exhausted by the first step.

"Don't stop when you're tired. Stop when you're done," I reminded myself.

We paused about thirty minutes in, and I pulled out my canteen for a drink. I looked up and saw a hundred thirsty Kurdish soldiers staring me down.

"What?" I asked.

"Sir Jeff, they are thirsty."

"Well, tell them to drink water."

"Sir Jeff, they have none."

"Are you telling me that they left on this twenty-six-mile foot patrol up this mountain with no water?"

"Sir Jeff, yes."

Chris and I offered our canteens and Nalgene bottles. The Kurds passed them around. We were out of water by mile five. I was struggling physically, but I didn't want the Kurds to see any weakness from me. Chris and I resolved to fight through the pain and exhaustion and complete the mission.

So we trekked. And trekked. Up and down. Up and down. Climbing mountain after mountain. I just kept telling myself, one more step.

We stopped at every stream and filled our canteens and Nalgene bottles. The Kurds would just shove their faces in the stream. Chris and I would fill our canteens and pop a few iodine tablets in to kill any bacteria.

As we moved up to the ridgeline toward the enemy positions, we prepared to see the aftermath of our AC-130 bombing run the prior night. There were a few dead bodies, but what stuck out to me were the body parts: arms and legs strewn about the mountainside like some sort of horrific amusement park. Every now and again, I'd see a head. The heads were fascinating to me. I thought, "That's the face of the enemy. That was the guy who wanted to kill me."

BOOM!

"Get down, get down!" I shouted. It sounded as if we were taking indirect fire. "What happened? Sayid, find Hayman and get me a SITREP (situation report)!"

"Sir Jeff, Captain Hayman says that we are surrounded by mines, and one of his men just stepped on one."

I ran up to the Kurdish soldier who had stepped on the mine. His leg was blown off. I flashed back to the Q Course, back to my training. He had a femoral artery compromise. I couldn't let his artery recede into his hip cavity. He screamed when I stuck my hand in his leg and wouldn't stop. I punched him in the face to shut him up. He didn't shut up. Even so, I got four fingers up into his leg and was able to find and tie a knot around his femoral artery with some 550-cord string.

"Sayid, tell those two Kurds to come here! I need them to take him down the mountain for help."

The two Kurd volunteers were more than happy to oblige my orders. They fashioned a makeshift gurney out of some sticks and a jacket and headed down the mountain.

We pushed forward. One more step, I continually reminded myself.

BOOM!

Another Kurdish soldier stepped on a landmine.

BOOM!

Another.

Chris and I began to treat each injured Kurd. We got into a routine. Slap on a tourniquet. Stop the bleeding. Send the guy down the mountain. All in all, eight Kurdish soldiers ended up stepping on landmines. I continued to operate on full autopilot, falling back on my training. Thank God I had sweated so much in training, I thought; it saved not only me but several Kurdish soldiers from bleeding out on this night.

When we finally arrived at the designated ridgeline on the Iraq/Iran border, my legs were numb. But there was no time to rest. We immediately started to receive small-arms fire.

"Chris, grab those Kurds behind you and follow me!" Seven Kurds followed us as we assaulted one of the dug-in positions from where the enemy was firing at us. From his position, Captain Hayman saw us running, and he sprinted through the entire open area and enemy gunfire to link up with us.

The sporadic gunfire we received ended up being from two half-dead battle-hardened Iraqi NCOs. We sent them to Valhalla and proceeded to clear the six artillery pieces on the ridgeline. We took note that those heavy weapons were aimed directly at our staging area.

Chris grabbed the radio and notified our captain of mission success. He ordered us to send our small, unmanned drone over the ridgeline to check for remaining enemy forces. The drone was immediately shot down. There was clearly still work to do.

We slowly took the remaining Kurds down the other side of the mountains. As we climbed down, we spotted enemy fighters digging in. I told Chris to take out his sniper rifle, and I began spotting for him.

He fired the weapon, and one of the enemy fighters dropped. The other fighters in the group froze. Chris took aim and fired again. Headshot. Another one went down.

Chaos. The enemy fighters dispersed in all directions. Chris was able to tag another one in his back, dropping him.

"We are going into that town. Get the Kurds," I ordered.

We directed the Kurds to set up a cordon and started moving through the city. The first house we entered looked like some sort of political building—possibly the mayor's office.

The Kurds entered first. Chris and I followed.

"Jeff, bottom floor clear. I am moving up the stairs," Chris relayed to me over his MBITR (Multiband Inter/Intra Team Radio) radio.

Something felt off. "Chris, cease movement." I quickly moved to Chris's location and opened a closet door. I saw an artillery round hanging on a quick-release string. I motioned for Chris to come over.

"Dude, three more steps and we would have all been dead."

We dismantled the bomb and continued clearing the house. I thought, "This is the wakeup call. This is what I have to look forward to for the next year."

I accidentally knocked a picture of an Arab emir off the wall. Turned out the picture was hiding a perfectly square hole, big enough for a man to fit through. We discovered a forty-foot tunnel with a light at the end of it. This is what nightmares are made of.

The hole smelled like death. A distinct copper-blood smell combined with excrement, sweat, and cigarettes. I took off my body armor and pulled out my pistol and tac-light. I took a deep breath and slowly blew it out in an attempt to slow my heart rate. Here we go.

Chris helped me fit through the hole, and I started low crawling through the tunnel. No sounds reached me from the other end, which made me feel a little better.

My mind started to wander. What the hell have I gone through today? When was I the closest to dying? Was it on the plane? The mines? The ridgeline? Crawling through this tunnel? I couldn't really say.

When I got to the end of the tunnel, I took a deep breath. Hopefully there was nothing in there that would try to kill me. I stuck my two hands and head out the hole, frantically scanning the room for any sign of enemy activity. Seeing none, I next searched for booby traps.

Clear.

I squeezed out and fell six feet to the floor.

I leaned my back against the wall and squatted. With my right hand on my pistol and my left hand crossed over it holding my tac-light, I scanned the room again. It was poorly lit, but I could make out black Islamic flags and several hooks attached to chains hanging from the ceiling. Cigarette butts littered the floor. A poorly made wooden table with newspapers spread across it leaned against a wall. The table was flanked on each side by small wooden chairs. I noticed streaks on the floor and ceiling. Upon closer inspection, I confirmed the marks were bloody handprints and footprints. There were bomb-making parts and children's dolls.

It was a torture cell.

I walked through the main room and found four tiny cells. Each was the size of a porta potty with a hole in the ground. Feces had been smeared all over the floors of the cells.

People clearly had died in here. What a miserable way to go. I wondered what was going through their minds when they were tortured to death. Did they know they were about to die, or did they have hope? If they did know they were going to die, what were they thinking?

I looked closer at the bloody prints on the wall. Fingernails were stuck in it, as though someone had been trying to claw free. I examined the ground. The tac-light gleamed off human teeth sprinkled among the dirt and pebbles.

"Jeff!" Chris called out through the hole. His voice seemed distant.

The noise startled me, and I pointed my pistol and tac-light toward the sound.

"Do you need me to come in there?" he yelled, but this time it was difficult to hear him.

"No, I'm good. I'm going to conduct a little SSE and get back," I shouted.

"Yeah man, let's speed this up, Captain Hayman was just on the radio, and he is reporting sporadic gunfire on the backside of the town," Chris told me.

I quickly conducted SSE and took pictures of everything I thought was important. There was no paperwork or electronics. I didn't see anything of immediate value to take, so I pulled one of the wooden chairs over to the wall and stood on it to crawl back into the hole. Before hoisting myself in, I dropped a chemlight to ensure that the enemy and future coalition forces would know we had been there. As I hopped off the chair and into the hole, the chair splintered and broke. I kicked my feet against the wall, slid through the hole, and low crawled back to the entrance.

I crawled out the other side and fell to the floor.

"Chris, get me a cigarette, bro."

He pulled out a box of Camels, and I grabbed a smoke. Chris lit the cigarette, and I took a nice long drag as I sat on the floor with my back against the wall.

"What did you see in there?" Chris asked.

"Fucking torture cell. Bloody handprints and footprints all over the wall," I stated matter-of-factly, blowing out a long puff of smoke. "Take a look at the pics."

"I'll have to look later, bro. Captain Hayman is losing his shit. We need to get to his location," Chris said, pulling me up from the ground. We exited the house and ran out into the street with some of the Peshmerga and Sayid.

As we ran, Captain Hayman approached us. He told Sayid to tell us that they had found more artillery pieces and had taken some prisoners.

"That's great. Sayid, take us to them," I told him.

The Kurdish soldiers led us through the town. Sure enough, a line of cannons and rockets were spread out in the sand. Bird cages, most of them with chirping birds still inside, sat next to each cannon.

"What are the bird cages for?" Chris asked.

"Detecting chemicals," I answered. "If one of their chemical artillery rounds starts leaking gas, the birds will let them know."

"How? Like the birds chirp or something?" he said.

"No, dude. They die. If the birds start dying, then you know you have a chemical problem."

I made the call to end the mission and motioned Captain Hayman to come over to me. "Captain Hayman, let's get back to your base. Your feast sounds pretty damn good right about now," I told him. Soon, we loaded into his Toyota Hilux trucks and left the objective. My first combat experience, and I had made it.

As I sat in the passenger side of the truck, my mind began to again turn toward Dostoevsky. I had stared death in the face in the last twenty-four hours. What did I think during that time? Did I find out what I valued most?

I turned back to Jason, finishing my story. He was digesting every word.

"Damn, Jeff. That's an incredible experience. I see why the major wanted me to speak with you. My mind is still trying to process everything you just told me," he said.

Chris spoke up. "Jeff, you never told me anything about that Dostoevsky stuff. What did you finally think about?"

I sank into deep reflection. I had been disappointed in myself until realizing that a thought never came to me because I never really thought there was any chance I would die. All I had really thought about was taking the next step.

"What the hell is wrong with you?" Chris asked with a look of admiration after I answered.

"What the hell *is* wrong with me?" I said. "A lot of people ask me that."

"Whatever it is, it makes you damn good at your job," Jason responded.

SOF to Science with Nate Last, Mental Science Officer

Nate has a master's degree in exercise and sport science with a specialization in the psychosocial aspects of sport from the University of Utah. He works as a mental performance trainer in private practice alongside youth sport programs, athlete development programs, and corporations to facilitate the development of elite performers. Nate is also a competitive triathlete.

We live in a world saturated with distractions and constant demands for our attention. Our personal and professional lives seem to be ruled by digital devices, social media, a twenty-four-hour news cycle, and the demands of other people. When we're in control of our attention, our focus is where it needs to be, when it needs to be there. These are the times when we're "switched on" by being present, positive, and productive. This is the "real" version of your best self. In contrast, the fake version is when you're distracted and your attention is directed toward negativity, criticism, comparison, and debilitative self-talk. It's in these times that we lose control of our mind's capabilities and attach ourselves to ineffective thoughts, emotions, and the uncontrollable, which keep us from a mission-focused mindscape.

As you read Jeff's story, you can see him executing a shift in his attention to stay focused on mission-critical and controllable tasks through countless distractions. Jeff is not only observant and aware of where his attention is at any given moment, a skill we call "being the spotter," but he is also able to orient his internal and external attention by shifting his focus to where it needs to be, when it needs to be there (Tolle & OverDrive Inc., 2010). Jeff does this by making a decision in the moment and acting and reacting according to the demands of each situation he encounters. The process that Jeff has come to master, that anyone can learn, is known as the Observe-Orient-Decide-Act (OODA) loop.

The OODA loop is a term developed by former air force colonel John Boyd to describe the reactions of fighter pilots in the Korean War. The goal for pilots was to both understand their own OODA loops and those of their adversaries. This is a transferable skill that can be applied to everyday situations in both personal and professional performance arenas.

The OODA loop is traditionally applied toward human reactions to external stimuli in a dynamic environment. However, the concept can be applied within our dynamic mental environment as well. We call this mental environment "the mindscape," and in this section, we are going to focus on utilizing this process to help you develop and practice an effective performance mindscape within a variety of Volatile-Uncertain-Complex-Ambiguous (VUCA) conditions and operating environments.

There are two common misconceptions regarding mental strength.

The first misconception is that the attentional aspect of mental performance is some ethereal and complex thing that cannot be controlled or harnessed and learned. Over one hundred years of behavioral science research and application suggests this is untrue. Just like physical skills, mental skills such as attention control require intentional and deliberate training through practice and quality repetition over time. In other words, mental skills are learned behaviors. Attention control training can be done anywhere, at any time, and it doesn't require any equipment or a gym. The reality is, controlling your attention is easy. It just takes a little bit of understanding of how your mind functions, and then a lot of work with quality practice within the process described below.

The second misconception is that our mind-set and mental state, which are conscious and unconscious patterns of thinking, are the by-product of environment, birthright (e.g. genes), or circumstance rather than our personal responsibility. If you are to develop any kind of mental strength, you will need to take responsibility for and own your mindscape, no matter what state you find it in. Our mindscape is our choice.

Mindscape is defined as an individual's mental or psychological scene where we can observe our mental space. Notice how Jeff goes into his head at points in his story and observes his mindscape. His ability to be the "spotter" of his mind gives him the capacity to see and be aware of his attention, self-talk, imagery, and emotional response status. This awareness enables him to assess and make adjustments to that mindscape accordingly.

It's evident that Jeff executes an effective process of managing his mindscape through the application of his knowledge, experience, and skills. In other words, mental strength is not an outcome or achievement that he has obtained by accident. **Mental strength is a process he intentionally practices daily.**

When Jeff is faced with a new mission to destroy enemy field artillery along the ridge line, his initial mental reaction was one of worry and stress. In the moment, he put his attention and thinking behind the what-ifs: mistrust in his team and the consequences of failure.

"If we did not complete our mission, the other teams would be hit with heavy artillery……If Chris and I don't succeed in our mission, our brothers will be killed. I hope we can trust the Kurds. I hope they aren't going to shoot me in the back…"

This is the point where we tend to get stuck. An activating event starts a negative mental and/or emotional response, and if we're not in control of our attention, it's easy to not observe or catch it in the moment. The reaction just proliferates into a doom loop of harmful or unproductive thoughts and emotions that can dominate our mental space.

But as you previously read, Jeff executes some real mental toughness in these moments. He "spots" his mind and finds it's going in an unhelpful direction with an unproductive pattern of thinking. In this moment, Jeff orients his reality and then deliberately shifts his attention to the mission-critical and controllable aspects in front of him. In a split second, he observes his mindscape, orients his focus to what is important, makes a decision, and then acts on it.

Sometimes we can be afraid of what is happening in our own minds. When we observe our mindscape, we can see our personal inaction, negativity, debilitative self-talk, and ineffective focus. Sometimes we just can't accept it all. We judge our mental space and shame ourselves, then run from that place only to get trapped in a downward spiral. This cycle not only affects *us* negatively, but also the people we are around. This is yet another aspect of our development where we have the opportunity to get comfortable being uncomfortable.

It may be uncomfortable, but you need to master the skill of mindscape observation first. Observe what is happening in your head. Become the "spotter" of your own mind. Once you can execute this ability to observe, you will be met with a new ability: to orient and manage your mindscape (emotional response, self-talk, imagery) and choose where you want your attention to be.

So What?

The US Special Operations Forces provide opportunities in training to develop the skill of being a spotter and shorten their OODA loop. They deliberately put candidates in situations where they will react with negative thinking, debilitative self-talk, fear, anger, anxiety, and misplaced focus. Explosions, rigorous physical training, and sleep deprivation provide the perfect environment to observe, orient, decide, and act on the mission critical and controllable. They are able to get thousands of reps every week over years and years of elite training, effectively shortening their loops.

Although most people are not faced with life-and-death situations, we are faced with decisions that affect our livelihoods. VUCA conditions and operating environments are all around us in the workplace and at home, consisting of deadlines, screaming babies, and the frustrations and fears that come with relationships and love. These moments become the best opportunities to develop and apply an effective OODA loop. How many times can you flex that mental muscle and move through your loop? Once you do look at your mindscape in these situations you can acknowledge that space and give yourself the chance to shift that focus and attention to the mission critical and controllable.

Now What?

Optimal outcomes

Intentionally practice this approach as it applies to your mindscape with quality reps so you become unconsciously competent at it. Close the loop faster and more intuitively in VUCA situations so you don't have to deliberately engage and think about it. Anticipate and react accordingly, freeing up your attention for higher-order thinking and the next target.

The OODA loop applied

OBSERVE-ORIENT-DECIDE-ACT

- Observe your mindscape and become aware of your thoughts and surroundings.
- Orient your thoughts toward productive self-talk and belief statements. Put your attention in a helpful place.
- Decide on the most important choices: the mission critical and controllable.
- Act and react according to the situation. Remain agile and flexible to changes.

1. Observe

Choose one event where a negative mental response occurred.

Responses might include any of the following: pressure, volatility, chaos, distraction, discomfort, decision-making, ambiguity, anxiety, stress, anger, frustration, inaction, competition, review, feedback, leadership scenarios, and so on.

Take a moment to place yourself in the event. Walk through the process that typically occurs in your mind. What happens mentally? Observe the thoughts, feelings, emotions, self-talk, and imagery that come up. Write the scenario and each of your reactions down in sequence. I MEAN ALL OF IT (helpful and hurtful)! You must take this time to be honest with yourself.

2. Orient

Once you walk through the scenario a few times, look at each piece of the sequence objectively and write down what you know are more effective responses to helping you achieve your end state. You may not know the best response to everything, but start with what you do know. We are working to find your ideal performance mindscape.

3. Decide

There will be many courses of action that you can take to reach the place where you want to take your mind. Choose one and execute it to the best of your ability!

4. Act

Rise up. Move! Act accordingly!

5. LOOP IT!

These is where you get reps.

Professional tip: Set a timer to run on a thirty-minute loop to remind yourself to observe your mindscape.

Initially steps 1 and 2 will take time to truly feel confident. Your loop will be slow in the beginning, but the more you rep it, the faster it will get. It is OK to find yourself within a negative, debilitative, ineffective mindscape. However, it is not OK to stay there.

Practical Application with Jason Van Camp

Mental strength is a process that you must constantly work on to execute consistently. It's not an achievement or outcome. So how does one become mentally strong? As Nate Last points out, it doesn't just happen to you; it's a choice that you make. You must *decide* to be mentally strong. By choosing to take "one more step," you magnify your perseverance, determination, and tenacity until your goals become reality.

Jeff Adams's story showcases the power of mental strength in overcoming adversity. In the chapter, Jeff wants me to know how deep he had to dig mentally in order to successfully complete his first combat mission. Jeff explains his thought process:

"I thought back to Special Forces assessment and selection. Our instructors would tell us, 'Do not self-assess!' They were warning us to stop critiquing ourselves. When we start self-assessing, we let negative thoughts creep into our minds, and it causes us to doubt. If you start to question yourself, remember to doubt your doubts before you doubt your faith in yourself. At other times, self-assessing gives us a distorted view of reality. We think we are greater than we actually are. This distorted view of reality causes an identity crisis that has the potential to be catastrophic to your mental well-being. In order to overcome the self-assessments, you need a wingman, a battle buddy, to provide you blunt, honest feedback in a way that resonates best with you. You need the ground truth. And you aren't the one to give that to yourself."

As I discussed in chapter 1, self-assessing feels similar to watching game tape after each football game in college: "You never played as bad as you thought you did, nor did you play as well as you thought you did."

Stop judging yourself, stop self-assessing and try moving through the OODA loop. Observe your mindscape, orient to the controllable, decide, and act!

Here's why developing mental strength is important for your team:
- It builds a better person from the inside out.
- You are not going to be present 24-7. When you are not around,

you want your people to make good decisions. Mentally strong people make good decisions.

■ It provides a framework for dealing with inevitable adversity. Instead of walking away from a problem, they confront it. The bad days become fewer and fewer.

■ It increases aspirations. They aspire to be better than they are. They work hard to improve themselves and their team.

■ It decreases inefficiency and wasted time. The number of personal and sick days taken decreases because people want to come to work.

■ It develops tough skin. They don't take offense as easily and become distracted by lingering thoughts and regrets.

■ It increases recovery time. They put things in perspective, stay focused on individual and team goals, and recover more quickly.

In business and sports, you are constantly being told how important mental toughness is for individual and team success. The problem is, mental strength is often preached but rarely taught.

In the NFL, you are measured in every physical aptitude test imaginable. Unfortunately, those tests aren't always the best predictors of future success on the football field. We don't have a tool that can measure how strong your heart or your mind is. In order to *be* mentally strong, we need to learn from others who *are* mentally strong.

Chris Long is one of the strongest, most resilient people I know. Chris was drafted as the second overall pick in the 2008 NFL draft out of the University of Virginia. He ended up playing eleven years in the NFL for the Saint Louis Rams, New England Patriots, and Philadelphia Eagles, winning two Super Bowls. Chris retired from the NFL in June 2019.

While still playing in the NFL, Chris created the Chris Long Foundation. His foundation serves four philanthropic causes: military appreciation, homelessness, youth, and clean water. At his invitation, Chris and I spent a few weeks together in Tanzania supporting one of his nonprofit organizations, Water Boys. We helped provide clean water to local villages and schools and then climbed Mount Kilimanjaro to raise awareness for Water Boys. The more I got to know Chris, the more impressed I became. There are certain people you meet in life who you know are special. It's just something that they possess that separates them from the rest of the pack. Some people call it the "it" factor. Whatever "it" is, Chris Long has it.

Chris was voted the Walter Payton NFL Man of the Year in 2018 after he donated his entire year's salary, well over $1 million, to charity. In addition, while refusing to kneel during the national anthem, Chris still chose to support his teammates by demonstrating his respect for the social justice cause and supporting the fight for equality.

Chris explains, "I thought it was important that athletes with my skin color stood up for others protesting for racial equality." Even former president Barack Obama recognized and praised Chris for his incredible work.

But Chris had to put the work in to achieve the mental toughness that he attributes to his success both on and off the field:

"My dad (NFL Hall of Famer Howie Long) is who eventually made me mentally tough. I was raised with every opportunity available to me. I didn't want for anything. When I was thirteen, I wasn't tough…at all. In order to develop my mental toughness, my dad hired Ben D'Alessandro, a basketball player from Providence, to kind of break me. Ben had me run suicide sprints until I reached that breaking point. I would collapse and tear up, but was encouraged to keep going. So I did. I wasn't forced to keep going; it was my choice, and I credit those workouts to developing the mental toughness that I was able to lean on throughout my career.

When I got to the NFL, I thought I was mentally tough. The thing is, I had no idea what was in front of me. I was the number-two overall pick to the Saint Louis Rams in 2008. It's kind of like walking into carnage, going to one of the worst teams the year before and knowing that you are going to have to grind your way to a winning record. You hope that the team is just going through a transition period, but for me, that wasn't the case. We went 2–14 my first year and 1–15 my second. In total, in the eight years I was there, we won thirty-nine games. That's averaging fewer than five wins a year for eight years while never making the playoffs. The heart of my career, my prime, was spent losing. There were many times when I wondered if I was a failure.

I knew I had to choose to change my outlook. I was determined to make the most of whatever situation I was in. I made that choice. I'd look at it like this: adversity is an opportunity. If we were down by forty points in a game, I was determined to be the guy who jumped off film. I wanted to be the guy people watched and said, "Is that guy crazy? He's got nothing to play for. They're 2–13, and he's playing the last game of the year like it's the Super Bowl."

I learned that this mind-set could help me fight through injuries. I had a severe ankle injury that kept me out of practice for eight weeks, but I would shoot the ankle up and play every single Sunday. For me, I was in the mind-set of "This is opportunity talking to me. Let's see how tough this can get." I wanted to see how much I could overcome. When I took the field, I was always playing for the respect of my peers. I've found the best way to earn respect is to overcome adversity.

In 2014 and 2015, the injuries became too severe, and I was put on the injured reserve list. I had ankle surgery one year and then broke my tibia the next. I was in the prime of my career. This was a real crossroads for me. I was on the wrong side of thirty, had gone through two season-ending injuries, and had experienced eight years of consistent, painful losing. I thought, "This is it. I'm going to retire. I'm going to quit."

I was feeling sorry for myself until I went into the Rams' defensive line room. Coach Mike Waufle, an old marine turned pro football coach, had this cartoon picture on the wall. It was a picture of two guys mining for diamonds. These two guys are side by side. You can see their progress, and one of the miners is just hammering away. They are making this hole, and although they can't see it, the diamonds are just a few feet away. So close. One miner is sweating, and he just kind of turns around and says, "Fuck it." The other miner keeps going and reaches the diamond that was just three feet away. That cartoon, as silly as it might sound, helped me to look at my situation and realize that you never know how close you are to your breakthrough. If you quit now, you might never know how close you were to realizing your goals.

For me, that turned out to be prophetic.

I made a choice. I could retire and be comfortable, or I could face discomfort. I deliberately chose the uncomfortable. I told myself, I overcame so much adversity already, I'm not going to quit; each obstacle in my path is an opportunity to earn respect. I realized that I could not be what I wanted to be by remaining what (or where) I was. I mustered up one last little bit of courage to keep going and signed with the New England Patriots. That was when I experienced winning football games. I became a Super Bowl champion in my first year with the Patriots. The next year, I signed with the Philadelphia Eagles. I became a Super Bowl champion again. For me, that was the defining moment of my career.

With the Patriots and Eagles, I'd watch players and coaches struggling with a little bit of adversity like a loss or an injury and I'd say to myself, "Are you kidding me? You don't know what hard is. You don't know what mental toughness is. You don't know what 1–15 is. You don't know what it's like to be down by forty points on a regular basis." I had to recognize and appreciate how much mentally tougher I was having gone through the adversity in Saint Louis.

It can be easy to slip from keeping things simple and positive to getting in your own head and overthinking things. For me, the big stuff was always easier to overcome than the little stuff. The easy stuff was on Sunday—game days. The little stuff, the stuff that you would think is relatively unimportant—the nutrition, the workouts, the practices—was harder for me. The stuff that maybe you can cut corners on or cheat on a little bit. That was where it got hard respecting and overcoming the little stuff. It's easy not to quit on the big things. But the little things—we make a choice to quit those every single day, and that's often the difference between winning and losing.

I learned to embrace adversity. I learned that everything you do, big or small, matters. I learned how to do hard things—to train with intention and subscribe to the mentality that every little exercise is a big exercise. I learned to find meaning in everything that I did. I learned to deliberately choose discomfort. Anyone who makes that choice internally and dares, wins."

Like Jeff Adams, Chris executed a shift in his attention to stay focused on what he could control despite countless distractions and internal negative self-talk. Chris was then able to orient his internal and external attention and shift that attention to where it needed to be. Chris's message resonates tremendously with me: "Mental toughness is forged in the dark times. You have to fight when you already feel defeated. You have two choices when things get uncomfortable: you can either fight, or you can quit. Humans are creatures of habit. If you quit when things get tough, it gets that much easier to quit the next time. On the other hand, if you force yourself to push through a challenge, the strength begins to grow in you."

Mental strength is not something that we achieve; it's a process that we execute. It's a choice. Being aware of and acting on your mental mindscape is critical for succeeding on the battlefield of life.

Remember:

- Mental Strength is a process that needs to be practiced daily.
- Practice the Observe-Orient-Decide-Act (OODA) Loop.
  - Observe your mindscape and become AWARE.
  - Orient your thoughts toward the ideal. (Put your attention in a helpful place.)
  - Decide on the most important choices. (The mission critical and controllable.)
  - Act accordingly.
- Embrace doing what other people resent or are reluctant to do.
- Don't self-assess. Doubt your doubts before you doubt your faith.
- The best way to earn respect from your peers is to overcome adversity.

5 The Fog of War

with **Joe Serna**

Joe is a retired US Army Special Forces (Green Beret) noncommissioned officer. He has earned one Bronze Star with a V device, two additional Bronze Stars, and two Purple Hearts during three combat rotations in the Middle East. He earned his BS in both business and accounting from Methodist University.

My mind wandered as I finished breakfast in the chow hall with my team, lost in my own personal demons. I knew I wasn't doing well, but hell, I'm a survivor. I get up, every single day, and fight my demons.

Still, it was a welcome distraction when our team sergeant turned the volume up on the TV, calling out, "You think they could stop putting these so-called experts on the news with their doomsday scenarios of how the terrorists might attack us? Because you get the sense they're only giving them ideas."

The report was on one of our Blackhawks that had crashed the night before in Iraq. But CNN wasn't reporting the whole story. We knew what had really happened.

The Iraqi locals had reached the crash site before the coalition Quick Reactionary Forces and recovery team. The helicopter crew was all dead except for the pilot, who was alive but badly injured. When the Iraqis reached the helicopter, a mob of men, women, and children stripped the pilot naked and dragged him from the back of a truck to the only bridge in town. They put a noose around his neck and tied him to the edge of the bridge. They whipped him, castrated him, then pushed him off, leaving his body to hang in front of the whole town. These were the same people we had been sent to protect and deliver freedom to.

I had a hard time figuring out how to process this. I just wanted to drop a bomb on the whole country. A lot of the other guys did too. Except for our captain. He said that we needed to "see the big picture." I scoffed at that idea. All I saw was what was in front of me. That was my reality. A reality that said that somebody needed to answer for what had happened last night.

"Hey, Joe, some captain is here asking for you." One of my teammates, Ransom, an African American from Fresno, California, was standing next to an officer I had never seen before.

"Staff Sergeant Serna," he said to me, extending his hand. "My name is Captain Jason Van Camp. Major Petit told me I should speak with you. Do you have a few minutes?"

"Hey, sir. Yeah, the major told me to expect you. Happy to help any way I can. I've got some time before the team heads back to the team room. Anything for Major Petit."

"Great," he said, some nerves showing through. He was young, but I'd heard he was squared away. I'd give him the chance to prove it.

"I appreciate it. The major told me that you've been through a lot. I don't want to be out of line, but I'd love to hear about whatever experiences you feel comfortable sharing with me."

"Certainly, sir," I answered. "What exactly did the major tell you to ask me?"

Captain Van Camp's discomfort seemed to intensify. He cleared his throat. "He told me he considers you one of the guys who make up the backbone of this company. I'd like to find out what makes you tick, what your motivations are, and why Major Petit thinks so highly of you. I want you to tell me how I can be the best commander I can be."

"Want to know how to *really* get to know someone?" Ransom asked. Without waiting for a response, he shouted, "Stormy Waters!" at the top of his lungs. More than half of the chow hall immediately looked up and stared at Ransom.

"Yell out a porn star's name in a crowded room. The guys who look up know. They know you know. And that's all you need to know."

"Got it," the captain replied.

Ransom grinned, happy with his demonstration. "So why are you talking to this cholo, sir?"

I interrupted. "Because the major wants him to learn about leadership, not how to pick up fat chicks at Parrot Bay."

Ransom scoffed. "Joe, you know once you go black—"

"You're a single mom," I finished.

Ransom laughed at my joke, which we both noticed caught the captain a little off guard.

Ransom turned his attention directly to the captain and asked, "Hey, sir, there are no black people in Iraq. How will you know who to shoot at?"

Jason's eyes went wide with shock. "Whoa," he said. "I'm not racist. And I don't tolerate racism either."

"Sir, he's just messing with you," I said, putting Jason out of his misery. "First thing you need to learn: there's no such thing as too familiar or over the line when operating on a team in the Special Forces. We don't have time to be offended by anything. Lives are on the line. Are you uncomfortable with that? You better learn to deal with racism, sexism, and *especially* homophobia. Everything goes. We make a choice to let everything fly and let everything go. Nothing is off limits."

"Why *especially* homophobia?" the captain asked.

"Well, you are gay, aren't you?" Ransom asked. He and I laughed unrestrainedly. The captain started to smile slowly and then finally laughed as well.

Ransom's face suddenly went serious. "Racism will always exist as long as people identify themselves by a race. Do you know how many times they called me a nigger when I first got to the team? Yeah, it bothered me a lot at first. I wanted to fight everyone. I felt disrespected. When the guys on my team saw that it bothered me, they said it even more. I got even more mad. It took a while for me to realize that I was letting them win. I was choosing to let them get to me. I was showing weakness. In the wild, sharks smell blood. Strong animals attack weak animals. C'mon, man. You learn this shit in kindergarten. If you show weakness, the other kids are going to attack you. That's unfortunately built into our human DNA. We've got to learn to stop arming our enemies. I was giving them a weapon. A weapon to use whenever they felt like hurting me or getting a reaction out of me.

"When I stopped caring, they stopped caring. They stopped calling me nigger. They weren't doing it because they were racist. They were doing it to test me. To test my mental fortitude. Was I going to let things get to me that didn't really matter? Let them affect my performance? It's about having the emotional dexterity to overcome those challenges. It's about not being offended, not being soft or weak or sensitive. It's about making friends out of your enemies. It's about getting comfortable being uncomfortable.

"Listen, I can't control anyone else but me. I can't control what other people say and do. I can only control how I react. My reaction is my strength."

The three of us took seats in a corner booth, and I could see the wheels turning in Jason's head. But it was Ransom's turn to aim the spotlight elsewhere.

"So the major wants you to learn about Joe's Mexican leadership, huh?" he asked. "First thing you need to learn is how to stop a Mexican tank."

Jason laughed "How's that?" he asked.

"Shoot the people pushing it."

I shook my head in disappointment. I knew he had better jokes than that. "Sir, enough from this non-swimmer. If you really want to learn something from my experiences, I'm going to have to get uncomfortable. I don't like being vulnerable, but if it's going to help one of our brothers become a better leader, I have no problem with it." I meant every word. "Let me ask you this. Ever been hit by an IED (improvised explosive device)?"

Jason shook his head. "No," he replied.

"I've survived a few. And some other things. That's the thing about me. I just…survive. Somehow," I said philosophically.

He looked at me curiously and asked I what I meant. I could tell he didn't want to trigger anything but was genuinely interested.

"Well, sir, during our last deployment, we lost some guys, some of the best. Somehow, I ended up surviving," I said quietly. I felt myself drift back to Afghanistan.

"We got word on the radio that one of our sister ODAs had a team member step on a landmine. As they were transporting the body back to Kandahar, the vehicle got stuck. Our team scrambled to assist. We threw on our body armor, helmets and shemaghs, slung our weapons, and raced to our vehicles. In preparation for movement, I started conducting commo checks on the radios in my RG-31 (a mine-resistant light armored vehicle), while our team sergeant took position in the passenger's seat. James, one of our senior weapons sergeants, jumped in the back with me, while Seth drove. The rest of the team found their positions in the remaining two RG-31 vehicles, and we rolled out.

It was dusk by the time we left the wire, so we drove under blackout lights with our night-vision goggles on. Despite the worry of hitting an IED, the convoy sped down a hard-balled dirt road toward our sister ODA's location. My vehicle was last in the convoy.

After about an hour, we began to slow down. I looked to our east and could make out headlights about three hundred meters off the road. It was our sister ODA. The plan was for us to provide cover while a wrecker towed their vehicle back to the FOB (forward-operating base). There had been no enemy ambush or counterattack, so we felt like the area was relatively secure for the vehicle recovery. The only issue was a deep, muddy creek running parallel between their location and ours.

We tried to figure out the best route to reach them. One of the other drivers spotted a well-constructed concrete aqueduct about a mile up the road. A pipe gushed dirty water into it from beneath a small bridge. The lead vehicle radioed that we would attempt to cross the embankment there.

The convoy followed a small dirt road to the aqueduct. The aqueduct was about twenty feet across and seven feet deep with water moving swiftly, fed from the open pipe. We had our doubts that we could make it across, but one by one, each RG-31 before us made it up the hill. Then it was our turn.

Once we started driving up the far bank, we realized we were in a terrible position. The dirt kicked up, browning us out under our night vision. We were completely blind.

As we slowly headed up the hill, I felt the front of the RG-31 give way. The road started to crumble beneath our truck. I was sitting with my back against the left shell of the vehicle, facing the middle. I was strapped in by a five-point release seat belt, in full kit, my pistol on my vest.

The RG-31 jerked left, causing the front left tire to slip. Up front I could see the silhouettes of Seth and the team sergeant. They were trying to shift their weight to the right of the vehicle to counterbalance the slide.

"What the hell?" I shouted, feeling us slide backward down the aqueduct embankment. Of all the places to slip, this was the worst.

The truck kept leaning farther and farther over, slowly tipping to one side. To make matters worse, everything in the truck started shifting to the left. We tried to brace ourselves, but ammo cans broke off their racks and equipment fell all over us.

"Brace for impact!" our team sergeant yelled.

Our truck flipped over, sending us back down the embankment. We smashed into the water on the side of the truck where I was sitting. An ammo can that had broken from its cargo strap hit me in the face, knocking me out cold.

When I woke, there was water on the top of my head and in my ears. I realized the vehicle was on its side in the aqueduct, and I was still strapped in. I started frantically pushing everything off me in an attempt to get to my seat belt. But I had so much gear covering me that I couldn't find the five-point release. I was stuck and getting frustrated. The water crept higher. By the time it reached my neck, I was starting to panic. I raised my head and shouted, "Hey, I need help! I can't get my seat belt off!"

Soon, the water touched my chin. From up front I heard the team sergeant yell, "James, help Joe!"

Suddenly, my entire head was submerged. I was completely underwater. Next to me, I could feel James reaching all over my chest, searching for the seat belt release.

I heard a click from the seat belt release, and suddenly I was free. I gasped for air and reached for James to lift me out of the water. I was able to get a deep breath, but any relief was short lived. As soon as he raised me up, the RG-31 flipped over. We were now completely upside down in the aqueduct.

At the same moment, the electricity in the truck went out. We had lost all power. No radios, no hydraulics, no lights. It was pitch black inside the vehicle.

James pulled me up and frantically looked around. "Dude," he said. "This is not good."

The only door—our only exit—was in the rear of the truck. It weighed at least six hundred pounds and opened with hydraulics. Of course, hydraulics require electricity.

We tried to open the door manually. I contorted myself upside down, trying to figure this damn door out. The water was freezing. It continued to rush in and was now up to my knees. I couldn't budge the door. I looked for something to hit it with. We found a hammer and a crowbar and hit the lock as hard as we could. It didn't budge. As we struggled to open the door, we realized the water had reached chest level. I couldn't actually see it rising because of the darkness, but I could feel it, which was terrifying.

"James, James, I don't know how you're going to find one, but I need a flashlight," I called out urgently.

James dove under the water. I couldn't see him, but I heard a splash, then silence. I had no idea how long he was gone, but it seemed like forever. Just when I began to think he wasn't going to make it back, he rose from the water with a helmet that had a flashlight attached to it.

I took the helmet from him and plunged underwater to look at the doors. Even with the light, nothing was visible but brown, muddy water. I was able to find the latch but couldn't budge the door before needing to come up for air. When I reemerged, the water was all the way up to my neck.

I was beginning to accept the situation.

"Bro, I can't go back down," I said. "If I go down, I don't know if there will be any air left when I come back up. It might be my last breath."

James said, "We need you to open that door, man."

I had to find the inner strength, the courage—*something* to drive my will to survive. I quickly realized what it was. *My family*. I had to survive for them. I decided that if this was my last breath on this earthly world, it would be used to go down fighting.

Just as I was thinking that, James said, "Joe, I can't feel my legs."

I wanted to be positive for my teammate, so I said, "Hang in there, bro. The water is going to stop rising."

But in my mind, I knew we were fucked. There was only a sliver of air left in the truck.

I looked over at James. Both of our heads were thrown back, eyes staring upward, our mouths kissing the metal at the top of the vehicle, which was really the floor. My eyes were almost covered with water. I took small breaths, exhaling tiny amounts of air. Although I could not see him clearly, I could make out James and his struggle in my peripheral. I heard him take his last breath and go under.

My mouth remained open, letting out small amounts of air through my esophagus. I was trying to buy as much time as I could before I went under too. I knew my team had to be doing everything they could on the outside, but I couldn't help but get pissed. "What the hell is taking them so long?" I wanted to scream.

My legs started to go numb. My lips did the same. I sucked what little oxygen was left and tried to relax. Any attempt at calm was interrupted by a nasty sound.

"Pop, pop, pop."

I noticed air bubbles popping all around my limited air space. The water smelled of diesel fuel. I started coughing and choking on the fumes. The fuel cans on the bottom of the vehicle must have broken and were now leaking diesel into the vehicle.

With my remaining air, I was inhaling those fumes.

I began to panic. My brain stopped working, going straight into survival mode. Throughout my entire life, I knew there were two ways I didn't want to die: drowning or burning. I couldn't go out this way, drowning without being able to do anything about it. I didn't want to suffer. I had always thought that if I was facing certain death and could get it over quickly, I would take that option.

I resolved to kill myself.

I stopped fighting and pushed myself down in the water. I reached for the pistol strapped to the front of my kit and pushed it against my forehead. I locked the hammer back, placed my finger on the trigger, and anticipated the gunshot that would end my life.

In that brief moment, I thought, "Do I have the courage to do this? If I love life so much, how can I pull that trigger?" Usually when people do this, they have already made their choice to end their life. In that moment, I realized how much I loved life. I looked forward to waking up each and every day. I enjoyed working hard so that my kids would have a better future. I looked forward to witnessing their milestones—the first steps, graduations, walking my daughters down the aisle one day. I was happy. Did I have the strength to blow my head off?

With the few seconds I had left, I made a decision. I let go of the helmet still clasped in my left hand. I watched its light softly diminish as it descended to the bottom of the RG-31. With my right hand, I lowered the gun. Once it got to my chest, I loosened my grip, dropping it. The gun felt like an enormous weight slipping away. I could barely make it out spinning to the bottom of the freezing brown water. The light from the helmet cast a dark shadow as the gun circled below. It was powerful and dramatic watching the pistol slowly rotate in the freezing water of the aqueduct, finally hitting bottom.

With all physical elements out of my control, I tried to accept whatever the outcome would be while praying for a better one. I told myself, "I'm going to make peace with the Lord, and then I'll be ready."

My body was still contorted in an awkward posture: torso arched forward, limbs flowing backward, my eyes gazing straight up to the floor of the RG-31. The water had completely filled the truck.

I started to make my peace. It was time for my last breath.

My heart pounded out of my chest. I slipped underneath the surface, completely submerged. It was a calm, peaceful sensation. I told myself that if I kept moving, I'd waste energy. So I stopped and prayed.

Instinctively, I began to flail my arms and legs desperately. My lungs were on fire. I gasped for air and in doing so inhaled the cold, dirty water. My mind was taken over by base, animalistic instincts. I had to survive. I spun around and around. There had to be a way out. But there wasn't. In my desperation, my body went limp, and all effort ceased. I just let go and floated in the water for a few seconds. Then I blacked out.

Suddenly, a burst of energy filled me. The will to get out of this predicament reemerged, along with the desperate flailing. I kicked my legs up to the top of the RG-31, even though I knew there was no longer room for air. I pounded my fists against the metal. It was hopeless. Soon all strength left me once again. My pounding grew weaker and weaker.

I don't remember the moment it happened, but once more I blacked out. The last thing I remember was feeling my body convulsing. When I regained consciousness, I wasn't in the vehicle anymore. I wasn't sure where I was, but my instincts told me it was a bad place. A sudden horrifying thought: "Am I in hell?"

It was hard to remember what had happened, how I had gotten there, but I forced myself to think. I remembered being in the RG-31, I remembered drowning. I accepted it—I was dead.

It was as if I were floating in outer space. It was cold and empty, and I was alone. As I floated, I felt something grab at my legs. I was too afraid to look down and see what it was, but I fought it. I kicked and fought to escape whatever it was.

A loud sound jarred me back to consciousness. I found myself still in the RG-31, completely under water, but my lungs were no longer burning. I thought, "How the hell am I still alive?"

My body shuddered. Then I blacked out again. I returned to the same place as before—outer space. I looked around, trying to assess the situation. With a renewed confidence, I resolved to pay more attention and not be afraid. In the distance, I could see a glowing orange ball. Slowly, as if by a powerful unseen force, I was being pulled in the direction of the little ball. I looked around and saw Earth to my right. As I floated closer to the orange ball, Earth got smaller and smaller. My velocity increased. I was moving faster.

In the silence of this cold place, I heard a deep voice with an ugly laugh. The voice said one word loudly: "FONG." I didn't know what it meant, but that word—*FONG*—kept repeating maniacally and cruelly. The more it was said, the more terrified I became.

I felt something grab my leg. Again, I tried to kick it away. But this time I was caught, and it was dragging me back to Earth. I felt like I was being dragged to hell.

A loud clang reached me, giving me comfort rather than fear. I couldn't tell where it had originated, but it wasn't from the alternate world in which I was hovering. I woke. It was the wrecker pulling my RG-31 out of the aqueduct.

My lungs were on fire. The rest of my body was numb and frozen. I was still fully immersed in water. For some reason I kicked my legs, propelling myself upward. The RG-31 was rising slowly, the water beginning to drain. As I propelled myself upward, a pocket of air appeared, and I opened my mouth to greedily suck it in.

I wasn't sure if I was alive. I struggled to find my bearings, still disoriented on diesel fumes. My head was pounding, my eyes exploding out of my head. I couldn't stop coughing and vomiting brown water.

One thought came to me: What had happened to my teammates?

As the water began to drain from the vehicle, I was able to get my feet on the ground. In a daze, I looked for James in the truck. There he was, lying on his stomach under the water. I grabbed him by the shoulders and pulled him out. As I held him out of the water, lights flashed against our waxen faces.

My brain still wasn't processing what was going on. I knew something was happening, but wasn't sure what. Slowly, I waded toward the lights. I found myself at the back door of the RG-31, my teammates shining their flashlights at me through the back-door window.

"Cholo! Cholo! Open up the door, man!"

I didn't understand. Nothing was clicking for me. I was completely confused and disoriented. I opened the small portal window on the door. One of my teammates, Nate, aggressively reached through the door window and grabbed me and pulled me to the window. "Breathe, Cholo!" he shouted.

I stuck my face out of the window as far as I could, my nose and mouth protruding, and took a deep breath. Suddenly, the lights came back on. I fell back inside the RG-31 and frantically tried to open the door. As soon as I unhitched the lock, the door swung open from the outside, and Nate pulled me out. Jeff went in and grabbed James. They dragged James out of the RG-31 and laid him on the small dirt road paralleling the aqueduct and began CPR.

I sat on the ground in my drenched uniform. I felt sick to my stomach. Every ten seconds or so I would vomit water, hitting my chest and the crotch of my pants.

"How long were we in the water?" I asked, shivering violently.

Ransom stood near me, pulling security. He looked over and said, "Forty minutes, bro. The worst forty minutes of my life."

I looked to the side of the vehicle and saw three bodies. Jeff and the medics were working on them. "Ransom, are they going to make it?" I asked quietly.

"I don't know, man. You guys were in that aqueduct for a long time. How are *you* even alive?"

I tried to speak but couldn't control the chattering of my teeth. Didn't matter—I had no answer for him anyway. Nothing I tried to say made any sense. I began to shake even more violently. I was going into hypothermia. Ransom rushed to my side with a blanket and some extra clothes.

"Joe, get up!" he instructed. "Get out of those wet clothes."

I rose and began peeling off layers. Ransom kept telling me jokes to keep me engaged and moving.

"Joe, how many cops does it take to arrest a Mexican?" he asked. "Eight. One to handcuff him and the rest to carry his oranges."

The laughter made it easier to move. I wrapped myself in a blanket and tried to get warm. My body stopped trembling, and I paced between the vehicles. I still didn't know if my teammates were going to make it.

Ransom looked over at me. "Hey, Joe, let me ask you something. When you were about to die, when death was imminent, what did you think about?"

"Brother, in all honesty, I think I *was* dead," I exclaimed.

"Jeff has been asking me that question for a few weeks now. It's been on my mind. I don't know what I would really think about," Ransom said.

"My family," I answered. "I thought about my kids."

Up ahead, our captain sat in the lead vehicle, on the radio. I walked to his location, tremoring, blanket still tightly wrapped around my shoulders. I didn't want to interrupt, so I stood outside the passenger door of the RG-31 and listened. He held the hand mic to his ear with his left hand, leaning across the open door to put his right arm around me.

"Glad you're alive, Cholo," he said, then went back to relaying traffic. "Roger, we need two Blackhawks immediately for exfiltration," I heard him tell our higher headquarters.

"Break, break, break," came back the major's voice, interrupting the captain's communication. "Grim Reaper 6, I need a SITREP."

The captain responded, "We have three KIA, drowned, and need an air MEDEVAC to return the bodies to base."

I realized then that I was the sole survivor.

I stopped my story there and looked up at Jason and Ransom. Jason was watching me with wide eyes.

"Joe, thanks for telling me that," he said. "Thanks for getting uncomfortable and vulnerable with your story. Wow. I understand why the major wanted me to speak with you."

"Like I said, sir, if my experiences can help you become a better leader, I am all for helping."

It was Ransom's turn to speak up. "Hey, sir, ask Joe about the time the Afghan he was interrogating pulled out a grenade and detonated it on him. That was the first of his two Purple Hearts. Great story."

"Another time, Ransom. We need to roll," I said, standing with my breakfast tray. "I'll leave you with this, Captain. I honestly don't know why the major wanted you to talk with me. I'm weak. It's tough for me to deal with what I've—we've—been through. I'm doing the best I can, but it's hard. The only way I survive is with the support of my team."

"Joe, I'm guessing that's exactly why the major wanted me to talk with you. Because you have the strength and courage to admit that."

SOF to Science with Dr. Sarah Spradlin,
Chief Emotional Science Officer

Sarah is a United States Marine Corps veteran who served as the first female principal staff director at US Marine Corps Forces, Special Operations Command, MRTC. She holds a doctorate in business administration (DBA) specializing in industrial organizational psychology from Northcentral University, an MA in criminal justice with a concentration in narcotics investigations from American Military University, and a BS in psychology from Virginia Tech. She is a leading expert in the study and application of emotional intelligence.

The "fog of war" is a term used to describe the atmosphere in war that promotes confusion and uncertainty in your situational awareness, resulting in crippled decision-making and a lack of action. It is critical to understand the importance of managing emotional information in terms of our ability to influence an optimal outcome, even when facing insurmountable odds under impossibly stressful situations. The fog of war is the recognition of the constant level of uncertainty one faces during battle. It's that notion of working under the confines of organized (or disorganized) chaos as everything you thought you knew to be true begins to change…and then change again. It's the unexpected requirement to communicate when a significant event impacts your ability to hear, see, or speak. It's the resolution to comfort a dying teammate while your own safety is at risk. It's the emotional regulation and decision-making process that ensues after waking from a head wound only to find yourself physically confined by a five-point harness in a vehicle flooding with water and toxic air. In the midst of the fog of war, we learn that we must keep calm, objective, and in control of the barrage of emotional information we are experiencing. By doing so, we create a pathway for self, social, and situational awareness to flourish, leading to effective decision-making.

It is difficult to process Joe's incredible real-life experiences as he braves the catastrophic results of his RG-31 vehicle rolling over into an aqueduct. We discover that this battle-hardened Green Beret was exposed to the ultimate perils of a precarious environment—all while expertly navigating the embodiment of what we formally refer to as the fog of war. Yet, throughout all this uncertainty articulated above, it was Joe's perceived control that he was not helpless and that the situation was not hopeless that facilitated his ability to persevere during his extreme exposure to the fog of war. Joe's unprecedented ability to efficiently identify and effectively manage emotional information helped guide his thoughts and behaviors to influence an optimal outcome from situation to situation.

When chaos ensues, self-regulation and specifically emotional regulation must prevail. Whether you're entrenched in the fog of war on the battlefield like Joe or you're combating stress, uncertainty, or conflict in the workplace, it is the ability to efficiently identify and effectively manage emotional information that will build a foundation to help guide your thoughts and behaviors in an effort to influence an optimal outcome. The capacity to efficiently and effectively identify, assess, and manage emotional information is called emotional intelligence.

So What?

In today's competitive business climate, change is the only constant. The ability to navigate the fog of war and combat change in the workplace requires leaders capable of adapting to and overcoming emergent challenges. These emergent and often unexpected challenges present an onslaught of emotional information that requires attention and skillful management. Yet these challenges can be masterfully handled when emotional intelligence (EI) is deliberately applied.

EI is your ability to identify, assess, and manage your own emotional information, as well as the emotional information of others, so that you can appropriately use this emotional information to help guide your thoughts and ultimately your behaviors in an effort to influence an optimal outcome in any given situation. As we learned from Joe, EI creates a foundation to evolve self, social, and situational awareness through the constant assessment and management of emotional information.

Research indicates that considerable problems may arise when leaders, who do not possess the necessary EI required to successfully manage the complex, dynamic, and diverse nature of today's inter-connected business environment continue to operate without a functional knowledge of EI. A lack of EI among leaders may result in diminished team performance; weaken leader-member exchange; reduce customer satisfaction, trust and loyalty; and foster a low aptitude for stress management and employee productivity. Likewise, a lack of EI among organizational leaders may impede innovative thought, disrupt a positive organizational culture, and ultimately hinder the organization's strategic ability to maintain the competitive advantage during times of uncertainty.

On the contrary, leader EI is positively correlated with a myriad of human performance outcomes that characterize high-performing employees and transformational leaders. For example, individuals who possess a highly balanced level of EI tend to display strong strategic decision-making, problem-solving and coping skills, and they have a heightened capacity for managing occupational stress.

Furthermore, a wonderful aspect of EI is that it can be objectively measured and developed.

One way to develop and refine EI is to evolve your locus of control.

Locus of Control

Recall that throughout all the uncertainty Joe faced, it was his perceived control that he was not helpless, and the situation was not hopeless that facilitated his ability to persevere during his extreme exposure to the fog of war. Even when Joe was faced with the ultimate decision to take his own life, it was his decision not to drown. When he changed his mind, it was his decision to concede to a higher being. In science, this is called our locus of control.

As our environment changes, our emotions ignite, decisions are made, actions are taken, and perspectives take shape. As humans, we are hardwired to self-justify, so we instantly begin to categorize our thoughts, decisions, and actions as either successes or failures. In doing so, we attribute success and failure either to those things we have control over or to those external forces outside our scope of influence.

The position we choose is known as our "locus of control" (LC) (Lefcourt, 2014). If you maintain the position that outcomes are derived from your own thoughts, actions, and decisions and believe you maintain full control of your own success and failure, you maintain what is called an internal locus of control (ILC). You see yourself as the director in the movie that is your life.

If you maintain a position that everything is out of your control, external variables are to blame, things like luck influence outcomes, and you have little to no scope of influence over your own success and failure, you maintain what is called an external locus of control (ELC). You see yourself as an actor in the movie that is your life.

However, the concept of locus of control is not absolute, it falls along a spectrum.

Now What?

Identify Your Locus of Control

First, in order to develop a healthy LC, you need to identify where you fall along the LC spectrum.

Ask yourself:

- Where do I fall along the LC spectrum?
- What is my dominant position?

Most people tend to fall somewhere along that spectrum based on different variables—location, emotional state, situational requirements, past trauma, availability of social support networks, emotional intelligence, and so on. Yet we all present a dominant position. For example, Joe's dominant position is to maintain a moderately strong internal locus of control (Mentalhelp.net, 2019).

Joe recognizes he is at the helm of his ship—his steers the course for his own destiny while adapting and refining his skills when he validates external influencers that may impact his course. He works hard to develop his knowledge, skills, and abilities across a wide range of performance outcomes. He works to evolve his emotional intelligence, and he is open to constructive feedback in an effort to manage his continued success. Having a moderate rather than fully right-sided strong ILC may help you identify, accept, adapt, and effectively manage situations that you simply cannot influence. A moderately strong ILC helps train your brain to become resilient and persevere during times of uncertainty.

Evolve Your LC through Goal Setting Analysis

Once you've identified where you fall along the LC spectrum, write down a few goals you want to accomplish. Review each goal separately and consider what factors (i.e. people, money, time, focus, forgiveness, impulse control, etc.) contribute to your ability to accomplish each goal. Be honest with yourself. Write down anything and everything that comes to mind; the good, the bad, and the ugly. Then ask yourself the following questions:

- Who appears to be responsible for my success? Am I in control of my future success, or am I holding external forces responsible?
- How does my list of contributing factors impact a healthy ILC?
- If I maintain an overly high ILC, is there an opportunity to ask for help in order to create efficiencies?

Practice Impulse Control and Objectivity— Take the Lazy Susan Approach

Now that you've considered the tough questions about who's in control of your success, it's time to take the Lazy Susan approach. The Lazy Susan approach helps you practice impulse control and objectivity in terms of managing emotional information, leading to a healthier ILC and refined level of EI.

EI requires a level of impulse control and objectivity that helps prevent us from making reckless accusations and rash decisions. It also helps thwart impulsive thoughts and behaviors (such as negative self-talk or even suicide) that could prove detrimental in the long run. As we develop the capacity to refrain from impulsive behaviors and consider problems objectively, we inherently develop a healthier ILC and evolve our EI.

The Lazy Susan approach is a simple method for building a foundation for efficient yet objective decision-making. Essentially, a Lazy Susan is a rotating tray placed atop a table that you can spin around to distribute different items to different people located at various positions around a table. As you spin the Lazy Susan, your perspective of the items on the tray changes. With each small shift in position, you get a new look at the same tray. The ability to consciously consider different perspectives before taking action empowers you—the more information you consider, the better equipped you are to influence an optimal outcome that benefits all vested parties.

The next time you're faced with uncertainty or simply a tough decision that requires you to make haste, consider taking the Lazy Susan approach:

First, visualize the problem set atop a Lazy Susan.

Next, assess your perspective of the problem along with all the variables that play into your decision-making process (if you have time, write down your thoughts).

Now, make a concerted effort to take a tactical pause in your decision-making process and just breathe.

Next, begin to spin the problem around to assess it from other vested perspectives (i.e., your boss, your peers, your adversaries, or your family) before you take action (if you have time, write down your thoughts and identify trends—both positive and negative).

The more you practice objectivity using the Lazy Susan approach, the more efficient you can become in your ability to analyze alternate perspectives that may prevent you from making rash decisions or acting impulsively. For example, Joe showed us a highly balanced level of EI coupled with a healthy ILC, which provided a foundation to mitigate rash decision-making—it ultimately prevented him from pulling the trigger.

Even when Joe had only a nanosecond to consider alternate perspectives, his healthy ILC and highly balanced EI allowed him to efficiently employ the Lazy Susan approach in his decision-making process. Although he naturally considered his own perspective first by asking, "Do I have the courage to do this?" Joe immediately spun the problem around to consider other variables. He considered his children, his family, their future.

Although very few of us will ever experience the fog of war on the battlefield the way Joe did, we all experience stress, uncertainty, and the requirement to make hasty decisions in our professional and personal lives on a daily basis. The ability to navigate the fog of war and combat change in the workplace requires leaders capable of adapting to and overcoming emergent challenges. These emergent and often unexpected challenges present an onslaught of emotional information that requires attention and skillful management. Yet these challenges can be masterfully handled when EI is deliberately applied. Your ability to develop your EI by cultivating a healthy ILC and practicing impulse control and objectivity will place you at the helm of your ship and guide sustainable success during times of uncertainty.

Practical Application with Jason Van Camp

This chapter is about emotional dexterity—from both internal (within ourselves) and external (how others see us) perspectives. As we've learned so far, it's difficult to perform any task at a high level and ultimately be the best version of yourself when you're not in control of your thoughts and emotions. When stress is added to any situation, whether it's in business, sports, or life, allowing your emotions to control your behavior versus you controlling your emotions can lead to trouble. Your ability and willingness to control your thoughts, feelings, and identity is what we call emotional dexterity. This process doesn't happen automatically or by accident, nor can you expect yourself or others to flip a switch and be cool, calm, and collected under pressure.

Considering Joe Serna's experiences under one of the most stressful and terrifying situations imaginable, he did a remarkable job regulating himself. By controlling his emotions in the moment and staying relatively composed, he was able to survive. Joe gripped on to the factors within his locus of control—his attitude, behavior, and identity. Had he become hopeless and not taken a moment to self-reflect, Joe might have committed suicide. Had he panicked and let his emotions take control of his behaviors, he very likely would have wasted precious energy and air and then drowned before he could be rescued by his teammates.

The reality is that Joe's ability to survive this situation and then inspire others through his story started long before he got in that RG-31 or even deployed to Afghanistan. His identity and the perspective associated with it began long before he joined the army. Like shooting, moving, and communicating as a member of a Special Forces team, Joe deliberately practiced and trained how he thought, how he controlled his emotions in all situations, and who he really was as a man of character. Through this training, Joe became subconsciously competent at self-regulation and emotional dexterity. These skills are what kept Joe alive when others in that situation might have died a tragic death.

You can practice emotional dexterity by making a choice to:

- DECIDE who you are, what you believe in, and what you're all about;
- CHOOSE to think in effective ways that generate energy, optimism, and enthusiasm; and
- RECOGNIZE your emotional triggers and actively regulate yourself through productive self-talk and reaffirming belief statements.

One of the leaders Mission Six Zero has worked with is Brent Dial. Brent was a West Point football player, army infantry officer and Ranger, Wharton graduate, and division CFO at Anheuser-Busch. He is now an investor in San Francisco.

Brent explains, "Business is personal. Our position in an organization is personal. Our performance is personal. Thus negotiating changes in these dimensions always comes at a personal cost—particularly to our identity. One of the biggest stumbling blocks to effectively communicating with someone is navigating their identity—how they see themselves. Whether you raise a conflict with someone's performance, status, self-worth, or judgment, you need to take stock of how effectively you are addressing the needs of their identity and the emotions that come with it."

On the other end of the communication, one needs to examine the relationship between their actions, status or position, and identity. A more malleable view of identity can be helpful in moving past emotionally laden conflicts and changes.

For example:

You lose your job—get laid off, fired, retired. Your job wasn't your identity; it didn't define you; it was just something you did.

You experience a traumatic injury. That experience doesn't define you; it's something that happened to you.

You get a divorce. Your divorce isn't your identity; it's just something you went through.

Brent continues. "When I went to my twenty-year high school reunion, I thought, 'I am six people removed from who I was in high school.' These former classmates didn't know me when I was Brent Dial, 'the West Point cadet.' Or Brent Dial, 'the college football player.' They didn't know me when I was an officer leading men into combat. They didn't know me when I was Brent Dial, 'business development director traveling and meeting with government officials in Mexico, India, or the UAE.' They did not know me when I became a divisional CFO at Anheuser-Busch. They knew who I was in high school, but who I am now is not who I was in high school. In each transition my identity (i.e., my relationship to colleagues, work, family, friends) was changed in some way."

Even verbal racial assaults tend to hurt most those whose identities are concentrated or dependent on the distinction of race. Brent explains that one of the most emotionally stressful situations an African American can deal with in this country is a white person calling him a nigger.

"I remember three separate situations in my life where someone called me a nigger," Brent said. "During each situation, I could have lost my control. I would have been justified to do so. Instead, I practiced emotional dexterity and was the better man. Racism will always exist as long as we identify ourselves with a race. That's not who we are; that's just the color of our skin."

Joe Serna has struggled with identity since the end of his military career and suffers from PTSD that can often be debilitating. Afraid of the repercussions in our Special Forces community, Joe kept quiet about those issues while still in the army. He was a Green Beret. He did not want to admit weakness. He did not want to get kicked off his team. He did not want to lose his career.

When he retired, Joe no longer had his strongest support system: his brothers-in-arms. His teammates understood his experiences because they had been there with him and gone through the same things. Now they were still actively serving their country while he was reclassified as a veteran. Still a part of the community, but no longer a door kicker. His purpose was no longer clear. Without a clearly defined identity, Joe discovered he had considerably more time to himself. With plenty of time to think, his mind turned to the past. There were demons.

Joe turned to alcohol to silence those demons and was arrested for a DUI. As part of his sentence, Joe was required to report to Judge Lou Olivera's Veterans Treatment Court in Fayetteville, North Carolina, every two weeks to take a urine test and prove he hadn't been drinking.

Luck certainly played a part each time Joe passed that mandatory screening. The truth was, he had been drinking quite a bit since his DUI. He rolled the dice one too many times and eventually came back positive for alcohol in his system.

Judge Olivera had no choice but to levy punishment for Joe's inability to follow the rules: one night in the Cumberland County jail.

But Judge Olivera struggled with the decision. He was an army vet as well. He knew of Joe's PTSD and how difficult it would be to spend the night in a confined ten-foot-by-seven-foot cinderblock jail cell with no windows. Joe had previously expressed his fear of being in a confined and claustrophobic space to the judge while recounting his story of the RG-31 rollover.

Judge Olivera wanted to help, but what could he possibly do?

The next day, Joe reported for jail. He walked into the facility and into a cell where a heavy steel door slammed behind him. He began to think of James and his team in Afghanistan. He began to think about being trapped and out of air in an overturned RG-31 as it filled with freezing dirty brown water. He began to take short breaths and panic. He began to cry.

Joe was on the verge of screaming for help when he heard the jail door open. In the doorway was Judge Olivera.

"Judge, what the hell are you doing here?" Joe asked.

"Joe, you never left a man behind. Neither am I. I'm staying here with you," Judge Olivera replied.

The jailer—also a vet—brought in another mattress before locking the heavy steel door behind them. Joe and the judge talked for hours about their service, combat, family, and life. Just after midnight, Judge

Olivera heard Joe's breathing get slower and deeper. The judge looked down and saw that Joe was asleep. Mission accomplished (Kiener, n.d.).

The judge had a choice. He could only control what he could control. He could have taken the comfortable path and stayed at home. But he deliberately chose the uncomfortable path and volunteered to stay the night in jail with a fellow veteran, someone he had sentenced, to help him triumph over his demons.

Remember:

- When chaos ensues, self-regulation and specifically emotional regulation must prevail.
- You alone control how you react. Your reaction is your strength.
- Locus of control:
    - You are not helpless, and the situation is not hopeless.
    - Visualize the problem.
    - Assess your perspective.
    - Take a tactical pause.
    - Assess it from other vested perspectives.
    - Take action.
- Practice emotional dexterity and be a master of de-escalation.

---

6 The Dragunov

with **Rusty Whitt**

Rusty served six years in the US Army Special Forces (Green Beret) as a noncommissioned officer. He earned his bachelor's degree in police science and administration from Abilene Christian University in 1994 and his master's degree in kinesiology from Texas in 1997. He now serves as a strength and conditioning coach at the United States Military Academy at West Point.

My morning had been thus far uneventful, spent walking the company hallways sipping coffee, chewing Big Red (gross, I know, but not as gross as the pounds of Copenhagen the rest of the guys consumed), and knocking on team room doors.

"Have you seen this new captain—Van Slyke or something—around?" I asked Captain Daniels, our temporary executive officer, who was sitting in the B-team room.

He didn't look up. "Yeah, he was just in the mess hall with Serna."

"Thanks," I said, moving in that direction, wondering just what exactly I should tell this new team leader about combat. I understood what the major was asking me to do; I just wasn't sure how comfortable I was talking about my combat experiences, even with a fellow Green Beret. There were plenty of grizzled, humble, and reflective men in my company who had done and seen more than I had. However, if the major thought it would make the company better, then I'd get it done.

I walked across the grass and over Bad Toe LZ Road and into the mess hall, still deep in thought. I asked myself, "What was I thinking about before my first deployment?" Like most people, I wanted to know what combat was going to be like. How would I act when the bullets were coming at me? What if I failed? What if I didn't have what it takes?

I remember looking up at my team sergeant, Rich, before our first mission. He had been working on the headspace and timing on one of the .50-caliber weapons in the Humvee and loading ammo cans in the gunner's turret, a burning Marlboro hanging from his lips. Rich had been a nineteen-year-old sniper during the first Gulf War and was the most battle-hardened pipe hitter on the team. I knew I didn't want to let him down. I asked him what he expected of me. Rich just looked down from the turret and said, "Remember your training, and keep your shit straight."

Good advice, I thought, scanning the nearly empty mess hall until spotting Joe and Ransom finishing breakfast with a young-looking captain I didn't know.

"What's up, cholo," I said, approaching the table. Joe looked up and slapped my hand while going in for the bro hug.

"Pendejo!" he said.

"I'm looking for Captain Van Slyke. Major Petit asked me to sit down with him," I said. Joe and Ransom stood with their trays, ready to leave. Their dining partner remained seated.

"Then let me introduce you to Captain Jason Van Camp," said Joe. "Sir, this is Staff Sergeant Rusty Whitt. We'll leave you to it."

I took the seat Joe had vacated and extended my hand. "Nice to meet you, sir."

"You too, Rusty. Thanks for spending some time with me. I just had a great conversation with Joe. Man, he's been through a lot."

I nodded and asked, "Did he tell you about the suicide bomber who threw a grenade at him while he was interviewing him?"

The captain didn't seem surprised by the question. "He didn't, but Ransom was just telling me how I needed to hear that one. He told me about when his RG-31 fell into an aqueduct and he drowned."

"Ah," I said. "I remember that night. I heard the whole thing over the radio. That was a bad day." I paused, and we let the story settle.

Then I said, "I've been thinking about what to talk with you about, what can help you lead SF guys into combat and succeed as a commander. I decided it's probably best to start at the beginning. So I'll tell you about my first combat experience and how all my training came together to keep me alive, if that's cool with you."

"Definitely," he answered.

"When we first deployed, I made a commitment to myself. I vowed that when I got into my first real fight, I would not be a coward. That I'd fit right in along with all the other brave, crazy SOBs on my team.

My first mission in Iraq was in support of a conventional infantry unit that had been ambushed by enemy forces after one of their Stryker combat vehicles hit an IED. Americans had been killed, and the bomb had been triggered from an area near a mosque under construction. We gathered in the former Iraqi military base being used as our compound for an intelligence briefing before heading out. While the team organized, I climbed up on a HESCO barrier that served as one of our watch towers and looked around. The compound was a pillaged and plundered ruin, artillery and mortar shells littered among twisted rebar and blasted slabs of concrete. I scanned the landscape, but there was only desert to see. Whirlwinds of sand would pick up from time to time in the distance, and I could just make out the old city of Baqubah. That's where we'd be heading. Our mission would be to clear the area the bomb had been remote detonated from. Our team sergeant, Rich, motioned for me to come down for the briefing. I climbed down the HESCO barrier, and Rich began talking. "Listen up," he told the assembled team. "The Stryker brigade guys got IED'd earlier today and got into pretty good gunfight with insurgents over in Baqubah. We're going in to clear the neighborhood." He explained that a group of insurgents had commandeered a backhoe and dug a twelve-foot by four-foot hole at a four-way intersection in Old Baqubah. They had stacked two large concrete drainage pipes on top of each other, then lowered two fifty-gallon steel drums packed with diesel and fertilizer through the pipes. The drainage pipes were to channel the blast upward, maximizing damage to whoever was positioned on the road above. It was a complex construction project and a large enough explosive to take out a squad-sized element and any type of vehicle in the US arsenal.

The terrorists had pulled twenty-four-hour shifts in nearby houses and rooftops, watching the street through bored-out holes and waiting for the chance to detonate the bomb. We didn't know how long they had to wait, but when one of our Strykers unwittingly parked right on top of the device, they had their opportunity. As troops began exiting the vehicle to begin a neighborhood clearing operation, the bomb went off, blowing the nineteen-ton Stryker into sharp, charred, wasted bits of metal. Four Americans were killed, and even worse, a sense of vulnerability popped into the minds of any crewman or dismount who worked out of heavy vehicles around the town.

"The explosion precipitated a sustained gunfight between insurgents holed up in a freshly constructed mosque and US forces," our team leader, Captain Gerald, informed us, taking over the briefing. "At this time, conventional US forces have pulled back. And they want us to go in," he said, raising the excitement level throughout the team. We immediately began putting on our kits of body armor and assault packs and prepping to go outside the wire.

Rich told us to load up with six magazines and to store seven more in our assault packs. With one magazine locked in the weapon, this "double basic load" meant each man would be packing 420 rounds of 5.56 mm ball ammo for his M-4 carbine.

As I geared up, I looked down and noticed that my knees were shaking. Normal nerves I had felt in the past—asking my fiancé to marry me, running the last leg in the mile relay—didn't compare with the true fear coursing through my body. As I put live grenades in my rig, I felt nauseous. I guess this is what it's like to truly be scared, I thought.

I looked around at the older guys as they prepared themselves. They all seemed calm, moving with confidence. I was impressed but not surprised. I told myself, "I'm going to act like these guys, even if I have to *pretend* to be as calm as them."

Rich was leaning across the hood of one of our Humvees, cleaning his sunglasses with an Oakley cloth. He had no sympathy or patience for me or my inexperience.

"Rusty, here's what to expect: West Baqubah is shit and occupied by Al Qaeda. North and east is shit. You are going to get shot at. You're going to get IED'd. You are going to be in a firefight. Got it?"

"Roger that," I told him, hoping he couldn't see my heart pounding through my body armor. I hopped in Rich's Humvee, taking the seat behind the driver. I was stuffed in the back of the vehicle, knees to my nose, my M4 rifle stuck between my legs, barely able to move. Ammo cans dug into my right shoulder, and the turret gunner's left foot jabbed into my right knee. We rolled out, everyone lost in their own thoughts, mentally preparing for a major fight.

Most of the team wasn't much on praying. Some guys were agnostic, and some didn't give a shit either way. A few grew up in religion but didn't see the need for it anymore. Some were probably like me and felt a little closer to God knowing it wasn't outside the realm of possibility that we could be meeting Him soon. Whatever the case, I began to hum an old country song by Don Williams, "Lord, I Hope This Day Is Good," as our convoy left the FOB gates.

The road we traveled, called Route Vanessa, was pockmarked with roadside bomb holes and resembled the surface of the moon. Charles, the gunner up top of the Humvee, would look down the road and call out IED craters to our driver. "Crater right!" "Crater left!"

We picked our way through the obstacles and into Baqubah. As we entered the city, we slowed our pace to 20 mph. "Hey, Rusty, you're going to get your CIB (Combat Infantryman Badge) in five minutes," Charles said, grinning down at me from the .50-caliber turret.

I took a few deep breaths but didn't say anything. I just watched the Iraqi kids running alongside our Humvee. "Mista, mista! Chocolate! Mista! Please!"

Charles threw an expended .50-caliber shell toward them. There was a time for dispersing candy, and it wasn't now. I recalled a conversation I had with our intelligence sergeant, Kevin. He had told me about the kids who would swarm your vehicle. Your first instinct is to be compassionate, but that could wind up getting everyone hurt.

We continued through the city at a slow, cautious rate, expecting contact at any moment. A nearby mosque was playing a tape in Arabic that ran on a loop, saying "The American and Iraqi soldiers are here. Leave your weapons unloaded on your porches, and you will not be harmed." We stopped, and the captain told us to dismount. Anyone not driving or manning a weapon in the gunner's turret hopped out. I was among the small element that exited the gun trucks. Over the radio, I heard that there was an insurgent who had been shot up in front of us.

We started to walk from house to house looking for evidence of insurgent activity, the Humvees following closely. No one our interpreter spoke to claimed to know the man who had been shot. This was a big clue that insurgents were shacking up in the area.

We moved back to our Humvees and pulled down the first alley. At the far corner, we saw a teenager wearing an Adidas jogging suit with a belt-fed RPD machine gun slung over his shoulder, casually walking across the alley. He was noticeably alarmed to see us and hesitated a split second, then adjusted the ammo hanging around his neck and defiantly raised the old Russian belt-fed gun to waist level. Simultaneously, Charles, in the gunner's turret, yelled "Contact left!" and hand cranked the turret rapidly to engage this kid. From forty meters away, the young insurgent fired, and bullets flew toward my window, splattering into the thick ballistic glass. The inside of the gun truck erupted as .50-caliber rounds blasted back toward him. He dropped the belt-fed gun, and it swung around his neck as he turned to run. I don't know why he didn't just go back around the corner of the building, but he made a break toward the open alleyway. As he sluggishly ran away from us, I saw a red tracer round pierce him in his upper right rib cage. He spun unnaturally and dropped to the ground. From the front passenger's seat Rich shouted, "Yeah, kill that motherfucker. Shoot him!" as he spat dip juice into an aluminum Rip It energy drink can.

In the back seat I was transfixed, inadvertently holding my breath.

Charles looked down and shouted, "I told you, Rusty! I told you!"

We continued to the objective. Our four-Humvee convoy moved into the neighborhood to take control of the target house. We dismounted, and several of us, along with the captain and a few of our Iraqi scouts, breached the home dynamically to conduct CQB. The trucks moved back to our southwest to prevent any insurgents from west Baqubah flanking us. That side of town was infested with Al Qaeda elements and would likely present targets.

Along with the gunners and drivers, this element consisted of our junior communications sergeant, Donnie, and two of our sniper-qualified senior team members. Chief Warrant Officer Tomlin would be spotting for First Sergeant Ryan with his M-24 sniper rifle. Both were graduates of the US Army's Special Operations Target Interdiction Course (SOTIC) and had acquired the highest skill sets of any sniper in the US military.

We were five hundred meters away from the support of our .50-caliber guns, but the good news was that we had two Apache gunships on station circling us in a wide arc. You couldn't see or hear them due to the trees in the distance and surrounding urban terrain, but it felt good knowing they were up there.

Upon entering the house, we encountered an unsuspecting Iraqi family sitting in their living room. We sat the man, wife, and children on the floor and checked them for weapons and bombs without incident. The wife had a crying infant in her arms, which increased the stress levels of everyone. As Bobby, our senior medic, and Murray, the junior commo sergeant, locked down the family, we began to inspect the house.

"Sir! Check this out," Jerry, our senior weapons sergeant, yelled to the captain. He had found a series of holes that had been drilled in the four external walls of the house, allowing them to sit inside and observe oncoming traffic. Looking through the hole in the east side wall, there it was—the remnants of the Stryker vehicle that was blown to hell. Jackpot on the IED source.

We finished clearing the house, and then Rich and I moved to the roof. Dusty gray tiles crunched underfoot. Dried-out dates baked in the sun next to broken clay pots. A large blue bucket to catch rainwater for bathing sat empty above the door. I wiped sweat, squinting into the never-ending blue sky, wondering when the last time was the bucket had afforded a shower. "Hot as hell out here," I lamented with no sign of relief. The area stank of raw sewage. Above, sagging electrical wires traversed the roof haphazardly.

I looked across the street to our north, taking in a mosque under construction. Its minaret ran about eighty feet high, with a few small windows near the top. I raised my weapon and used my 4x power ACOG scope to scan the windows. Nothing there.

"Damn, perfect sniper's perch," I commented to Rich. I looked down and noticed a bored-out hole in the damaged, incomplete wall that ran the edge of the rooftop. The hole was the size of a Coke can and faced west. I squatted down and looked through it, viewing the westbound road dotted with one- and two-story concrete houses on either side. I noticed a pile of debris on one roof, about three hundred yards away. My "Spidey senses" started tingling as I made out the classic glint of a sniper scope.

"Hey, Rich, I think I just saw something," I said, now kneeling behind the wall.

"What's that?" he asked just as another flash of light crossed my vision, like the sun hitting a tiny mirror. Simultaneously, the air snapped over my head, and I heard the crack of a gunshot.

"Sniper!" I shouted, eating the gray tiles. Particles of the concrete wall, splintered by the sniper's round, dropped down my shirt and body armor. Rich joined me in the prone, scrambling for cover. The small wall provided it, just barely, and we paused to regroup. We needed to identify the distance and direction of the sniper and return fire.

It was 130 degrees, and we were almost out of water. The air was thick and quiet except for the popping sound of one of our Iraqi scouts' weapons below. He was emptying an entire box of two hundred rounds through his M249 squad automatic weapon at ground level.

We couldn't help but notice that the mosque's minaret towers were higher than our rooftop. That was an additional stressor for us. Rich and I both put our M-4s over the wall, firing in the sniper's direction. Standing to fire properly would have almost guaranteed a rapid end to our deployment. There was nowhere for us to go.

Snap.

Another round flew right over my head. I could feel the air breezing past my forehead as the bullet whizzed by. It was a strange sort of exhilaration.

"I can guarantee you that motherfucker has a Dragunov SVD. He can send ten rounds at a time." Rich was a former senior weapons sergeant and knew a few things about guns.

With no display of panic, Rich jumped on the radio to inform the team in the house that we were pinned down. Then he called in our quick reaction force of twenty-five terrified and unmotivated Iraqis for support. I radioed our captain, telling him we needed air weapons on scene.

"Rusty, you lucky bastard!" Rich grinned at me. "You already got your CIB today, and now you have a chance at a hog's tooth!"

I low crawled toward him and asked, "What's a hog's tooth?"

"We got a sniper trying to kill us." Rich exhaled as he explained. "If you can kill him before he kills you, you eject the chambered round from his weapon. That round was intended for you. That's a hog's tooth." I could tell he was glad I asked him the question.

Snap.

The next round impacted the bricks just above my head. I stuck my cheek into the ground and stayed low. Rich and I alternated putting the barrels of our rifles through the bored-out hole and returning fire. There wasn't much else we could do, or anywhere we could go. We would have exposed ourselves to the mosque's minaret tower if we made a break for the staircase. We expected the insurgents to move to the minaret's windows to gain the upper hand if they hadn't already. So we traded shots the best we could, hoping to keep the insurgents from closing the distance between us. We needed those Iraqi soldiers to clear the mosque. Good thing we had brought in extra ammo.

The first few seconds were adrenaline filled, but after around ten minutes, Rich was pretty animated about having the Iraqis step up and do their job. "Damn it, get those Iraqis out there and clear that building!" he barked over the radio, the snipers' bullets hitting close and in rapid succession as he spoke. He must have been trying to send rounds through "our little hole" we were firing out of.

A sudden burst from a belt-fed weapon echoed off the walls around us. We guessed that it had come from the same area as the sniper. By this time Jerry, Charles, Murray, and Bobby were downstairs in the house, firing from windows and engaging the insurgents. The 40 mm grenades from Charles's M203 exploding down the street emboldened me, giving me the confidence that soon we would take the upper hand from these bastards. But for now, we would wait on the rooftop and not make any mistakes.

Rich and I remained in the prone position, staying patient, just looking at each other. The sun beat down on us from directly overhead, and I felt the back of my neck burning. I was thirsty as hell, and my sweat-drenched uniform was soaking up the sand from underneath me. I watched Rich crack a smile and look at his Sunto watch.

"They're trying to bait us to come down that dirt road, man," he said. "They want to piss us off, make us lose our temper, and get us on that dirt. We do that, and somebody else is getting blown up. But that's not happening. None of us are getting hit today."

He flipped onto his back and belly laughed into the sky. "It's 156 degrees on the roof. I'm out of water. I just pissed myself, and we are pinned down by this motherfucker. Another beautiful day in Iraq."

Captain Gerald radioed back to inform us that the Apaches would not engage a mosque or any building connected to the mosque's external walls. Great. More bullshit ROEs that valued a building over my life.

Two more of Charles's 40 mm grenades exploded farther down the road. Then, finally, I saw movement. We were engaged in a chess match of urban warfare with this sniper, and he had just lost. He had grown impatient and mistakenly revealed his position to me.

"I can see the sniper!" I reported. He wasn't in the mosque. He was now on a rooftop about fifty meters closer than from where he had initially engaged us. "He's covered in a tarp with debris all around him."

"OK, if he's not in the minaret, then we can move," the team sergeant said.

"Not in the mosque," I confirmed. "He's about 250 yards out. Our rooftop level." Another round slammed into the wall right by my head. Now that we knew the sniper's position, we could try to break for the staircase and get off this damn roof.

Rich's voice raised in pitch. "Let's get to the stairs," he said.

"Let's do it," I answered, rising slightly, preparing to move.

In order to reach the staircase that led off the roof, we would have to expose ourselves to the minaret's windows. Just because I saw one sniper, that didn't mean there couldn't be another one in the minaret. There also was a gap in the wall encircling the roof where we'd be left unprotected when we made a break for it. I radioed our plan to my teammates.

"Hey, some of you guys put a barrel on that minaret and cover our ass," I instructed, getting ready to move.

"Rusty, get to the stairs, and I'll cover," Rich ordered. I nodded in agreement. He raised his M-4 and began counting down: "One, two, three, go!" He then dumped a magazine on full auto through the hole in the wall. I made a break for the stairwell and dove face-first, launching myself down the stairs.

Smack, smack, smack! Bullets from the enemy belt-fed came fast and furious as the gunmen realized what we were doing. I flipped over to my back and began checking myself for bullet holes. I felt OK but couldn't be sure because my adrenaline was in overdrive.

I lay on the stairs for a few seconds confirming I was alive until I felt myself being pulled inside the house. I looked up and saw Charles dragging me to my feet by the strap on the back of my body armor.

"Thanks, buddy," I said as we got inside.

"You bet. How was it?" he asked me casually.

"Uncomfortable," I replied, hustling down the next set of stairs and into the front room. Murray, Jerry, and Bobby were still sending rounds out the windows, covering Rich's break for the stairwell.

"Rusty, want a Rip It?" Murray asked me, aiming his M-4 out the window and popping off a few rounds. Our junior communication sergeant was a world-class smart-ass.

"Hell no! Are you kidding me? My heart is already beating out of my chest," I shouted.

A few minutes later, I trotted around the outside of the house. I stopped at the corner, where I could fire down the road and help cover Rich's exit from the roof. That was when I saw him rolling down the steps of the staircase.

Rich landed soaked in sweat, his sunglasses filthy and Peltor headset crooked on his head. His pants were sliding down his hips, and his pistol rig was near his knees. He looked disheveled and definitely pissed off.

"Can we get some MOTHERFUCKING IRAQIS to support us?" Rich shouted as he stormed into the house. Bobby handed the team sergeant a plastic two-liter water bottle. He set his back against the wall of the house and slid down to the floor to drink. He downed the entire two liters and asked for another.

"Hey, the Apaches had a bead on the snipers but lost them," Captain Gerald yelled from an adjacent room. "They don't want to light up a house with noncombatants."

We traded glances, but no one wanted civilians targeted. We'd have to root the bad guys out on foot. I went back outside to get another glimpse down the street. At the corner, I saw one of our scouts, a young Iraqi soldier, leaning against a doorway twenty meters away. Suddenly, he dropped to ground, clutching his wrist. His AK-47 fell, clacking against the concrete floor. Simultaneously, a series of gunshots rang out. One of the snipers had put a round through the Iraqi soldier's wrist. The soldier lay in the doorway screaming as arterial blood spurted from his arm. He was panicking and kicking his feet out, back and forth, trying to get his body inside the house.

"Medic!" I shouted. "Bobby! Medic!" I took a step toward the street and the injured Iraqi, a burst of machine-gun fire spattering in front of me.

"Dude, you want me to go get him?" I called out to Bobby.

Bobby looked at me through his sweaty, scratched-up Oakleys. "No! That's my job. I'm the medic!" he yelled out, never letting his sarcasm journey far. Then, unexcitedly: "I always wanted to say this…"

"What?" I asked.

"I'm going in!" he blurted, sprinting across the street through the machine-gun fire. One of his 9 mm magazines popped out of his kit as he high-stepped across the road. I threw a smoke grenade to cover his dash, firing a dozen rounds toward the threat until Bobby reached the injured Iraqi. He grabbed him by his shitty, ill-fitting South African body armor and dragged him into the house. A few minutes later, Bobby was waving at me. He radioed that the young soldier had a tourniquet on his arm and could not—or would not—walk.

Over the radio, I heard Captain Gerald report, "I've got three fuckers roof hopping toward us." I clicked my radio channel to the air weapons team. The pilots were already talking to each other. With all the calmness I could muster, I said to the pilots, "Red Wolf Seven, this is Havoc Nine-Two Mobile. Do you have eyes on the insurgents and clearance to engage?"

On the horizon, we could make out three faint silhouettes moving toward us, popping up and down on the rooftops. One hostile had a belt-fed machine gun, one smaller man an undiscernible weapon, and another a precision rifle slung over his back. With the sun to their backs, the insurgents had no idea that behind them two Apache helicopters were sitting in the tree line, the sunset covering them.

Captain Gerald put his hand against the wall of the house. "Hey, Rich, let's do this," he said simply. The captain's rational mind mixed with the first sergeant's calculated aggression made for an effective dynamic. They decided that with our casualty and unknown number of civilians, a complex urban assault was not the right call.

"Let's take a small element with Bobby and get the wounded kid back to the checkpoint," Captain Gerald instructed. "The rest of us will cover and then follow them out. If the enemy sniper team pursues our exfil, the gunships will take care of them."

The plan went out to the whole team over the radio, and we got ready to move. Bobby broke out his Skedco stretcher, and six of our Iraqi scouts ran to help while we provided covering fire from both ground level and windows.

Peering into the sun, I saw one of the insurgents jump from a low roof about three hundred yards away and run parallel to us, toward another building connected to a five-story grain elevator. I raised my M-4, and before I could touch the trigger, I heard my teammates firing toward him. The insurgent appeared to stumble but made it to a low wall surrounding the adjacent building. He reached out with his AK-47, using the wall for cover, and was about to fire on us, not realizing his fatal error:

He had run into the field of view of our Green Beret sniper team.

His AK fell and his head bounced off the ground, the .308 round from roughly five hundred meters away doing its work.

"Who got him?" Charles asked over the radio. "I don't think we did."

"We did, you fuckers," came First Sergeant Ryan's reply over heavy static.

At the same time, the flat, deadpan radio voice so familiar to Special Operators broke over the air weapons frequency: "Havoc Nine-Two Mobile, this is Red Wolf Seven. Uh, yeah, we have eyes on three armed combatants. Wait one, we're getting clearance to engage...uh, checking their vicinity to the mosque. OK, we are engaging."

We all scrambled to the window to watch the show. Two Apaches swooped down from out of nowhere. A Hellfire missile squirreled off one, impacting the building the snipers had been staging from. The remaining hostiles ran through the smoke toward the five-story grain elevator. The Apaches trained their Hellfire missiles on the grain elevator and let loose, firing about six missiles in total. The high-explosive, copper-lined warheads were powerful enough to burn through the heaviest tank

Jason Van Camp as an 18-year-old cadet during West Point summer training (Buck-nam).

Captain Van Camp leads his team in High-Altitude, High-Opening (HAHO) parachute training in Arizona.

Captain Van Camp with a Kurdish Peshmerga soldier before leading 4,000 Kurds to liberate a city in northeastern Iraq.

Captain Van Camp prepares his Iraqi counterparts to conduct a mission in support of his ODA.

Steve Mueller

Steve shows off his bruises during Hell Week as he attempts to become a Navy SEAL.

Steve as a young Navy SEAL in the Philippines conducting Foreign Internal Defense.

Captain Steve Mueller conducts High-Altitude, Low-Opening (HALO) parachute training just three months after breaking his hip. He has had both hips replaced.

Captain Mueller shows off a pirated copy of a *Navy SEALS* DVD he purchased in a black market in Sadr City.

Captain Chaney prior to departing on a combat operation in Iraq.

Matt, his wife Sonya, and his three boys.

Major Matt Chaney speaks to West Point cadets about leadership.

Jeff Adams

Master Sergeant Adams conducting operations in Iraq.

Jeff and his young family.

Master Sergeant Adams burning holes through souls.

Jeff Adams and his family in Colorado.

Sergeant First Class Joe Serna and his ODA posing for their team photo during pre-mission training in Nevada.

Sergeant First Class Serna saluting the memorials for his fallen comrades in Afghanistan.

Sergeant First Class Serna and his team sergeant hours before the mission that would take his team sergeant's life.

James through the open turret in the same RG-31 that he would drown in hours later.

Rusty Whitt

Staff Sergeant Rusty Whitt and a teammate after a mission.

Rusty conducting Foreign Internal Defense training with a tiny Iraqi man.

Staff Sergeant Rusty Whitt and a teammate at the range outside their Forward Operating Base in Iraq.

Staff Sergeant Whitt training Iraqi soldiers.

Andy Riise

Petra Kowalski

Sean Swallen

Nate Last

Sarah Spradlin

Tyler Christiansen

Mission Six Zero

Mission Six Zero flamethrower training as a part of our custom program.

Jason presents to the University of Texas football team.

Mission Six Zero CEO Jason Van Camp provides Tim Tebow feedback on his performance during a leadership evaluation exercise.

Mission Six Zero team-building tank driving experience.

armor in existence and completely decimated the grain elevator. The sight, thunderous sound, and smell of the explosions was something that I'll never forget.

"Dammit, Rusty, you missed out on getting your hog's tooth," Rich said to me as the smoke cleared. "That shit finger took his rifle in the silo with him. Well, you'll get another chance tomorrow." The grizzled team sergeant sighed and slapped me on the back of my body armor.

"And that, Captain Van Camp, was my first combat operation," I finished. I had almost forgotten he was there.

"What do you think the catalyst was for your success?" Captain Van Camp asked.

"We rise or fall to the level of our training," I answered. "I believe that the intensity of our training had exposed the team to enough stress that everyone was able to maintain their cool, communicate, and problem-solve in a chaotic environment. The key is understanding what is going on inside your body during those stressful moments and learning what you need to do to keep your composure in order to operate at your optimal level. This all goes back to preparation, right?" I asked rhetorically.

Jason nodded. "Thanks for a great conversation, Rusty," he said, rising to shake my hand. "I appreciate your willingness to help me out. I would love to reciprocate the favor sometime. Anything you need, I got you," the captain said.

"I will 100 percent take you up on that offer, sir."

SOF to Science with Tyler Christiansen, Physical Science Officer

Tyler is a human performance director who works with a multidisciplinary team of operational psychologists, physical therapists, strength and conditioning coaches, dietitians, and athletic trainers in the Special Operations community. He was recognized as the National Strength and Conditioning Association's 2019 Tactical Strength and Conditioning Practitioner of the Year. He also served as an infantryman for eight years and physically trained SOF operators for the last fifteen years.

When you are in "the suck," you need to be prepared. Preparation does not start the day of; it starts now.

We don't rise to the occasion, we rise to our level of training. Rusty had not been in combat before, but he had trained (practiced) day in and day out to be prepared physically (and mentally and tactically). Had Rusty and his teammates cut corners in their training, the end of this mission might have been different.

Did Rusty practice that exact scenario? No. But he had the fundamentals of combat instilled in him through years of practice. Rusty was in a Volatile-Uncertain-Complex-Ambiguous (VUCA) environment and handled it perfectly with the use of Observe-Orient-Decide-Act (OODA loop).

As we discussed in chapter 4, the OODA loop describes rapid decision-making in a dynamic environment. Think of your personal situation here: You *Observe* your environment and gather all the facts or data you can. *Orient* or analyze your data to make multiple courses of action based on the data to develop your path forward. Then *Decide* on your course of action or path. Then it is time to take *Action* and execute the mission. Being that this is a loop, you must continue this process along all steps of your journey. As they say in the military, the terrain will dictate your mission, and the enemy gets a vote. You must always be prepared to adjust.

One does not have to train to the extreme, but you do have to practice the fundamentals day in and day out to be able to adapt to the stressors put before you. Rusty experienced exposure to "little doses of venom" through his prior training that prepared him for when the snakebite came. Picture what Rusty went through in his first battle. Knees shaking, heart pounding through his kit, mentally preparing for what to expect... Have you felt this way before? Now add in 130-degree weather on top of an Iraqi house with little water, sweating your ass off, and bullets snapping over your head while you lie behind an unstable wall.

So What?

Many people think of the physical strength domain and focus purely on working out and good nutrition. Working out and great nutrition are important factors, but they do not act alone. This thought process discounts the importance of chemical balance within the body. Let's discuss what happens inside you when you are confronted with stress.

Remember the acronym EDSOC:

E—**Endorphins** (Greenberg, 2017)

Endorphins kill pain.

Positive effects:

- We can run farther.
- We can work harder.
- We can endure more extremes (hot/cold weather).

Negative effects:

- Too many endorphins cause panic. Your body expects pain that never comes.

D—**Dopamine** (Greenberg, 2017)

Dopamine acts as a reward.

Positive effects:

- Reaching goals
- Learning
- Getting better at something

Negative effects:

- Highly Addictive (eating survival foods like sugar— highly addictive)
- Too much causes bipolar or schizophrenia, binge eating, etc.

S—**Serotonin** (Greenberg, 2017)

Serotonin inspires leadership and pride.

Positive effects:

- Satisfaction

- Creates strong communities "esprit de corps"
- Makes you want to make your coach or parents proud
- Better Memory
- Increases confidence
- Increases cohesion between team members

Negative effects:

- Too much causes confusion and agitation

O—**Oxytocin** (Uvnas, 2003)

Oxytocin inspires love, trust, friendship, relationship

Positive effects:

- The reason we spend time with friends and family
- Feeling of safety
- Causes bonding
- Inhibits addiction, inflammation
- Increases creativity and higher thought process

Negative effects:

- Too much causes oversensitivity to emotions.

C—**Cortisol** (Greenberg, 2017)

Cortisol is commonly referred to as the "bad" drug. That's not accurate. Although cortisol triggers the stress and anxiety chemical, it also triggers your immediate survival instinct, known as the stress response to "fight, flight, or freeze." Cortisol is supposed to be in and out, not the constant drip that is prevalent in modern society.

Positive effects:

- First step in flight, fight, or freeze
- Heightens the five senses (sight, hearing, smell, taste, touch)
- Injects glucose into the muscles to get ready to act (fight or flight)
- Increases heart rate (gets blood to the muscles)

Negative effects:

- Shuts down oxytocin. You become selfish, self-interested, and don't care about others. It makes people less empathetic and less generous.
- Increases paranoid behavior
- Inhibits immune system

Both:

- Infectious with others around us
- Shuts down all the other chemicals for good or bad
- Shuts down nonessential systems
- When it kicks in, higher thought drops and the reptilian brain takes over
- We go into survival mode

Now What?

Imagine the endorphins surging through Rusty's body as he lay there in 130-degree heat in full combat gear. Imagine the dopamine as Rusty finally threw himself through the door to a relatively safer spot. Imagine the serotonin when Rusty's teammate joined him in safety. Imagine the oxytocin that was released after successfully completing the mission. How would you react in Rusty's situation? How would you prepare and perform?

Rusty prepared and armed himself with his "layers" of physical and nutritional bases. Just like getting prepared for cold weather, we advise you to put on your base layer.

Physical Base Layer

Do something physical every day. It doesn't really matter if it is CrossFit or yoga or whatever; do what works for you.

Sanitation Base Layer

Cleanliness is next to godliness (keeping your body and the area you live in clean creates a healthy environment).

Nutrition Base Layer

Take vitamins and minerals. If you are drinking diet chemical garbage, you are compromising your health. If you consume sugar (simple carbs) in great quantities, you are causing inflammation and health issues.

All three pillars (physical, sanitation, and nutrition) are your armor against stress.

Practical Application with Jason Van Camp

Companies and sports teams often ask Mission Six Zero to "help them succeed." When we ask them what success looks like, they frequently struggle to quantify it. Only after several intense conversations do we usually come to the same conclusion: success for them is defined as happiness.

Happiness is the precursor to success. Not the other way around. In order to find the success that you are looking for, you need to find your happiness first. Every time you think, "I will be happy when (fill in the blank)," you need to realize that happiness is a choice as opposed to a response to circumstances.

Mission Six Zero believes that true happiness comes from *serving other people.* Many of our clients ask us, "How is your training making me a better player or better at my job?" We tell them it's not. It's making the person next to you a better player. That's the mind-set that you must have in order to truly be happy, which in turn will lead to success in all facets of life.

Jeff Kirkham is one of the most service-minded people that I know. It's no surprise that he is also one of the happiest and most successful people you'll ever find. Jeff is the owner of three successful businesses: Black Rifle Coffee Company, RATS Tourniquet, and Readyman. If a Neanderthal, James Bond, and Tony Stark fathered a baby, it would be Jeff. In service to his country, Jeff spent twenty-nine years as a Green Beret with just over eight years "boots on the ground" in Afghanistan and Iraq as a member of a counterterrorism direct-action unit. Somehow, he has managed to study six foreign languages, earn a bachelor's degree of science, write three books, earn multiple registered patents (one of which is the RATS tourniquet), and manage his passion project, Readyman.

"Everyone has the same chemicals in our body: endorphins, dopamine, serotonin, oxytocin, and cortisol," Jeff explains. "Dopamine helps us to achieve—to reach our goals. Serotonin inspires pride and esprit de corps, and oxytocin inspires love and bonding. What can we do to maximize those three chemicals? I'll tell you what—it's service. We are operating at our optimal levels when we are in service to our fellow man. Therefore, we have discovered the trifecta of happiness, and it's not as if we just invented it or discovered it; it has been around for thousands of years. If you read the sacred texts of all the major religions, it really comes down to one thing: service."

The trifecta of happiness:

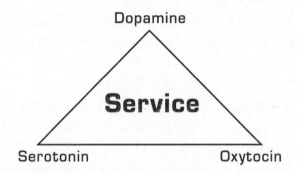

How do you find happiness and achieve success? You don't make it a goal. The more you chase it, the less you will find it. Viktor Frankl explains brilliantly:

Don't aim at success. The more you aim at it and make it a target, the more you are going to miss it. For success, like happiness, cannot be pursued; it must ensue, and it only does so as the unintended side effect of one's personal dedication to a cause greater than oneself or as the by-product of one's surrender to a person other than oneself. Happiness must happen, and the same holds for success: you have to let it happen by not caring about it. I want you to listen to what your conscience commands you to do and go on to carry it out to the best of your knowledge. Then you will live to see that in the long-run—in the long-run, I say!—success will follow you precisely because you had forgotten to think about it (Frankl, 1962).

Lose yourself in service to others. Only a life lived for others is a life worthwhile. When you focus on serving the men to your left and right, the more personal benefit you will find.

During a team-building exercise with the New York Jets, I asked one of the participants, Matt Slauson, an all-pro guard, what he thought of the exercise. Matt told me, "This is exactly what we need." I then asked him why that was.

Matt was silent for a few seconds and then pointed to one of the players a little way off from where we were standing. "You see that guy?" Matt asked.

"Yeah," I responded. "That's Jeff Cumberland."

"Jeff and I have been on the same team for three years now. He's a tight tend. I'm a guard. We both play offense, and we line up almost right next to each other."

"OK," I responded, confused by the direction of the conversation.

"The first time I ever said a word to Jeff was five minutes ago."

I thought to myself, "I just walked out of a meeting where the team referred to one another as brothers and as a family. They talked about fighting for the men to their left and their right. But how can they call one another brothers and family if they don't even know who their teammates are? Why would you fight for the men to your left and to your right if you don't even know who those people are?"

There is meaning and purpose behind "family," and the Jets didn't get that yet.

Too often, words like "family" get thrown out indiscriminately.

At the time, the Jets wanted to be a family; they just didn't know how to do it. After our event, we stressed the importance of adjacent unit communication with the team. The art of building true relationships and getting to know one another on the field, in the locker room, and off the field. The key to high performance is not in the content of the team's discussions, but in the manner in which it communicates.

As a result of our work, the Jets enjoyed career seasons from players along their offensive line, most notably Matt and Jeff. Jeff especially increased his productivity by catching five times as many passes and several more touchdowns than in the previous year. Jeff became more comfortable with the improved communication. Matt's deliberate choice to build a relationship with Jeff was a significant factor in Jeff's quantifiable improvement on the football field.

Recently, Matt and I talked about how our training impacted his career. Matt explained, "I was young and still new in the league when you came to train us. Your curriculum really helped bring me out of my comfort zone. You nurtured my leadership abilities and encouraged me to step forward. I was able to continue that further in my career. I was immediately thrown into a leadership role when I was at the Bears, Chargers, and Colts. I really believe it all started during the Mission Six Zero training. It got to a point where teams were bringing me in not because of my play on the field, but because of my leadership abilities."

How do you live a life of service to others? You must do things that are, at first, uncomfortable. Here's how:

1. Start.

The first step is always the most uncomfortable. In order to start, all you have to do is show up. The battle is half won if you just show up. If possible, make the decision to start on your own rather than have someone make that decision for you. Whenever you start something, it sucks. You start a diet, it sucks. You start working out, it sucks. Once you start, you are going to want to quit immediately.

2. Don't quit.

You've decided to start. You're not seeing results. It's difficult. You want to quit. It's OK. That's normal. You're going to start thinking of a way out where you can quit and save face. Don't do it. Don't give yourself an out. Just don't. Don't give yourself any options. Either you succeed or you fail. No excuses. Remind yourself that you made a decision. You are already committed, and there is no going back. The point when you are just about to give up is the precise moment when the other guy gives up. At some point, you are going to ask yourself, "Why am I doing this?" You had better have an answer. What is driving you? Is it a challenge? Is it something that you have to prove to yourself? Is it pride? Whatever the answer is, it had better be powerful.

3. Push yourself past your comfort zone.

At some point, you are going to say to yourself, "I've never done this before" or "I don't know what I'm doing." We've all been there. Here's a trick: Don't say it out loud. Just pretend to be confident. Fake it till you make it. It's scary, but I promise you this: When it's over, you are going to say, "It wasn't as bad as I thought it would be." Fear kills more dreams than failure ever will.

4. Embrace "the suck."

The situation is bad—deal with it. And don't just deal with it—open your arms and welcome it as you would an old friend. You know him well. Just when you think things couldn't get any worse, he shows up. "The suck" is here to make you tougher. He's a friend who has arrived to make you better. Instead of complaining, celebrate the blessing that is the suck. If you are embracing the suck by yourself, laugh at how ridiculous the situation is. You are building your mental and physical toughness points. If you are embracing the suck with others, you've just made new best friends for life. Embracing the suck in a group is a powerful bonding experience.

5. Create a support network.

Talk about your experiences. The worse the experience is for you, the better the story will be to everyone else. Soon you will be seeking uncomfortable experiences to share with your friends. Be a good storyteller.

6. Recognize your improvements.

Track your progress. Revel in it. You are now a changed person. You know it because you see it. Build your confidence by going back to what before was uncomfortable, and go through the experience again. You are seeing your progress in real time. By nature, you are going to want to push the envelope to find out your boundaries. You will find yourself saying, "I wish it would suck more." It's our human nature to want to know what we are able to overcome.

7. Rinse. Repeat.

There's an old Russian saying, *povtorenie mat ucheniya,* which means "repetition is the mother of learning." The more you perform the same activity, the more confident you become. Confident behaviors are a tangible thing—they come from practice and repetition.

Remember:

- You rise or fall to the level of your training.
- Quality repetition during training inspires confidence.
- EDSOC: endorphins, dopamine, serotonin, oxytocin, cortisol.
- Put on your base layers! (physical, sanitation, nutrition).
- Service is at the center of the trifecta of happiness.

---

7 The Dilemma
with **Dan Quinn**

Dan served ten years in the US Army, mostly as a US Special Forces (Green Beret) officer. He earned two Bronze Stars during three combat rotations in the Middle East. He graduated from the United States Military Academy at West Point and has an MBA from the University of North Carolina.

This wasn't easy for me. The rest of my team had just started preparation for a deployment to Iraq, and I was sidelined. In fact, I was more than sidelined—I was waiting for my clearing papers. I was being kicked out of the military for what happened in Afghanistan. As much as I didn't want to leave my brothers, I didn't regret a thing.

As I had just explained to Captain Van Camp, I had been relieved of my command and sent home from Afghanistan on our last deployment for beating up an Afghan commander who had kidnapped a young boy, chained him to a bed, and kept him as a sex slave while raping him repeatedly.

These male child sex slaves are supposedly badges of honor in their culture, and the practice is especially prevalent in the Afghan military. I had witnessed it several times in country and was fed up with turning a blind eye. So I did something about it, and our leadership decided that what I had done was egregious enough to send me home and kick me out of the army.

"How can they let our supposed allies get away with that?" Jason asked, shocked at what he was hearing. "What can we do about it?"

"There's nothing we can do," I told him. "I got fired for doing something. I may even get a dishonorable discharge for this. But I couldn't let this type of behavior continue on my watch. I believe in what I did."

I explained that the US military's official stance on *bacha bazi*, or "dancing boys," is to not get involved. It's supposed to be a local Afghan legal issue, but they did nothing to stop it. I could see on Jason's face that he was having a hard time comprehending what I was telling him. I couldn't blame him.

"Let me start at the beginning of that deployment. I took over as team leader after my team had already been in Afghanistan for some time. Their commander had suffered a broken back and leg, and three other guys had also been hurt badly, so it was a tough situation to walk into.

"I wasn't sure how the guys were going to react to a new team leader. They had just lost a quarter of their team, and I didn't know what their mind-set was going to be. They could either want to get back in the fight or just ride out the rest of the deployment. Luckily, it was the former.

"For the first two weeks, I watched how the team operated. I decided I needed to make a change and fired the team sergeant."

Jason was taken aback. "Damn. With everything that had already happened to that team, that was a bold move, Dan," he said.

"It was definitely tough because I didn't know how the guys would react. The team sergeant was a great guy and I liked him personally, but he was just a little too fast and loose. Not conducting proper training—things that could get guys hurt. It wasn't like he was a bad guy or doing anything illegal. I mean, I wish he had been a turd. That would have made it easier. But he wasn't. I felt the team needed a change. People had gotten hurt. I didn't want to continue with that cowboy mentality. I got the sense the team craved a little more structure, and it wasn't going to come from him.

"It was a six-month deployment with only a couple months left when I took over. I wanted to make sure we maximized that time, got the most out of the deployment, and accomplished our mission. That started to happen. Right after I got there, we just turned up the volume. We really started to take the fight to the Taliban.

"We were doing great, and both the Afghans and our chain of command took notice. General Petraeus came to our team house to tell us that we were doing a phenomenal job, and he recognized us as the most effective team at building stability operations he had seen in northern Afghanistan. After that, every general and colonel in our chain of command visited us and commended us for our performance.

"The problem, at least in my eyes, was multiple incidents of sexual abuse by our Afghan partners."

Jason had a serious look on his face. "Man, I can't even imagine witnessing that. How can you work with people who do those types of things? That's not what we signed up for."

I nodded. "Absolutely not. I'm a Green Beret—our motto is To Free the Oppressed. How could I stand by and not do anything?"

"Exactly," Jason said. "That's why I went Special Forces. So I don't have to stand around and watch injustice. What about you, Dan? What was your reason for going SF?"

"I went to West Point, like you. Played sports there, like you. For me, it was basketball. Honestly, that's the only reason I went. They were the only D1 school that recruited me. So I went, sat on the bench, and ended up with a commission. I didn't love the school, but I loved the opportunity that came afterward.

"I've always felt that if you're going to do something, you might as well do it right. If I was going to be in the army, I was going to be in the best unit there was. I just wanted to surround myself with the best people I could. When you grow up playing sports and being on teams, you want to keep that feeling going. That's why I was attracted to the Special Forces."

"Funny. That sounds like my story," said Jason.

"And we didn't put in all the work to join an elite unit and then sit back when shit like that was going on right in front of us. At least I didn't. I asked one of my Afghan interpreters, Mohammed, about bacha bazi. He told me that he had been one. His mother and siblings had been killed, and his father sold him to a master who agreed to take care of him. His master told everyone that he was his adopted son. Then at parties, he'd be put on display while the other masters vied for who had the most attractive boy. He said eventually his master fell sick and died, and his service was over. He had nowhere to turn, no marketable skills, so he had to become a new person, someone who wouldn't attract attention. A part of him had to die so that he would not feel pain. He began to read books. He was fascinated with languages and began to study English, eventually getting hired by us as a translator."

"That's terrible!" exclaimed Jason. "And then he had to still be around it?"

"Mohammed would see the boys being taken. He could see the pain in their eyes, feel their scars from the rape and violence. As he spoke with me, he began to cry and said the trauma had killed a part of him."

"How can you go into combat with people who do this? How do you train them and trust that they're going to keep you alive?" Jason asked.

"It was hard. One of my Afghan commanders forced his men to give him their wages, and he spent it in a dancing boys club. Another commander violently raped a fourteen-year-old girl as she worked in the field. He was sentenced to one day in jail, and then the fourteen-year-old girl was forced to marry him because she wasn't suitable to marry anybody else. We reported each incident up our chain of command, and each time the response was 'Don't interfere.' I get it—we can't be the judge, jury, and executioner of Afghanistan. We aren't there to impose our will on the people. But there must be a line for what we will tolerate. It's infuriating, because as a soldier, when you see injustice you want to do something about it. It finally got to a point where I said, I'm done just reporting this. We've got to do something different to stop this. I'm not just going to keep turning a blind eye.

"One day a young mother came to our front gate in tears. Mohammed got me and Charles, my new team sergeant. When we arrived, we could see that she had been severely beaten.

"Mohammed told us that her twelve-year-old-son had been kidnapped from their home by our top militia commander, Mohammed Rahman. She said her son had been held for two weeks, chained to a bed, and repeatedly raped by this commander. When she went to Rahman's house to beg for his release, she was beaten, and the commander continued to rape her son.

"I told her I'd deal with it and had Mohammed escort her off base. I needed to make sure the accusations were true before doing anything. Charles and I called four of the top Afghan lieutenants in the area and asked them what they knew about the incident. Each one admitted it was true. They said it happened exactly as the mother reported and that the commander was bragging about it.

"I remember just looking at Mohammed and saying, 'Bring him in.' Mohammed called Commander Rahman and told him to report to our base. No reason was given. We weren't sure what we were going to do, but we knew we needed to make it clear that this type of behavior was not going to be tolerated.

"Mohammed led Commander Rahman through multiple layers of security and into a tent to wait for us. When we arrived, Charles and I stood in front of Rahman, arms crossed. He smiled at us but did not get up.

"Mohammed ran up and whispered to me, 'Sir, the commander has released the boy.'

"I nodded, then turned to Rahman.

"'These are serious allegations against you,' I told him.

"Rahman continued smiling at me while I outlined the charges. He was about forty, maybe 5'10" and 150 pounds soaking wet. He took off a dusty beret to run his fingers through freshly cut black hair, then stroked his short beard over and over. He was smirking at me like a child caught in a white lie. When I was done outlining the allegations, he laughed. We did not.

"'Yes, it's true.' He grinned, shrugging. 'I'm sorry.'

"His laughter, his attitude, could not be tolerated. I picked Rahman up and threw him on the ground with a thud. That got his attention. Then Charles grabbed him and tossed him around a few times. As Charles approached Rahman again, Rahman's eyes flashed in my direction, a silent plea to save him. When Charles stopped, Rahman seemed to recover and said with a satisfied smirk, 'It's just a boy.'

"We'd had enough. I pushed Rahman, and he fell back onto a bunch of pallets. He put his hands up in surrender, but I slapped them away. It made me think of the twelve-year-old boy he had abused. I'm sure the boy had tried to surrender and beg for mercy. I looked down at Rahman, and he slowly tilted his head back to look at me. He smiled again.

"I picked Rahman up and body slammed him on the pallets. He tried to get up, but he tripped and just lay there, hoping that if he was still, we'd leave him alone. Charles picked him up again by the back of his uniform and told him to get off our base. For some reason, he declined.

"I decided that if he would not leave of his own volition, we would have to escort him out, our way. Charles body slammed him, throwing him outside the compound. He began to mumble something over and over. We couldn't understand him in his own language, but I'm sure it was a plea similar to what the boy had been uttering over the past two weeks.

"Finally, Charles tossed him into the burn pit outside of the gate. Unfortunately, it wasn't lit.

"'Mohammed, tell him that's where he belongs,' I spat.

"Commander Rahman crawled out and looked at us in confusion and anger.

"Before he could say anything, I shouted, 'Listen to me! You're done. You're fucking done. Don't you ever come back!'

"He sat up gingerly, both of his legs extended. He grabbed the back of his head and began rubbing it as Charles and I slowly walked through the outer gate and back into our compound.

"We never saw him again.

"That night, I got a call from the infantry battalion commander in my area.

"'Hey, Dan, we just got a crazy report that you slapped around an Afghan commander,' he said.

"'Yes, sir. It's not crazy. I did it.' Then I told him why. He was sympathetic but said he'd have to report it up the chain of command. I told him I understood, and to do what he had to do.

"The next call was from my company commander.

161

"'Dan, is everything OK?' he asked.

"'Yes, sir,' I said.

"'We got a report that you beat up an Afghan commander and then confirmed it with the infantry battalion commander in your area of operations.'

"I confirmed the report and told him what had happened. He was not happy.

"'Dan, my Afghan commander counterpart called me and informed me that one of his regional commanders checked himself into the hospital and is in critical condition. He's unconscious, on life support, but he woke up for a few seconds to name you and Charles as the people who attacked him.'

"He went on to inform me that Charles and I should pack our bags. A Blackhawk helicopter would be picking us up to take us to battalion headquarters, where I would be facing an AR 15-6, an army procedure for investigating officers.

"We were told that Charles and I would be treated like criminals. They even wanted to handcuff us, but our company sergeant major wouldn't let the MPs do it. We found out that we lost our team and our positions. Our chain of command threatened to pull our Special Forces tabs from us. At one point, we were told that we were going to jail. Our lawyers tried to get us to say we had PTSD and we were temporarily insane, but neither Charles nor I were going to go that route. We owned up to what we did because we knew it was the right thing to do."

Jason was wide eyed. "I heard about that, but I had no idea it was you," he exclaimed. "I can't believe the command treated you like that."

"I knew what I was doing. I don't want you to think it was just a reaction or emotional outburst. I *chose* to send this commander a message. I don't want it to sound like I was a guy who couldn't control myself, because that's not the case. Our superiors said that we couldn't get involved in cultural Afghan affairs. I disagreed. So I decided to do what I did. And now my career is over. I'm looking at a less-than-honorable discharge."

I made sure to look Jason straight in the eyes before I finished. "And I don't regret a thing."

SOF to Science with Shelley Smith, Social Science Officer

As a certified professional culture curator (CPCC), Shelley has developed and implemented plans for both large and smaller corporations to manifest stronger company cultures throughout her thirty-plus-year career. She is the author of five books, including Brass Ovaries, Own Yours: Master the Mindset, Change the Game *and* How to Avoid Culture Big Fat Failure (BFF).

What is unacceptable in one society can be considered normal in others. Culture is made up of people—how each of us socializes, builds trust, influences, and negotiates through conflict with positive outcomes. Understanding who we are (self-awareness) and how we all fit together to form a healthy trust of one another is essential to achieve results.

To achieve positive results, we need to learn how to best influence one another and to negotiate through conflict. That all begins with understanding our own behavioral needs and those of others. The relationships in society, individually and culturally, branch into our day-to-day communications, economics, history, health, and sociology. In the modern world, our differences, biases, and (in)tolerances are more intertwined than ever—they are inescapable. Being a good human, a good steward of mankind, is now tested on a daily basis.

In this chapter, the differences between cultural norms are unbearable. When boundaries are crossed, they appear dark and unclear. However, when our personal ethical and moral boundaries are attacked, the differences suddenly become clear and intolerable.

So What?

Three main social (culture) references to digest from this chapter include:

1. Dismissal of a leader

Removal of any leader is always a tough decision, especially when the leader is deemed "a good guy" and has been in place for a long time. In combat, there are goals that must be met because lives are at stake. The leader in this case didn't fully recognize the needs of his team. He was driven by taking risks, and his team needed processes, rules, and boundaries. His approach did not motivate and engage his team. For your team's talent to be optimized, an intentional alignment to the company's mission, vision, values, and core must be nurtured. A leader without followers is not a leader at all.

Seek to fully understand your own natural behaviors and those of your team members in relation to the business objectives. Hire intentionally—make sure there is alignment with the right job, right team, right person, and right fit. Business objectives are met through an intentional design, proper hiring, and ongoing inspiration—that's what allows for the results you seek to accomplish.

Many times, our teams are handed to us. When you come into an existing team and there is dysfunction, as the leader you must first assess (diagnose) what is going on. What is working and what isn't working and why. Once you analyze and get to the root—then and only then do you begin to formulate how to curate the opportunity and finally create the real solution. In the case of Dan, letting go of the team sergeant was a tough call that many wouldn't have taken, but it was the right thing for the team and the mission. Dan knew the team needed new leadership. Due to overwhelmingly difficult circumstances, his existing team sergeant wasn't able to change, shift, or pivot to get better results. Tough call, but the right one.

2. Core values, ethics, morals crossed

When a company's core values cross our personal values, ethics, and/or morals, it becomes difficult if not impossible to turn it off and look away. Self-awareness and personal beliefs should align with the company's mission, vision, values, and culture statements. If not, the situation produces stress, lack of engagement, turnover, increased costs, and lack of growth. The culture becomes misaligned and often toxic and unrecognizable. In years past we have read about those toxic workplaces, those with ongoing harassment, discrimination, bullying, theft, and more. How do you distinguish the lines? How do you keep self-preservation out of your culture? How can you ensure everyone is safe, seen, valued, and heard? It starts with clarity, focus, intentions, and culture norms. Everyone on the team must understand what defines success and failure. Gray should not be tolerated. We hold ourselves and others accountable with ease when expectations are clear and acceptable. We all have lines we will not cross—making sure we are aligned is also a moral and core value we must be in touch with—so self-preservation does not take over our personal morals, ethics, and values.

Make sure your team, your department, your division, and your organization are all clear on successful actions and behaviors, and what is and what isn't acceptable. The more that is in writing, the better. The more support given to recognize and reward good behavior, the better. We are quick to call out poor performance at times, but how quick are we at defining good behavior and rewarding for it? Example: If accountability is a part of your mission, vision, values, or culture statements, then every employee must know what it feels like, sounds like, looks like. What do they say, do, feel? How do they act as it relates to accountability? Place all your values into action statements.

3. Own it; repercussions

Dan and Charles were fully aware of their actions, meaning they could take action to do *nothing* or take action to do *something*. Their choice was to do *something*. As Dan said, "And I don't regret a thing."

Could it have been handled differently? What would *you* do? What *do* you do?

Have you ever stood up for something that got you suspended or fired? Have you ever chosen to ignore a fellow coworker doing something morally or ethically wrong and act as if you didn't see it, hear it, or thought it was none of your business—yet you knew it was wrong? How do you handle the struggle inside when you don't agree with the actions of your company, your team, or your supervisor? When do you stand up for another human being?

Taking a stand is what Dan and Charles chose to do. It is up to each of us to decide when, where, or if we will rise to the occasion. As owners, managers, leaders, and human beings, how do we help our employees make a stand for what is right while protecting them or helping them move on through termination? It starts with a deep-rooted trust that you truly have an open-door policy and are willing to listen and provide feedback to assist all parties in the final decision-making process. Trust is at the very foundation of all relationships, and it's critical for healthy and strong teams.

There is a reason why we discussed TRUST in chapter 1. It all begins with trust.

Now What?

1. Think about your workplace environment. How aligned are your mission, vision, core values, and culture statements to one another? Do they have a clear thread to one another?

2. If you asked your team to describe your workplace culture on index cards, would the individual responses be the same? Do they align and match what is already in writing in your handbook, on the walls, and on your website? Are they describing the culture you envisioned? Are they in unity? Will these responses aid you in achieving your goals?

3. Are you rewarding good behavior that is aligned to your envisioned workplace culture? Are expectations clear? Are you motivating your team as you need to be motivated or as the members individually need to be motivated to achieve your business objectives?

4. The last time you onboarded a new team member, did you explain why you chose them, how they fit into the big picture? Did you paint a clear picture of the expectations of success? Were you clear on culture boundaries? Why they matter? Did you make yourself a resource if they became concerned or questioned those boundaries?

5. When was the last time you checked in—really checked in—with your team members to make sure they were engaged and truly at peace with their roles and expectations?

6. How would you describe your culture of accountability? Transparency? How do you give feedback, help others pivot inside your walls or into another company when alignment is no longer there?

Practical Application with Jason Van Camp

Cultural differences can be shocking and at other times appalling. I think back to conducting humanitarian aid missions to villages in Iraq where we passed out soccer balls, Gerber baby food, etc. We were conducting much-needed rapport building and providing assistance to the locals, but in reality, we were gathering as much intelligence as we could to help us in future operations.

One day, when we returned to a particular village, I was surprised to see the floor of one building strewn about with little glass bottles of Gerber baby food. In one of the glass bottles, I noticed an adult-sized spoon. I was curious, so I walked around the house looking for an explanation. I opened one of the doors to a room in the building and found an elderly man lying on a bed of flat, dirty mattresses eating out of a jar of Gerber baby food.

"Are you fucking kidding me?" I said out loud. I called in my interpreter over my MBITR radio to join me. I lifted the old man up from his bed, grabbing the front of his dishdash and pinning his back against the mud wall of his room. The old man's body went completely limp, which made him annoyingly heavy and made me rethink my decision to get him out of bed.

"You've been stealing the food we gave the mothers for their babies, you selfish son of a bitch!" I shouted while my interpreter translated.

The old man was terrified and began to softly and rapidly blurt out his response in Arabic.

"He says that the mothers gave him the food," my interpreter said.

I ordered my interpreter to find the women whom we had given the baby food to during our last humanitarian aid mission and bring them to my location. My interpreter quickly returned to the room with six of them.

I lined the mothers up. "Has this man been stealing baby food from you?" I asked as nicely as I could muster. I could tell these women were terrified and confused.

I instructed my interpreter, "Tell them that the baby food was meant for them to give to their babies so they could live. Although this man claims that you gave him this food, I know he is lying. I want to protect you so you can get the food you need to take care of your families."

One of the mothers started speaking quietly. "We gave the food to the man—he is the village elder."

"Bullshit. They are trying to protect him. Translate that," I responded.

The mothers all fell to their knees and began pleading in Arabic.

I told my interpreter, "Tell them that I am not going to hurt them. I want to protect them."

Another mother spoke up. "We gave our elder the food. He needs it in order to live. Our tribe will suffer if our elders die."

I picked up one of the glass Gerber baby food bottles and pointed to the baby on the label. "The food that we gave you is intended for your children. We want your children to live," I explained. I could sense that they were confused.

My interpreter explained. "They don't understand you. They want to know why you want their children to live over their elders. This woman says if the children die, they'll just have more. But if the elders die, they take with them years of experience and knowledge."

"They would rather have their children die than their elders?" I asked.

My interpreter asked the mothers my question, and I didn't need a translation. I could tell by their body language that that was exactly what they would do.

I explained my thoughts out loud to my interpreter. "In America, when someone gets old, we put them in an old folks' home. Someone takes care of them, and they eventually die. We all say something like 'This person lived a long, healthy, and happy life.' We tend to cope with that scenario pretty well. But if a child dies, it is catastrophic."

He began to translate what I said to the mothers, and they looked at me through their head scarves with judgmental eyes and disgust. They began whispering one to another. The mother closest to me spoke up again, "If that is how you treat your elders in America, YOU are monsters."

I walked out of the house and headed back to my Humvee. I thought, "We're living in a foreign country in a culture that has zero awareness of America. Conversely, I'm an American with zero awareness of what they're all about."

Why do different cultures think so differently? Who is right in their thinking? Who is wrong? How can we listen to them and understand them while withholding judgment?

What is truth for us is not truth to them. How does that make sense in this world?

Captain Dan Quinn found himself in an incredibly difficult and uncomfortable position: he not only was joining a new team, but he was responsible for commanding that team. He had to earn their immediate respect, learn the team SOPs, train and rehearse with the team, and bond with them. On top of that, he was replacing a team leader who had just been seriously injured, he fired his team sergeant, and he was dealing with serious moral, ethical, and cultural issues from his top Afghan commanders. All while in combat. That's as difficult a situation as there is.

Dan's story produces a lot of mixed emotions from the SOF community. When Dan's situation is brought up, most operators I've talked to say, "Man, that's a tough one. I'm not sure how I would have handled that. I wouldn't have risked getting thrown out of the G-base, (guerilla base, where allied indigenous forces live and operate) but I also wouldn't have tolerated the rape of a child." Regardless of your opinion, one thing is clear as a leader: not knowing (or ignoring) what's going on around you is the precursor to failure.

Dennis Allen, the former head coach of the Oakland Raiders, hired

Mission Six Zero to help him solve a unique problem. When I sat down in his office, Coach Allen was blunt.

"Jason, my job is on the line this year. I need to win or I am gone. I know that. Management knows that. The team knows that. This off-season we had a lot of salary cap space, so (general manager) Reggie McKenzie and I spent that money bringing in veteran players who have been successful and produced for other organizations. Here's the thing—I don't know these guys. I didn't develop them. I don't know what their motivations are. Are they going to be there for me in the fourth quarter when the game is on the line? Are they going to give up if we go on a three-game losing streak? I need you to help me find out who the guys are on the team that I can count on, that I can trust. I need you to help me figure out what is going on around here."

Before I left his office, Coach Allen opened up to me: "If anybody is going to have a hard time during your events, or is going to quit, it's going to be Pat Sims…I don't think he is going to be able to make it."

I asked why.

"It's just consistency and effort," Coach Allen answered. "Pat plays like an all-pro on first down, but he doesn't put forth any effort on second or third down."

"Why do you have him on the team, then?" I asked.

"I've come close to releasing him, but I just can't do it," Coach Allen said. "Pat plays well sometimes, and cutting him would cost us millions of dollars. Not to mention we'd have to find a replacement, which would also cost us millions of dollars *and* a high draft pick."

During practice, a specially selected Mission Six Zero instructor provided his feedback on Pat Sims. "When not engaged in a drill or other team activity, Pat simply appeared to be lethargic or disinterested. If my commander told me 'that guy' was coming to my A-team, I would order a sleep study for him first thing Monday morning. If the sleep study turned up nothing conclusive, I would consult a nutritionist or counselor to figure out if there's a legitimate cause for Pat's apparent fatigue." We found our answers a few days later during our initial event.

After taking Pat through a day-long individual actionable decision-making scenario, one of our instructors sat down with him for the out-brief, where Pat opened up. They talked for an hour nonstop.

Our instructor asked, "What's your pregame ritual?" Pat said he "pretty much just chills out." When the instructor asked what that meant, he explained that he just hangs out and watches movies and TV shows on Netflix. He asked Pat how late he stays up doing that, and he replied, "Until about three or four o'clock in the morning—just like most nights." The instructor smiled. His suspicion had been validated. Pat didn't sleep. Pat was tired first thing every morning. And he just went downhill from there.

As our instructor moved beyond the formal evaluation feedback, he began to dig. He learned that Pat's family and friends were all back east and that he was isolated from those closest to his heart. When asked where he lived, Pat told him that he lived at the Extended Stay hotel within walking distance of the practice fields. Pat had been living at this hotel for nearly a year! A multimillionaire NFL player living at a hotel for over a year doing nothing but staying up until 4:00 a.m. watching Netflix every night.

Furthermore, Pat explained how he hadn't connected with his teammates. He said that they openly talked negatively about him, but he had heard that sort of thing his whole life. Our instructor relayed, "I've learned to detect when a teammate is down, when things aren't quite right. I can tell when someone on my left or right is in need, and Pat was in need."

He didn't stay up late throwing marathon Netflix parties for one because he was that into movies and television. He was watching Netflix because it was something he could do alone, something with which he could occupy his time, since he knew he was going to be awake anyway. Television just filled a void for Pat. And that was why he was sleep deprived every day. That was why he seemed disinterested and unmotivated. That was why Pat underperformed even though he was such a physically gifted athlete.

A few days later, we presented our findings to Coach Allen and some of his coaching staff. As we went through the players one by one, we arrived at Pat Sims. We asked, "Do you know where Pat lives?" There were crickets in the briefing room. A coach asked, "No. Where?"

I pointed across the street to the Extended Stay.

"Pat lives there. He's been living there for over a year." We then went on to explain our findings. We addressed Pat's chronic sleep deprivation and the contributing factors to his lack of sleep. We talked about how Pat started his days "on empty," which was siphoning off his physical energy, mental toughness, and possibly his emotional resiliency. We discussed Pat's lack of peer support, personal friendships, and general happiness. We suggested that they consider possible depression. We explained that everything we discussed were issues that were solvable: rest, security, and social interaction (camaraderie).

After the overall assessment, one of the coaches said, "I can't believe that about Pat, I had no idea. We were just discussing cutting Pat today. Knowing what we know now, we definitely won't be doing that. You guys literally just saved us millions of dollars and wasted time spent on paying his owed salary, finding someone to replace him, and spending money on *that* player's salary!"

With so much confusion and uncertainty going on around you, it's important to go back to the basics, to your foundation, to help you make the right decision. In the Special Operations Forces community, we hold five truths as foundational and sacred. The SOF Truths are an important part of social strength:

SOF Truth 1: Humans are more important than hardware.
People, not equipment, make the critical difference. The right people, highly trained and working as a team, will accomplish the mission with the equipment available. On the other hand, the best equipment in the world cannot compensate for a lack of the right people. One person can make all the difference, both for good and bad.

SOF Truth 2: Quality is better than quantity. Build a room of the right people. When you have a bunch of good people working the problem, there are few things that you can't solve. In combat, a twelve-man ODA performs the work of a thousand-man conventional unit.

SOF Truth 3: Special Operations Forces cannot be mass produced. The cookie-cutter or canned approach will never lead to an elite outcome. A unique problem requires a unique solution.

SOF Truth 4: Competent Special Operations Forces cannot be created after emergencies occur. As a leader, you must slowly grow quality. You can't take shortcuts in a crisis. You cannot expect your people to step up their game and perform when an emergency occurs. In those moments, your underperformers usually perform even more inadequately or simply quit. You need to hire the right people, take the uncomfortable leap of faith to believe in them, and then develop trust by training them the right way, from day one. Competence is proactive, not reactive.

SOF Truth 5: Most Special Operations require non-SOF assistance. Check your ego. You can't do everything by yourself. Sometimes you need to rely on others to do their jobs so you can do yours.

A leader must have a foundation on which to build. In the SOF community, we use the SOF truths as our foundation on which to build an effective culture.

Remember:

- Define your line for what you are willing to tolerate.
- Everyone on the team must understand what defines success and failure.
- Gray should not be tolerated—inaction is unacceptable.
- Go back to the basics, to your foundation, to help you make the right decision.
- Not knowing or ignoring what's going on around you is the precursor to failure.

The Suicide Bomber
with **Flo Groberg**

Flo served six years in the US Army Infantry as an officer. He earned the nation's highest award, the Medal of Honor, when he tackled a suicide bomber in Afghanistan. During two combat rotations, Flo also earned two Bronze Stars and a Purple Heart. He was born in France and grew up in Chicago before his family settled in Potomac, Maryland. He attended the University of Maryland, College Park (UMD) and graduated with a bachelor's degree in criminology and criminal justice.

It was well into the evening by the time Captain Jason Van Camp entered my office. I rose quickly to shake his hand, making sure I didn't wince or show any sign of pain while doing so. Since the president had awarded me the Medal of Honor for my actions in Afghanistan, I'd noticed that people looked at me differently. Not judging me, necessarily, but certainly examining me closely. I never wanted them to see any weakness.

My body was always in pain, a fact I couldn't escape. And it always would be. But experience had taught me some time ago that there was no point in feeling sorry for myself, so I no longer wasted the energy.

"Flo? It's an honor to meet you," the young captain said.

"You too, Jason. Welcome to Fort Carson."

"Glad to be here. And thanks for taking the time to speak with me. Major Petit thinks highly of you and thought your experiences on the battlefield could help me be a more effective leader."

"Happy to help. You're the third new captain he's asked me to speak with, and I've found that I usually learn more from them than they do about me." I offered him a tin of Copenhagen. He declined.

"I understand you're going to deploy in a few weeks," I began. "How are you feeling?"

Jason answered quickly. "I feel good. I've met with some real badass dudes over the past week who have passed along some great lessons, and I'm just ready to meet my team and get over to the sandbox."

"Good," I told him. "But it's normal to be apprehensive. You're going to be leading men into war. That's a serious task. I certainly had fears going into combat."

"And you clearly were able to put them aside and perform under fire. I know you have to tell the story all the time, but would you mind talking with me about the day you earned the Medal of Honor?"

I nodded. Naturally. Everyone wanted to hear about the Medal of Honor. But it was the worst day of my life. Imagine having to talk about the worst day of your life every single day.

"Sure," I said. "It's a tough story because we lost some amazing people that day, but I tell it because I want what those men did to live on. It was Afghanistan for me, the second time. I was taking over Dagger Fourth Platoon out of Jalalabad. I had been hand selected by Colonel James Mingus to lead the personal security detail for him and Command Sergeant Major Kevin Griffin. My job was to keep them safe.

"Our area of operations (AO) was designated "green," which meant that in general, it was supposed to be a safe area with few threats from the enemy. But as I continually reminded myself, this was Afghanistan, and we were in a combat zone. Every time I stepped out of the wire, I made sure I was 100 percent locked in. The Taliban was really good at identifying your weak points, those soft spots where you think you are comfortable; exploiting them; and creating damage. In my AO, the Taliban focused on creating spectacular attacks. So, no matter how "green" it was supposed to be, I couldn't let my guard down.

It was supposed to be a simple patrol, one we had done plenty of times before. We'd be traveling on foot to the provincial governor's compound for a security meeting in the Kunar Province of eastern Afghanistan. As the personal security detail commander, I was leading a dismounted movement consisting of several senior leaders. We're talking VIPs, both from the US and the Afghan Armies.

I felt confident heading outside the wire. I had walked that route plenty of times and knew it well. So when we approached the compound and something didn't feel right, I decided to change the configuration of the element. I couldn't pinpoint exactly what was off, but there was just a strange feeling in the atmosphere. We were walking in a diamond formation, and I decided to position myself at the front of the element and put one of my soldiers, PFC Eric Ochart, in the "eye" position.

That's an incredibly important position, because if something happens, the eye is responsible for doing whatever it takes to protect the commander. I looked at Ochart and told him that if anything happened, I didn't care what anyone said to him, get the boss to safety.

As we approached the compound, two motorcycles sped at us from a close distance. One of our Afghan National Army (ANA) soldiers raised his rifle and started screaming and gesturing at them, forcing them to dump their bikes and run away. The Afghan soldier sprinted after them, not noticing the man walking out of a building to our left. But my platoon sergeant and I did. We made eye contact with each other, a nonverbal "Hey, man, are you tracking this?" It was a civilian Afghan national walking backward and parallel to us. He was between eighteen and twenty-two years old, no beard, with nicely trimmed black hair and wearing man-jams.

I yelled at him to stop.

Suddenly, he spun around and started running toward our formation. We realized the motorcycles had been a diversion, designed to draw our attention away from this guy. I left my position and sprinted toward the Afghan, who was now a threat. I could see in his eyes that he was crazed, probably drugged. As I reached him, I noticed a bulge under his clothing. But I didn't see a weapon, so I couldn't shoot him. I didn't want to end up on CNN, charged with murder. Escalation of force is a very real thing. In this case, my escalation of force was to yell at him, hit him, grab him, throw him to the ground, and hope no one got hurt. So that was what I did.

When I hit him across the chest with my rifle, I discovered what the bulge was. A suicide vest.

"Bomb! Bomb! Bomb!" I shouted at the top of my lungs. My only thought was to get the suicide bomber as far as possible from our group as quickly as possible. I threw him, knocking him to the ground, where he landed chest down. His dead man's switch fell from his hand, releasing as he fell.

Boom!

His bomb went off with me standing over him. When it detonated, I felt absolutely nothing. It completely knocked me out, and I can say that if I had been killed, I would have died without pain. But I somehow survived. Four others didn't.

I woke to a chaotic scene. Call it the fog of war. I saw one of my soldiers, a twenty-two-year-old specialist, working to save my life. He had a blown MCL and PCL and a concussion, yet there he was, in a ditch stopping me from bleeding out. I watched my platoon sergeant take over the entire scene. He leaned over, telling me, "I got this, sir. You fought your fight; you are done." These men were at their absolute best even while operating under one of the most stressful moments imaginable."

Jason cut in here. "Flo, that is amazing. I think we all think about jumping on a grenade or tackling a suicide bomber to save our platoon, but you actually did it," he said.

This was where I got uncomfortable. I didn't like to talk about my actions that day. "I made the decision to do my job just like everyone on my team did," I told him. "I was the closest guy to the bomber, and I wanted to do everything in my power to protect the boss. They were counting on me to do my job. As it turned out, the blast from the first bomber caused the vest of a second suicide bomber to detonate prematurely with minimal casualties.

"The next thing I knew, I was being loaded onto a MEDEVAC. I later learned that the suicide bomber killed four members of the formation: Command Sergeant Major Kevin Griffin, Major Walter Gray, Major Thomas Kennedy, and Ragaei Abdelfattah, a volunteer worker with the

US Agency for International Development. Fourteen others, including me, were severely wounded.

Little did I know what was in store for me. The bombing was just the beginning. I was flown to Landstuhl, Germany, then stateside to Walter Reed. I would undergo thirty-three surgeries and lose half of my calf and the hearing in my left ear. I have no feeling below the knee in one leg, and the ligaments in my feet are all fused together. I couldn't move for four months.

I was not a happy person the first four months in the hospital. Nope. Absolutely not. I was angry, I was devastated, I had horrible survivor's guilt. Every night, when the visits were over and everybody went away, it was just me and my thoughts, alone sitting on a bed. All I could think was, why am I here? Why did I live? How is it possible for me to have survived when a guy blew up at my feet and four incredible men who were fifteen feet away died? I didn't get it. I didn't want people around me, I didn't want to rehab, I didn't want to be on the medications. Thoughts of suicide came across my mind.

I went around with that crappy attitude for a while. Then one day Travis Mills, a quadruple amputee, walked in my room on his prosthetics. Travis heard that I was sort of a hard case and nobody could get through to me, not even my family. I needed some motivation and a good talking to, and he was just the guy to deliver it.

Travis came in and said, "Hey, sir, what a great day to be alive. What a great day to be an American. How are you doing? By the way, your Chicago Bears suck at football."

After fifteen minutes in that room with Travis, everything changed. Travis let me know that I was not suffering alone. He believed in me. He challenged me in an unconventional way—by helping me understand that I could and would get through my injuries, but I needed the right support system. That was the moment when I made a decision to be absolutely done with the negativity. I knew I had to earn the right to still be on this earth, and my job while on it was to honor the memories of my fallen brothers. I needed to stop complaining. I had to be a better human being. Everything you just heard about my injuries is nothing compared to what so many of our guys at Walter Reed go through. Here was a man who had lost all of his limbs coming into my room and telling me to suck it up, to stop being a crybaby, be respectful, and earn the right to stay on this earth. How could I say no?

It was during this time when I was when rehabbing that I started to hear rumors about receiving the Medal of Honor. I was conflicted. Did I deserve it? Did I even want it?

One day I got a call from the Pentagon. "Is this Florent Groberg?"

"Yes."

"This is Colonel Slaney from the US Army Headquarters Pentagon. I'm calling to let you know that a senior high-ranking Pentagon official will call you on Monday, five days from now, between the hours of 1400 and 1430. Is this a good phone number for you?"

"Roger that, sir."

"Good. Florent, you cannot miss this call. Be ready for the phone call."

And he hung up.

All I could think was, "What did I do? Either I'm in trouble or this is something about the Medal of Honor." I decided that whatever happened, happened. I had no say in the matter. Monday would once and for all put an end to the medal debate, and I could move on with my life with whatever medal they decided to give me.

When the day for the call came, I was sitting in my apartment with my girlfriend, Carsen. 1400 came around, then 1410, then 1415. Still nothing. At 1425, the phone rang.

"Hello?"

"This is the White House. Would you mind holding for the president?"

That was the moment I knew I would be receiving the Medal of Honor. It was also the moment that I realized I didn't want it. I guess I had been hoping that the call would be about investigating some crazy stuff we did in Afghanistan (which really wasn't anything), or getting the Distinguished Service Cross, which is the medal they had initially pushed for me. I was getting comfortable in my own life and wanted to move on from August 8, 2012. More importantly, I thought the families also wanted to move on from it. This call would change that.

"Hey, Flo, this is the president of the United States." I recognized the voice immediately. I was surprised at how normal he sounded. It seemed like any other conversation.

"Yes, sir. How are you, Mr. President?" Little did he know how badly I was shaking, sitting in my apartment wearing a Cubs T-shirt. Or maybe he did; I don't know.

"Flo, we're going to award you with this nation's highest honor, the Medal of Honor." President Obama went on to tell me his expectations of me, and then he gave me a direct order: "Do not tell anyone about this yet."

When he hung up, I wasn't happy or excited. I was confused. I was sad. I was scared. I was ashamed to call the Gold Star families to tell them that I had just received a call informing me that I would be receiving the Medal of Honor.

I didn't want to do that. I wanted to call them and tell them I was sorry that they were giving me this medal. That I was sorry I couldn't bring home their loved ones. That I needed them to come to the ceremony because the medal didn't belong to me; it belonged to their husbands and them, the true heroes. I was just a courier.

Carsen was waiting to hear what had happened on the call. I told her, "I just got a direct order from the president not to speak about this to anyone, but if I don't tell my mother, I probably won't make it to the ceremony." I called my mother and disobeyed President Obama within minutes of his order. Don't tell him.

The thing is, after a phone call like that, you go back to life. Carsen sat on the couch and clicked *Ellen* back on. I continued writing a grad school paper. That was it. That was the rest of the day.

Later, I called the families of the soldiers killed during the attack. I felt blessed that each family member was so proud, so excited to hear the news. The Kennedys were like, "Can we bring his mom, his dad, his brothers?" I replied, "Bring everybody. This is your day."

I told them, "Every time I wear this medal and speak, people will hear about your husband. This is his Medal of Honor, not mine. It's not possible for a human to own this medal. It represents something much bigger. In my case, it represents Command Sergeant Major Kevin Griffin, Air Force Major Walter Gray, Major Thomas Kennedy, Ragaei Abdelfattah, and their families: Americans, patriots, men who sacrificed it all.

"And I promise you one thing: If they were here today, they would do it all over again. They believed in their mission, they believed in their country, and they are all heroes."

I hope that when it's all said and done, people talk about me and say, "You know what? This guy—he did right. He was a good person, good husband, good father, good colleague, and also, at the end, he served his country honorably."

That was where I always stopped the story. I wanted it to be about those men, not me.

"Flo, after an experience like that, what did you learn about yourself?" Jason asked.

"I learned that bullets and combat didn't scare me. I was in control of my emotions during firefights. Most importantly, I learned that I would do anything for my soldiers. Day in and day out, night in and night out, I was willing to die for them, as they were for me. I also learned that combat isn't difficult. A lot of it is just being lucky or unlucky. Even though the enemy was never as skilled or well-equipped as we were, you can't control the path of a bullet flying through the air. The enemy sprayed and prayed that their rounds would hit us; on our unlucky days, they did.

"I learned that the real world isn't all roses. It's people from different backgrounds who are merely trying to live their lives. Even the enemy. They wanted us out of their country, and I'm pretty sure that after a while they didn't even know why they were still fighting us, other than we were there. A smart Taliban would have allowed the US to rebuild the country, provide them resources, and go. Of course, after we left they would have taken it back. Instead, they chose to fight, and that's how our world functions. Too many egos, too many emotions, too many chiefs.

"Jason, I'm not alone in these thoughts. I've got a friend I'd like to introduce you to so you can hear his story. He's another Medal of Honor recipient I've gotten close to named Leroy Petry. Interested in setting up a phone call with him?"

SOF to Science with Dr. Michael Gerson,
Chief Mental Science Officer

Michael is a professor at John F. Kennedy University and San Jose State University, where he teaches sport psychology–related courses. He was the lead performance enhancement specialist at the Army Special Warfare Command (Fort Bragg) and Drill Sergeant School (Fort Jackson). He was also the director of mental skills for the Seattle Mariners.

Values are internal signposts that help us navigate the challenging world we live in. Think of them as our systems shorthand that can influence everything from internal events (thoughts, feelings, physiology) to outward actions. The principles we uphold, such as perseverance, compassion, and teamwork, are the core of who we are, and provide us guidance on what choices to make. People like Flo Groberg, who are clear about their values and committed to them, are able to draw upon them during uncomfortable circumstances and use them as performance catalysts.

Operating from these personal and professional tenets has its benefits. Not only does it enhance the quality of our confidence, concentration, and composure, but it can signal us to select choices that are in line with our moral compass. All too often, we have the proclivity to allow the situation or transitory feelings guide our decision-making process. This is why values are vital to our day-to-day operations in all aspects of life.

Inherent in Flo's story are the values he developed in childhood that would later help him make the decision to join the army. Principles such as loyalty, integrity, and personal courage were his calling card. These criteria for thinking and behaving were forged through personal experiences and then instilled and nurtured over many years by parents and other members of Flo's support system (i.e., teachers, coaches, mentors, etc.). These internal standards of living and doing were then reinforced, refined, and expanded upon while he went through the army's indoctrination process. Flo demonstrated these military ideals when he said, "I was the closest guy to the bomber, and I wanted to do everything in my power to protect the boss. They were counting on me to do my job." Flo's sense of duty was honed to habit until it became so ingrained that he could move seamlessly from assessment to action. He said his actions were instinct—instincts honed from living true to his values. This is the beauty of values: they answer the question, What would I do in this situation?

Flo attended one of the most rigorous military courses in the entire US military—the United States Army Ranger School located at Fort Benning, Georgia. The purpose of the course is to learn to lead while enduring the mental, emotional, and physical stressors of combat. During these "sixty-one days of suck," as it is routinely called by soldiers who go through the grueling process, Flo's values were put to the test. Not only were his values put underneath a microscope, but they were also put on display and then further fortified—the result of the Rangers' value-enrichment and enhancement program embedded in the eight-plus-week course. This moral strengthening method stems from the rigorous mental and physical training that takes place as one progresses from Average Joe to GI Joe. It is also developed through the Rangers' cultural transformation process that takes place during the grueling program. An important component of this training is the introduction to the Ranger Creed.

The Ranger Creed is a set of clearly established beliefs or guiding principles that are read, repeated, and rehearsed. Members of the Ranger community recite the Ranger Creed during formations, ceremonies, physical training activities, and upon graduation from the Ranger Indoctrination Program, the Ranger Orientation Program, and the US Army Ranger School.

The creed is plastered on walls, carried in Ranger rucksacks and smart books, branded on plaques of retirees, and forever engraved in the mind of any Ranger-tabbed soldier.

What's the importance of the Ranger Creed? Aren't they just words? Hardly. The US Army uses creeds as a tool to define its soldiers and for the soldiers to define themselves.

The Ranger Creed states what a Ranger as an individual will stand for and what he will do for himself, the unit, others, and country. It is simple, clear cut, and powerful. That is its strength.

The Ranger Creed:

Recognizing that I volunteered as a Ranger, fully knowing the hazards of my chosen profession, I will always endeavor to uphold the prestige, honor, and high esprit de corps of the Rangers.

Acknowledging the fact that a Ranger is a more elite soldier who arrives at the cutting edge of battle by land, sea, or air, I accept the fact that as a Ranger my country expects me to move farther, faster and fight harder than any other soldier.

Never shall I fail my comrades. I will always keep myself mentally alert, physically strong and morally straight and I will shoulder more than my share of the task whatever it may be, 100 percent and then some.

Gallantly will I show the world that I am a specially selected and well-trained soldier. My courtesy to superior officers, neatness of dress and care of equipment shall set the example for others to follow.

Energetically will I meet the enemies of my country. I shall defeat them on the field of battle for I am better trained and will fight with all my might. Surrender is not a Ranger word. I will never leave a fallen comrade to fall into the hands of the enemy and under no circumstances will I ever embarrass my country.

Readily will I display the intestinal fortitude required to fight on to the Ranger objective and complete the mission though I be the lone survivor.

Rangers Lead The Way!
— *Ranger Handbook SH 21-76*

So What?

1. Values influence action

The words that make up the Ranger Creed are interwoven like steel thread throughout the fabric of Flo's story. One example of this can be seen when he says, "As I continually reminded myself, this was Afghanistan, and we were in a combat zone. Every time I stepped out of the wire, I made sure I was 100 percent locked in." Combat necessitates that soldiers hone their focus so that they can perform complex tasks in extreme environments and do so without error. This mentality to be dialed-in relates directly back to some of the creed's striking statements about being an elite warrior: "I will always keep myself mentally alert." To Rangers like Flo, the Ranger Creed is more than just lofty words. It is a tool used for tightening up things like values, beliefs, thoughts, emotions, and actions.

2. Values transport across various situations and challenges

Flo not only displayed the attitudes that make up the Ranger Creed in training and on the battlefield, but also in the hospital with arguably his toughest fight. This hero, who saved the lives of many in an act of duty and love, had to contend with the aftermath of war. No longer able to fight, Flo faced a new enemy, one that was entrenched deeply in his mind and that tested his Ranger values. Dealing with severe anger and crippling remorse, Flo was left with trying to make sense of it all. In fact, it wasn't until a fellow soldier who lost all his limbs burst into his room and reminded him what it meant to be a Ranger that he finally snapped to attention. At that moment, it was as though the final line in the Ranger Creed came to life and took on new meaning: "Readily will I display the intestinal fortitude required to fight on to the Ranger objective and complete the mission though I be the lone survivor." It was time for him to live the Ranger Creed by honoring the memories of his fallen brothers. Flo's mentality allowed him to once again embrace his ideals by changing the way he looked at his situation and to live out a new mission. Flo's life story brings to light the importance of what it means to connect, live, and operate by a creed or system of fundamental beliefs. A set of guiding principles and deep core values that keeps us on course even in the darkest and most uncomfortable of situations.

3. Values lead the way!

Mike Ditka once asked, "How many successful people have you ever heard say, 'I'll just make it up as I go along?'" His answer: "I can't think of one." High performance does not happen by accident. Instead it is an outgrowth of building, connecting, and drawing upon one's values with deliberate intention. Most military units have creeds to outline these values. They have found that a standardized, written statement is effective for setting the motivational tone of doing and achieving. They have drawn strength from this powerful elixir, rising to the occasion in harrowing situations by using values as a springboard to action— especially those that are steeped in discomfort. One way to be truly effective in your pursuit of excellence is to develop your personal creed or philosophy of professional practice.

4. Putting the comfortable in uncomfortable

A creed can provide clarity and consistency to yourself, others, and your mission. It is a philosophy that will inspire your efforts and that you in turn will aspire to live and uphold. Just as Flo utilized the Ranger Creed to make the uncomfortable more manageable, your personal creed should be your "formula for success." It should be unique to you; a set of affirmations that you can commit to over the ensuing years.

Now What?

How can we put this Army Ranger doctrine with all its morals and methods, traditions and techniques, philosophies and procedures into practice and play in our own lives? The purpose of this section is to lead you through a creative creed-building process that results in a clear understanding of the key values that will guide you in your chosen profession and/or life. Just like the Ranger Creed, your personal creed will be a set of traits, beliefs, affirmations, and actions that you will commit to.

STEP 1: Make a list of at least of at least ten personal values.

Note—Below are a couple of ideas to help you brainstorm.

1. First, think about a team that you have been a part of. How did you contribute to its success?

2. Or, if someone were to describe you, what would they say about you? What makes you unique or special?

STEP 2: Condense the large list into five key traits that will serve as rallying points for future success. The five traits you have selected are the keys, guidelines, and charter for the way you will BE and how you will ACT.

They can be five of the top values that define who you are or a combination that includes values that you believe you need to possess in order to accomplish great things.

Note—If you are struggling to make eliminations, then here are a few tips.

1. Go to someone who knows you well and ask them to help you whittle it down by having a conversation about your character.

2. Look carefully at the list and see which traits could be included in others or which ones are redundant.

STEP 3: Define the five traits that would be the most useful and beneficial for your future. The ones that could have the greatest positive impact on you.

Note—Search for a textbook definition that fits for you.

1. Search various sources to find the functional definition that you agree with most and write it down.

2. Next, put the definition into your own words.

STEP 4: Prepare a list of actions you will commit to.

Note—Give an example of this trait in action (i.e., as an outsider, how would I know if you really were operating from your values?). Get as specific as possible.

1. Decide on three to five behavioral indicators for each key trait.

2. Another idea, in addition to the action statements, is to assign one affirmation, quote, or belief sentence to each value.

STEP 5: Decide on a title, a slogan, and a background.

1.   Choose a title for your creed.

2.   Come up with a slogan for the ending. For example, the Ranger Creed says, "Rangers Lead the Way!"

3.   Last, think of a background for your creed. Something that represents and symbolizes the entire document.

Practical Application with Jason Van Camp

Of all the creeds that I had to internalize in the military, the Ranger Creed is the creed that has impacted me the most. During our six-month Ranger School train-up (pre-Ranger training), after each daily 120-minute physical smoke session, our team stood at attention while one of our teammates stood in front of the rest of the team and recited the Ranger Creed verbatim. We were inspired to repeat each line of the Ranger Creed as a group as loudly and patriotically as we could. I remember vividly when one of our instructors stated that the Ranger Creed is "the greatest assemblage of words next to the Bible."

Whenever someone made a mistake when reciting the Ranger Creed, we all dropped to the ground in unison to execute a painful physical penalty. Only after the punishment could we attempt to recite the Ranger Creed again from the beginning. This creed inspired me to want to become a Ranger—someone who is expected to move farther, fight harder, shoulder more than their share of the task, never leave a fallen comrade, and complete the mission though they are the lone survivor. During the dark and painful times in training or combat, I would often recite the Ranger Creed in my head or whisper it to myself. This repetition helped me to find my mental courage and fight through the difficult times. As we discussed in previous chapters, mental strength is not something that we achieve; it is a process that we execute.

A creed will:
- Establish a team mind-set, identity, and culture;
- Inspire buy-in to new strategies and initiatives;
- Provide a framework for communicating with customers, employees, and investors;
- Promote understanding and action;
- Embolden you in difficult times; and
- Answer the question, "Why?"

In the NFL, the New England Patriots, under Bill Belichick's leadership, have consistently proven the value of having a creed. They call it "the Patriot Way." It has come to define everything about the New England Patriots' excellence in the twenty-first century: eighteen consecutive winning seasons, sixteen AFC East Division championships, and six Super Bowl Championships.

Former Patriots' defensive end Rob Ninkovich represents everything good about the Patriot Way. As a two-time Super Bowl champion, Rob is a beloved sports icon in the city of Boston. But success wasn't handed to Rob; he had to fight for it every step of the way. Rob and I talked about his incredible journey and how he transformed himself into a perfect fit for the Patriots:

"I didn't have the easiest path to a successful NFL career. But I was mentally prepared to do whatever it took to make it. So that's what I did.

That road to mental toughness started when I was young. In my house, you never gave up, and you never quit. Once you started something, you were going to finish it. I didn't realize it at the time, but those lessons my parents were instilling in me allowed me to start developing my own creed at an early age.

Growing up, I fell in love with football. It was all I thought about, and my world revolved around the game. There were plenty of kids who were more athletic than me, but I always outworked them. It started in the weight room and on the practice field, so that when game time came around, I would be better than everyone. I was adding to my personal creed: hustle, hard work and determination were now included with my never-quit values.

At the end of my senior year, I earned All State as a defensive end. It was time to pick a college and play big-time college football. College recruiters came to my high school. They saw a 6'2", 185-pound defensive end who didn't take care of his academics and spent his time chasing girls. They didn't see a Division 1 football player.

I had missed my opportunity.

I decided to go to Joliet Junior College. When I got there, I started to set goals and write them down, a skill I learned from my dad. I became laser-focused on school and doing the right things. One day the Purdue recruiter attended our practice. He was scouting another player, not even looking at me, and I was pissed off about that.

When I went home, I told my dad. He said, "Do something about it." So I did. I called the head coach at Purdue, Joe Tiller. I called him twenty times. I'd leave a message. Then I'd call again. Leave another message. Call again. Finally, he called me back and said, "Hey kid, just send me your tape." So I sent him my game highlight tape. He called me back the next day and said, "Will you be able to come out to school next weekend for an official visit?"

Hell yeah, Coach.

I quickly won over the coaches and enrolled at Purdue, which was where I had always wanted to go. That first year, my junior year, I didn't start but still ended up leading the team in sacks. I wasn't a starter until the last six games of my senior year. At the end of my senior year, I wasn't sure if I had a chance to get drafted or would even get an invite to the NFL combine, but I trained like I would.

I did get invited to the combine and performed well. On draft day, my phone rang from a 504 area code. I picked it up, and Sean Payton, the head coach of the New Orleans Saints, was on the other end. "We're going to take you at 135," he said. I remember just being happy that my dream of playing in the NFL was coming true.

I led the team in sacks during the preseason and made the team as a rookie. Then, in our first home game since Hurricane Katrina, I was running down the field on a kickoff. I got hit, and my foot got stuck in the ground. My ACL, MCL, and PCL ligaments were all torn. It was a big-time knee injury, with nothing but my LCL holding my knee together. I told myself, "I'm going to get back here. I don't care how hard I have to work, but I'm going to get back here." I worked my ass off rehabbing and returned to the field next season. Then, early on in training camp, I tore my MCL again.

That one was tough.

Once again, I rehabbed the entire year and made it back for training camp the next season. Then, at breakfast before a preseason game, Coach Payton sat me down and said they were cutting me. My agent called the next day and told me that a few teams had claimed me. Since the Miami Dolphins had the worst record of those teams, the rules stated I would be going to Miami.

Miami was awful. We went 1–15 that year. But even on a 1–15 team, I couldn't get on the field. I asked the head coach, Cam Cameron, "What do I have to do to play?"

He just said, "We have the guys on the field that we think give us the best chance to win."

I responded, "We're 0–10. Anything would be better than that." Predictably, in the offseason, everybody got fired. The whole coaching staff, the GM, everybody. In came Bill Parcells to run the show. One day I was in the weight room when he walked in.

"Ninkovich, right?"

"Yes, sir."

"Purdue, right?"

"Yes, sir."

He put his hand on my shoulder and said, "You're an inside linebacker now."

I'd never played inside linebacker in my life. Once again, I found myself on the practice squad, now trying to learn a new position. After ten weeks of that, my agent called and said the New Orleans Saints were interested in bringing me back. They had two guys (Will Smith and Charles Grant) who were going to be suspended the last four weeks of the season. They needed help at defensive end.

I left Miami the next day without telling anyone. Upon arriving in New Orleans, I learned that a judge had overruled Will Smith and Charles Grant's suspensions. There went my playing time. I was placed on the roster for the last four weeks of the year but would not be allowed to play.

The next season, Coach Payton walked up to me and said, "Rob, you're never going to make this team as a defensive end. You'll never play defense here. The only way you can make this team is if you if you become a long snapper."

I looked at him incredulously. "A long snapper? You think I'm a long snapper?" I couldn't believe it. But I swallowed my pride and dove into it. I remembered my personal creed. I decided, "I'm not going to quit. I'm going be the best damn long snapper and cover guy I can be."

I snapped hundreds of footballs a day while peeking over at the defensive ends doing their drills. "Man, being a snapper is not me," I would think, then snap another football.

When I got out of my car on the first day of training camp, a guy was waiting for me. "Coach Payton wants to see you," he said. I knew what that meant.

I went to Sean's office. He told me, "We had something come up, and we're gonna have to release you today." I almost flipped his desk over, I was so mad.

I went out in New Orleans that night and got hammered drunk.

The next day I went golfing. On the second hole my phone rang.

It was the New England Patriots.

"Hey Rob, Bill Belichick here," he said. "We're two weeks into training camp, and we need a body. If you can get here today, that'd be great."

"All right," I said. "I'll get there." I left the golf course and drove straight to the airport.

I arrived at camp the next day determined to turn some heads. I wanted to go against their best Pro Bowlers and dominate them. I walked right to the front of the line on my first drill. Guys were taunting me, saying, "OK, go up there and get your ass kicked."

I found myself one on one with Matt Light, one of the best Patriot tackles ever. Tom Brady's blindside protector, a multiple Pro Bowler, and three-time Super Bowl champion. Didn't matter. I didn't care who he was, how big he was, or what his status was. I was going to beat him.

On my first rep against Matt Light, I beat him clean off the edge with a double swipe. The offensive line coach lost it. "Matt! Who just beat you? I don't even know this guy's name, and he just beat you! Do it again."

We lined up again. I acted like I was going to do the same thing, but instead countered inside. Matt flew past me. The offensive line coach yelled even louder. "You've got to be shitting me! One more time."

We lined up again. The first time I had won with speed. The second time with a countermove inside. The third time, I figured I would just put my head down and try to run him over. And that was what I did. Matt almost fell straight over, and I ran right past him. The offensive line coach blew his whistle and shook his head, saying, "I can't believe this."

At the end of each practice, we had team meetings. During those meetings, Coach Belichick would show highlights and lowlights. It didn't matter who you were; he'd call you out and put you on a lowlight if you deserved it. Likewise, a highlight. That day, when Bill showed the highlights, he said, "Look at this. This kid just got here today. This Ninkovich kid. This is what we're looking for. Rob, good rush. Keep it up. By the time we're done with you, you won't know what you're doing."

To this day, I have no idea what he meant by that.

I ended up making the team by playing special teams. I went on to become a starting defensive end for the Patriots and played for the next eight years, winning two Super Bowls. I attribute it all to developing a creed in my youth.

I learned a lot playing for Bill Belichick and the Patriots. Bill talks a lot about foundation. He'd tell us, "You can have a beautiful home. It can look awesome on the outside, but if the foundation isn't strong, it doesn't matter how great it looks. Eventually it's going to crack, and it's going to fall down." That's how he builds his teams. With a strong foundation.

Bill comes from a military background. His father coached at the Naval Academy for years, and he takes that military mentality to building a team. That's why practice is so important to the Patriot Way. Training in the offseason sets the foundation for the season. It's where you go through hard times and build chemistry with your teammates. For me, it was messing around with guys like Dane Fletcher, Ross Cintron, and Julian Edelman. The harder it is, the closer the relationships. Like in the military, you're not playing for yourself. You're playing so you don't let down the guy next to you. Bill would tell you that New England wasn't the easiest place to play. He was going to ask a lot of you, and there wouldn't be much praise. Bill wouldn't say, "Good job." Instead, it was, "That's what you're supposed to do. That was your job; you did it."

The Patriot Way is Bill's creed. We say, "I'm going to come in every day. I'm going to be the best I can be. I'm going to be attentive. I'm going to work hard. I'm going to put the team first, and that will be my mentality every single day." If you're going to work out in New England, you have to buy into that creed.

My creed helped keep me on course in my darkest times. My creed helped me to define myself: I was a guy who would never quit, always hustled, was persistent, and was going to win one way or another. My creed gave me confidence during uncomfortable times. It helped me make the hard choice to deliberately choose the path of most resistance. When my career was over, I looked back and thought, "I surprised a lot of people, but I never surprised myself."

Remember:

- Every time you step "outside the wire," make sure you are 100 percent locked in.
- Values are internal signposts that help us navigate the challenging world we live in.
- A creed is a set of clearly established beliefs or guiding principles that are read, repeated, and rehearsed. Use your creed to help define yourself, your team, and your team to define themselves.
- Make the decision to do your job just like everyone on your team does. You're not special for doing your job.

9 The Final Battle

with **Leroy Petry**

Leroy medically retired from the army in 2014 with fifteen years of active duty service with the 75th Ranger Regiment. He earned the nation's highest award, the Medal of Honor, for his actions during combat in Afghanistan. Leroy has also earned the Legion of Merit, two Bronze Stars, and one Purple Heart during his two tours to Iraq and six tours to Afghanistan.

It was still dark out when I got up for an early-morning workout. I checked my phone and saw I had missed a late-night text from Flo.

"Yo Leroy!" it read. "There's a new SF captain that I'd like you to talk to. One of Major Petit's guys. I gave him your number and told him to give you a buzz tomorrow."

"Cool," I thought as I sweated out leg day at the gym. "But what advice should I give this guy?"

After each set, I would lie down for a short moment and allow myself a breather. These moments of relaxation were my reward for hard work. But they didn't last long. In fact, the shorter I let myself relax, the more intense my workout became.

I'd come to realize that while being uncomfortable is something you need to strive for in order to improve, it's only a plateau. A beginning, not the end. You should remain comfortable just long enough to take a breath and acknowledge your growth and hard work, and then immediately put yourself back into another uncomfortable situation. That's how you continue to grow and improve.

As I was walking down the stairs to the locker room, my phone vibrated in my pocket. A 703 area code—must be Flo's captain.

When I answered, a gruff but friendly voice said, "Hey! This is Jason

Van Camp. I'm looking for Leroy Petry. Flo Groberg asked me to give him a call."

"Hi Jason, this is Leroy. Flo gave me the heads-up. What can I do for you?"

"Awesome. I've got to tell you: Flo's experiences and advice were incredible. I'm taking command of an SF team and deploying to combat soon. I'd like to get your advice and understand what I should know and do to help my team succeed over there."

"I can't tell you what to do and what not to do, brother," I told him. "But a good place to start is with your definition of success. And only you can answer that. The only thing I can do is tell you about what success means to me."

"That would great," Jason said. "I'd love to hear about it."

I took a deep breath. Though I had to tell the story quite a bit, it was never easy.

I was on my seventh deployment and fifth tour to Afghanistan. We were pulling so many missions that I lost track of time and wasn't even paying attention to how many months we'd been over there.

One night, we got pulled in by leadership and told that a high-value target (HVT) was moving around our area. All Special Operations Forces in theater were put on standby and told to hold all other missions because there was a chance this guy was going to pop up on the grid. Whoever was closest was going to action on it. Roger that. Hope we get the call.

The next day, I walked into our TOC to check my email. A few minutes after I had logged on, the officer on duty jumped out of his seat and yelled to me, "Leroy, wake up the pilots and all your guys!"

I didn't even ask what for—I just ran out and started getting everyone moving.

The rumors started flying. The high-value target had popped up. He was in our area, and we had been selected to go after him.

We scrambled to prepare for the mission. I did a precombat check on my weapons and personal equipment, then put on my body armor.

At the last second, I ran into the chow hall and shoved some packets of beef jerky and lickies and chewies into a pouch on my kit for the boys in case we got stuck out all day again. Soon we were loaded on Chinook helicopters and heading toward the objective, which was in a very rural area of Afghanistan.

When we were within three hundred meters of the target, our helo banked hard and put us down in a field. As soon as we ran down the ramp, an enemy combatant started shooting at us. I was running with the platoon leader and command element, and we maneuvered toward the gunfire to neutralize the threat. As we were clearing the body of the enemy combatant, I heard over the radio that one of our younger squad leaders was at the wrong compound. I knew this squad leader needed help, so I told my platoon leader that I would link up with him to provide overwatch and guidance.

I was kind of a free floater at that point because I was the weapons squad leader and had attached all my guns to the other three squads in the platoon. So our platoon leader told me to go for it. By the time I caught up to the squad in trouble, they were already stacked on the corner of a walled mud compound and about to enter. I fell in as last man in the stack, which consisted of seven guys preparing to breach the door to the compound.

Unfortunately, the squad leader was young, and he recklessly sprinted diagonally across the compound's courtyard with his guys to begin clearing a two-story structure. It was the wrong move, but once they committed, I ran with them. We should have locked down the courtyard first, but when they skipped that, I had to back my guys up.

I stood in the doorway of the two-story structure. In the sequence of clearing, we moved toward a smaller one-story structure, which we called a "chicken coop" because it looked smaller than the rest of the buildings in the area. As soon as we started moving toward the chicken coop, we started receiving small-arms fire. We broke the corner and heard the familiar pop of an AK-47. It was clear that the enemy combatant shooting at us was not well trained and firing from the hip like an amateur. Even so, I felt a thud against my leg.

My body bucked like a deer that had been shot. I knew what had just happened. I had been hit in the left thigh with a 7.62 mm round from an AK-47.

"OK," I thought, "I'm fine. The bullet lodged in my leg. I can keep going." I knew I needed to get our guys out of the kill zone, so I led one of them, Private First Class Robinson, behind the chicken coop. Everyone else was in the two-story structure.

"Hey, give me a battle damage assessment!" I yelled at PFC Robinson.

I discovered that Robinson had been hit just below his left shoulder in the side Kevlar plate of his body armor. Fortunately, it just hit his plate and not his body. We found out later that the bullet lodged about a quarter of an inch from where it would have punctured his lungs, heart, and other vital organs.

My focus shifted to the volume of fire coming from around the corner of the chicken coop. "Posture on this corner," I told PFC Robinson while prepping a grenade.

I threw the grenade at the attacking enemy and heard it explode on the other side of the chicken coop. A lull in the fire allowed Sergeant Higgins, one of our team leaders, to run over to us. "How can I help?" he shouted.

"Help Robinson watch that corner!" I yelled back.

Sergeant Higgins ran over to support Robinson. As soon as he reached him, he yelled back, "What the hell is that?"

The words were barely out of his mouth when the first explosion went off. They were enemy grenades. Robinson, Higgins, and I were all instantly hit with shrapnel from the grenades. Another grenade detonated near us. It sounded like someone clapping their hands together with such force that my ears exploded.

"They're throwing grenades!" I called out. "Keep your heads down, and keep watching that corner!"

I stayed on the radio informing higher of our situation while watching my corner. Every few seconds I would turn to check on the status of my guys. I moved into a squatting/seated position because my leg was really starting to throb. I just happened to look down and saw a pineapple grenade lying right behind Robinson and Higgins.

It's funny what goes through your brain in a moment like that. I thought, "Hey, we haven't used pineapple grenades in years. That can't be one of ours." Then: "That's *not* one of ours!"

I grabbed the grenade and cocked my arm back to throw it as far as I could. As soon as I opened my hand to release it, the grenade exploded.

I was thrown back toward the wall of the chicken coop. I sat up and looked at my right hand. It was completely gone. It looked as if someone had taken a circular saw and cut my hand off at the wrist. The radius and ulna bone were sticking up about a quarter of an inch. What was left was oozing blood pretty good. I grabbed my forearm and held it tight, but in my mind, I was thinking, "Why isn't blood shooting three feet into the air like in the movies?"

"Snap back to reality," I reminded myself. I had to take care of this.

I reached down with my left hand to grab a tourniquet off my kit and tie it around my right arm. I checked in on Robinson and Higgins. They had both received minor shrapnel and were in shock a little, but they were fine.

I switched my rifle from my now-nonexistent dominant right hand to my left and returned fire. We continued to hold the position and battle it out with the enemy.

Our first sergeant got on the radio to tell me that he was leading a group to our position for support. When he arrived, he grabbed me by my kit and said, "Come on. We're getting you out of here!"

I pushed his arm down and looked directly at him. "I'm good," I said. "I'm staying here. You guys need to stop this volume of fire they're laying down on us." First Sergeant looked me over. I could tell he was making a decision. Eventually he realized that I had already administered initial self-aid and was coherent.

"We'll be back for you," he said, and took off running.

We continued fighting and holding our position for another fifteen minutes or so. Every so often, I would sling my rifle and throw a grenade over the chicken coop with my left hand. Hey, what goes around, comes around. Eventually, there was another lull in the fire. I grabbed onto another Ranger and helped Robinson and Higgins run to the casualty collection point.

When we arrived, I saw a number of our guys getting treated. What shocked me was the blood. It was everywhere.

Our senior medic came running up to me. "Petry!" he shouted.

I glanced over at him.

"Hey, bud, we need to have a look at that arm."

"I'm good. I put a tourniquet on it," I replied. "Help those guys." I motioned to some Rangers on the ground bleeding.

"We got people helping them. We need to take a look at you. Dude, your legs are bleeding too!" he said.

I looked down at my legs for the first time since realizing I had been shot. My pants were soaked with blood all the way down to my boots.

What I originally thought was a bullet lodged in my left thigh was actually two different rounds that had penetrated my upper left thigh and exited through the right. Miraculously, the bullets had missed both bones and arteries.

In my mind, I didn't want to leave the fight. I wanted to contribute however I could, whether it was staying on a radio or just comforting the guys. But after what seemed like hours of fighting, I could feel my body running out of juice.

I acquiesced to the senior medic. "OK," I told him and sat down.

He cut off my pant legs and started prepping me for medical evacuation. They got me on a stretcher and tied me down. I remember one of my guys took my rifle and laid it next to me on the stretcher. I appreciated that. I couldn't really see much else because I was lying prone and strapped in, but I was aware of my surroundings.

As we started to make our way up a hill to the helicopters, a medic handed me something. "Here, man, take some fentanyl pops," he said.

I had never actually seen a fentanyl pop before, though we always joked about them with the medics. I assumed it was just a sucker with medicine and flavored like lime or lemon. He handed me what looked like a dipping stick. I bit off the end of the stick and threw the plastic end away.

When we were halfway up the hill, the medic looked down at me. "What did you do with the pops?" he asked.

"I ate them and threw the sticks over there," I replied.

The medic smacked me in the head and said, "You're supposed to suck on them, idiot."

He gave me a couple more pops and started explaining what to do with them, but stopped suddenly. "I have to go," he said quickly. "They lost the vitals on one of the guys."

As we continued up the hill, things started to slow down. I could make out our guys pulling security from a rooftop. Guys kept running up to me and saying, "Hey, man, you're going to be all right."

Each time I'd think, "Great, thanks. Now get the hell away from me." I felt helpless being out of the fight, and my biggest fear was that one of our guys was going to get shot while attempting to comfort me.

At one point I remember looking up and seeing all these guys with beards. I recognized a few faces. Navy SEALs. The ground force commander told them, "Hey, we don't need you guys here."

A few of the SEALs smirked under those damn beards. "Hey, man, we're just here to provide blocking positions for you."

I laughed out loud and said, "Really? How does it feel, assholes?"

The SEALs laughed with me, knowing that we were usually the ones being asked to provide blocking positions for them.

A Chinook landed, and they loaded me up the ramp. Before we took off, Higgins came running up. "You saved our lives, man," he said.

"Higgins, hurry up and get on the damn bird," I responded. The area wasn't secured yet, and the comforting words were superfluous.

We flew to a nearby airfield on FOB Sharana. They unloaded my stretcher and laid me on the side of the airfield while the helo took off to continue supporting the mission. We still had guys out there. I immediately started thinking about who else was hit.

While I was lying there, I watched as medics from our unit ran around working on other guys. I was later told that one of those guys was Specialist Christopher Gathercole.

Specialist Gathercole's team was on their way to support us when an enemy combatant hiding behind some brush started firing on them. Specialist Gathercole was hit in the head just below his helmet and was killed pretty much instantly. His death hit me like a brick.

Within twenty minutes of landing at FOB Sharana, a bunch of us wounded were put on a fixed-wing aircraft. By this point I was heavily sedated and lost consciousness. I woke up a couple of days later in Germany.

When I woke up, the nurses came in and asked me if I needed anything. The only thing I could think of was some shaving cream and a razor. I had to keep up the standard; what if a colonel or general came in to see me? I didn't want to be the Ranger with beard stubble.

When they arrived with the shaving cream and razor, I reached out with my right hand.

"Oh yeah, my right hand was blown off," I reminded myself. I'd have to learn how to shave with my left hand.

I lay in that hospital bed in Germany and thought about my wife and my kids. I thought about the rear detachment (Rear D) soldiers going to my house to tell my wife that I had been injured. I thought about how worried and concerned my family must be. My wife told me later that she and my mother-in-law were still in their nightgowns having coffee and getting the kids ready for school when there was a knock at the door.

She went to the peephole and looked out. She saw soldiers dressed in fatigues and knew that I wasn't dead, that I was just injured. If a soldier is killed in action, the notifying soldiers arrive in dress uniform. She told her mother to take the kids upstairs and opened the door. The Rear D soldiers explained to her what had happened, and then she waited for my phone call.

When I was finally able to call, she told me, "This has been the worst day of my life."

I lifted up my arm and replied, "It wasn't my best day either, honey." I let her know that I had been shot through both legs and lost my right hand at the wrist, but that I was OK.

The phone went silent.

"The good news is the junk is still there," I said, grabbing my crotch and ending the story.

Jason laughed. "Hey, Leroy, be honest with me. Were you afraid?" he asked.

"I get asked that question all the time. And the answer is, absolutely. Every single day I was afraid. It wasn't the fear of dying; it was a fear of failing those around me. Of not catching an IED in the road before one of our vehicles hit it or not catching a shooter in the window. My biggest fear was to come home and hand a folded flag to a family member of one of my guys.

"But I turned that fear into fuel. I turned that fear into awareness. I trained my guys harder. I did extra work with them. I let the fear serve as motivation. It drove me to train my team harder, and we became faster, stronger, and better."

"Leroy, you asked me earlier about success. What is your measure of success?" Jason asked.

"My definition of success is measured in knowing that your kids are going to be contributors to society and not a drain on it."

"Love it. Thanks for that, Leroy" Then: "What ever happened to the HVT you were going after on that mission?"

"We got him, but it was years later. He had fled the compound before we got there that day. The Taliban fighters that we were engaged with were the soldiers the HVT left behind. I heard that he was caught in Saudi Arabia and then extradited to the US. When he got to the US, he squealed like a canary and gave up a number of other HVTs."

"I know that feels good. What are you up to these days?"

"What do you mean?"

"Like, what do you do for a job?"

"Jason, I'm still in the military. Just because the president gave me the Medal of Honor and I lost an arm doesn't mean that I can't continue to serve."

SOF to Science with Casey Van Camp,
Chief Developmental Officer

Casey has served in the public and private sector for over fifteen years and has advanced degrees from Utah State and Penn State Universities in development, training, staffing, and leadership/management. He has led transformation efforts to redefine the developmental culture across offices within the federal government and Fortune 500 companies.

Leroy Petry's story showcases the power and fortitude of the human spirit as the foundation for optimal human performance. Leroy maintained control under the most volatile, uncertain, complex, and ambiguous circumstances by tapping into the power of the human spirit to make a choice.

That choice was based on his core beliefs of loyalty and determination to overcome overwhelmingly intense physical pain. His choices enabled him to interrupt the stress response, better known as "fight, flight, or freeze," as he needed to continue the fight. Leroy's spirit empowered him to find comfort in discomfort, to ignore the pain and fight on until his unit won the battle, when others might have quit (Benson, 1975). Recognizing and leveraging the power of your spirit can sharpen your focus and determination and can access the body's untapped potential to achieve truly exceptional feats.

It is critical to have a strong, well-nourished spirit to overcome the natural human response. You can nourish your spirit through preparation, embracing fear, setting goals and expectations, and finding a team. With a strong, well-nourished spirit, every person can overcome fear and achieve greatness. Humans are continually bombarded with internal and/or external stimuli known as stressors. A common misconception is that stress is negative. Negative stress, or distress, can be harmful for the body. However, stress can be productive in ways that help mobilize our attention. Dr. Carol Dweck's research suggests that positive stress is a fundamental building block to growth as an individual performer and as a team.

When humans interpret threats or opportunities through our senses, our brains spring into action and immediately release neurotransmitters such as cortisol, adrenaline, and norepinephrine. These (Herman et al., 2003) neurochemicals drive our bodies to the stress response known as "fight, flight, or freeze." For primitive humans, the stress response was critical to our survival as a species because it allowed us to quickly respond to the threat of predators, gather resources, and hunt prey.

While humans are no longer faced with threats such as saber-toothed tigers, our natural response to real or perceived threats or stressors has not changed. The good news is that we can control this process in part by relying on a well-nourished spirit. While the brain and body work to balance themselves to allow for decision-making, it falls upon the well-nourished spirit to give us the strength to perform beyond oneself when under pressure.

Despite continual sensory inputs from his environment telling him he should run or seek help for his injuries, Leroy chose to stay with his team to continue to fight for as long as he was able. His indomitable warrior spirit, grounded in his core values, beliefs, and purpose, created a dominant pattern of thinking by which he prioritized the needs of his fellow soldiers over his own needs.

So What?

- Spirit and external stressors: Spiritual power drives you to continue to fight through exhaustion and pain. A strong spirit allows you to interpret what is going on internally and externally and determine the body's reaction to external stressors. The human body continually takes in information and makes choices on a subconscious level. Many of our systems are automatic and beyond our conscious control. For example, you don't tell your body to breathe in and out. However, when faced with stressful situations, the body produces high levels of neurotransmitters leading to our fight, flight, or freeze response (Benson, 1975). The brain is conditioned to act/react to stimuli that can lead to rash decisions that may be satisfying in the moment but ultimately destructive. Leroy advised Jason to turn fear into awareness. Fear is antithesis of a strong spirit. Fear stands between action and inaction. "Our fears are grounded in self, time, and space. But when all three vanish at once, something far more incredible occurs: our fear of death—that most fundamental of all fear—can no longer exist" (Kotler, 2014). When the spirit is strong, it will ultimately overcome fear.

- Purpose, values (core beliefs), and passions: Each one of us has a core belief system, the essence of how we see ourselves, other people, the world, and the future. These core beliefs develop over time through experience. They exist to help us make choices in the face of external stimuli. Leroy's advice to "let the fear turn into motivation" means that as you work, you will face fear and be in uncomfortable situations. But if you make embracing fear a part of your core beliefs, you will be prepared to rise above and overcome fear (Shpancer, 2010). Don't fear your fear—appreciate it and use it as a tool. Leroy chose to support others, to fight back when his environment and injuries urged him to flee. His spirit allowed him to choose to fight, ignore his pain, and endure longer. It is the ability to overcome base instincts and make a choice that defines the power of the human spirit.

- Limits: Leroy said, "In my mind, I didn't want to leave the fight. But after what seemed like hours of fighting, I could feel my body running out of juice." Even when the spirit is strong, willing, and eager, you need to be aware of your own limits. Your spirit can push you beyond your perceived limit. In the office, you can work long hours, cover for others, or do two people's jobs. A strong spirit can get you through this for a while, but eventually you will be exhausted. As outlined in chapter 3, Leroy was in a flow state. But that can only last for so long.

"As focus tightens, the brain stops multitasking. Energy normally used for temporal processing is reallocated for attention and awareness (Kotler, 2014). Instead of keeping time, we are taking in more data per second, processing it more completely, and, perhaps—though great debate rages around this point—processing more of it per second."

Leroy entered a state of flow, overcoming tremendous physical pain, until his spirit knew it was time to stop the fight.

Now What?

- Be prepared: There is no way to remove stress from your life, but there are ways to be prepared for it.
    - Control the controllables: Understand what you can control—grip forces—and what you can't control—gravity forces. Focus your time, energy, and effort on grip forces and let gravity forces fall by the wayside.
    - Study: It's more than likely that you're not the first person to deal with this situation or circumstance. Talk to others and do your homework to learn best practices.
    - Imagine: Use as many senses as possible to create vivid, personal, and powerful images of you executing your performance perfectly before it actually happens. See yourself from both the inside, in terms of what you're thinking and feeling, and what you want that performance to look like from the outside.

- Embrace fear: The more you embrace fear, the more comfortable you will be challenging the unknown and overcoming being uncomfortable. As Leroy said, "Every single day I was afraid. It wasn't the fear of dying; it was a fear of failing those around me." Don't let fear prevent your success; let fear strengthen your spirit.

- Goals and motivation: Set high and hard goals that get you and others on your team excited. Establish and communicate a clear and detailed plan that is focused more on benefits through the process rather than the product and achievement. Leroy told Jason that he needed to start with his own definition of success. When creating your goals, first ask yourself, Why am I embarking on this journey?

- Feed your spirit: The spirit is powerful and enduring, but it is not without its limits. You will need to take time to strengthen and feed your spirit. You could feed your spirit by hiking in the mountains, surfing on the beach at sunrise, playing with your kids, or reading Holy Scriptures. Find what feeds your spirit and do it consistently through quality repetition. As Leroy proves, a strong spirit can help you overcome anything and take on any challenge.

- Find a team: You need someone to "have your six." Everyone needs a support structure for when the spirit falters, they lose the way, or they need to overcome colossal challenges. Be around like-minded individuals. There will be times when you need someone to motivate and encourage you. Other times, you are going to be the one to support the members of your team. Remember, if you want to go fast, go alone. If you want to go far, go with a team.

Practical Application with Jason Van Camp

Spiritual strength is not about religion. It's about recognizing and tapping into a private, transcendent, sacred force that each of us possesses. I've heard it said that "religion is a person sitting in church thinking about kayaking. Spirituality is a person sitting in a kayak thinking about God."

Having spiritual strength will help you overcome personal hardships. It will help you keep faith in yourself and believe in an inevitably positive outcome. Spiritual strength does not come passively. You achieve spiritual strength through pain and suffering (both internal and external), so you can be dedicated to your beliefs and certain about your competencies and skills.

Leroy Petry's story showcases the power and fortitude of the human spirit as the foundation for optimal human performance. Recognizing and tapping into the power of your spirit will sharpen your focus and determination and will access the body's untapped potential to achieve truly superhuman feats.

The most dedicated and self-confident person I know is Mike Moone. Mike is an incredibly accomplished businessman who started working at Procter & Gamble (P&G) immediately upon graduating UCLA in 1962. During his time there, he would go on to transform the way the company recruited new employees. He later joined the wine business, purchasing Beringer, Stag's Leap, and Chateau St. Jean before selling Beringer for $1.6 billion in 1999.

Mike is also an extremely spiritual person. He explains how he has leveraged his internal spirituality and certainty about his competencies and skills to find incredible success in life:

"Achievement is in my bones," Mike says. "I believe that most people don't have a conscious awareness of their inherent ability to achieve."

In the mid-1960s, when Mike was working for P&G in Cincinnati, his boss, Bill Coleman, called him into his office.

"Mike, I don't have anything for you. I don't need you. I'm going to let you go," Bill told him.

His underling's reaction was not what Bill was expecting. "You *do* need me, and I'll tell you why," Mike responded confidently. "Your food division, Duncan Hines, is like the Siberia of P&G. They have a high turnover rate because they hire five guys and only promote one of them. I have the ability to fix it," Mike said.

Interest piqued, Bill asked, "What do you suggest we do, Mike?"

"Recruit the right people, and fewer of them. No one should be recruiting at college campuses if they are not properly trained to do so."

Bill couldn't believe the audacity of this young, soon-to-be-fired salesman. "We have a system in place, and we do just fine with it."

"No, you don't. It's more complicated now. We need to hire more African Americans and more women. The people who represent our company must represent the people who buy our products. I'll tell you what I'm going to do. I'm going to hire two hundred African American salesmen and two hundred women in the next three years."

Bill's jaw hit the floor. But he agreed to consider Mike's suggestion and let him keep his job. For the time being.

A few weeks later, Bill called Mike back into his office. "Mike, I'm going to allow you to do it your way. You can go recruit at the University of Tennessee on a trial basis. But I'm sending one of our top decision makers to supervise. Oliver Hughes will decide if your proposed course of action is feasible."

Mike quickly learned that Mr. Hughes wasn't impressed by him or his approach. When they arrived at the University of Tennessee, Mr. Hughes didn't even want to interview in the same room with Mike, so they set up different interview stations.

On their second day, Mr. Hughes burst through the door as Mike was interviewing a candidate. Out of breath, Mr. Hughes interrupted. "Mike, I need your help!"

"What's the matter?"

"I'm in a bind, and this is going to look bad for P&G. A beautiful black girl just walked into my interview room."

"OK..."

"I told her, 'This room has already been cleaned.' Mike, she was an interview candidate!"

"Shit."

"Tell me about it. Oh man, this is going to be terrible for P&G."

Mike told Mr. Hughes, "I'll take care of it."

This was an opportunity for Mike to make things right with this young lady, prove himself, and win over Mr. Hughes. He walked into the interview room and found a justifiably furious candidate.

"Pardon me, miss, what's your name?" Mike asked politely.

"Eliza Marcus. And I'm not the cleaning lady. I'm one of the top academic students at this university, and I was considering P&G. But now I'm considering going to the newspaper to report how racist a company you represent."

"Ms. Marcus, I want you to know that this is my fault. The person who was supposed to interview you was not trained properly. He was not trained on what we are trying to do. I apologize and take full responsibility. If it's appropriate and you are willing, I would like to personally conduct the interview with you."

She agreed, and Mike gave her a proper interview. He found her to be an incredibly powerful candidate and offered her a job on the spot. She took it.

When Mike returned to Cincinnati, his boss called him. "Mike, I misjudged you. You were right with how we were recruiting. This thing is a whole lot more complicated than I thought. Oliver told me what you did for him. I'm impressed."

"So, do you think you need me here?"

"Most assuredly, yes. In fact, I'd like you to create a one-pager outlining your vision and present it to the board."

Soon, Mike was in front of the top executives in the company—a table full of "grumpy old white dudes." And he was proposing changing P&G's entire recruiting strategy. After the presentation was over, the CEO said, "So we're hiring blacks and women now?"

Mike explained his strategy. "Yes. Our customers are not just white men. If we aren't hiring women and minorities, the people who make up our customer base, then we're going to fall behind. I want to go to college campuses and recruit people in leadership positions. The student body presidents, the captains of athletic teams, the football players who aren't going pro. I'm looking for achievement. I believe that a person's past shows what their future will hold."

Mike was sent to the University of Texas to test his belief. He spoke with then Texas Longhorns head football coach Darrell Royal.

"Coach, I know you want to help your players after their careers here are over. I've got a way for you to do that. I want to hire a guy who's a leader on your team, who's smart as hell, and who doesn't have the skill set to go pro. I want that guy at P&G."

After a few days, Coach Royal presented Mike with a list of those types of players. Mike set up interviews with each of them. When they showed up, Mike told each of them, "Your coach tells me you're a natural leader. I want to hire leaders. If you come to P&G, you'll start out in sales for two years. After that, we'll move you to a management position."

Mike would also look for former military officers in college who were taking advantage of the GI Bill. He would tell them, "Look, I know you feel like you're behind. You are a little older than your peers here, but we want you at P&G because you have proven leadership ability. You are competitive, and your skills apply to what we do."

Mike hired so many military vets that he got interviewed by the *Wall Street Journal*.

"Why do you like these officers out of service?" they asked.

"Because Vietnam is winding down, and the guys coming back have experience leading people of all ages, races, colors, and creeds. They have everything that we like at P&G. Whether you believe it or not, the military uses people very intelligently. They don't put dummies in leadership positions. They put people in the right positions to get the job done."

"Wouldn't you rather hire an MBA instead?" the reporter asked.

"No, I would rather hire a military guy," he answered. "There are some really smart MBAs here, but they can't park their bikes straight."

Of course, the subheadline in the *Wall Street Journal* article read, "Moone hires officers out of the military because MBAs can't park their bikes straight."

Mike left P&G after eleven years with the company. He had made millions of dollars for himself and billions of dollars for the company. He was the top salesman for years and was a well-known and proven commodity. But he decided to join a small company called Beringer Wines.

"Nobody bought their wine; sales were less than $2 million a year. But they had great promise," he explains. Under Mike's leadership, Beringer went from $2 million in sales to $250 million in five years. During those five years, Beringer had three number-one wines in the world, which no one had ever done before. Mike exited at $1.6 billion.

Mike credits his successes to a deep desire to achieve combined with a willingness to take risks and deliberately place himself in uncomfortable situations. Mike added, "The reason I am successful is that I embraced doing what other people resent or were reluctant to do." These are Mike's keys to success:

1. Be direct. When you are a leader, tell me what you think, and tell me what you want me to do. I don't want you to use *we*. Say "I." I want to hear what YOU think. What do you think I should do, and what do you want me to do? This mind-set puts people in an uncomfortable situation. It turns people's brains on. It's how I achieved billions.

2. Make a personal commitment to each employee. Ensure the same commitment from them to you. I never let anyone down when I was doing what I said. I always gave at least as much as I asked.

3. Be clear with your vision. I made sure the team understood where we were going and how we were going to get there. The team knew our goals and understood the effort required to achieve them. This is where we are, this is where we are going, and this is how we are going to get there.

Remember:

- Comfort is the enemy of achievement.
- Spiritual strength is achieved through pain and suffering (both internal and external), so you can be dedicated to and certain about your beliefs.
- Spiritual strength will help you overcome personal hardships.
- Voluntarily putting yourself in an uncomfortable position means that you are willing to achieve.
- Complacency kills.

---

10 The Long Walk

with **Joey Jones**

Joey is a retired US Marine Corps staff sergeant. During his eight years of service, he worked as an explosive ordnance disposal (bomb) technician, deploying to both Iraq and Afghanistan on separate tours. During his last deployment to Afghanistan, he was responsible for disarming and destroying more than eighty IEDs and thousands of pounds of other unknown bulk explosives. He currently works as an analyst for Fox News.

I was pretty happy when I looked at my caller ID and saw that it was Jason calling. We had been friends for a few years, and I was proud that he had recently passed the Q Course and was officially a Green Beret. I knew he was headed back to combat, this time in charge of an SF team, operating in more dangerous environments and responsible for far more important missions. For a second, I thought to myself, "I wish I could go." Then my other side quickly spoke up. "Been there, done that," it reminded me.

"JVC, what's up man?" I answered vigorously. "You still owe me one of your football jerseys for my home gym!"

"I know. I'll get it to you," he promised. "I would think you'd be more embarrassed than anything to have that hanging on your wall."

"Bullshit. Hard-charging Green Beret war hero. Be an honor."

"Please, man, we all know there's only one hero on this phone call, and it ain't me." Jason paused, and I could tell he had something serious on his mind. "Listen, Joey. I'm having a serious conversation with my boss later this week and want to ask you something before I do."

"Sure. What's on your mind?" I had a feeling I knew what he wanted to discuss.

"It's about after you got blown up," he said.

That was what I figured. When you don't have legs, even for other combat vets, it's a touchy subject. But one I was obviously used to discussing. "You've never really asked me about that before," I said.

"I was kinda afraid to. But my new boss has opened my eyes to a few things, and I would love to hear your thoughts, if you're willing."

"Of course, man. Shoot."

"Thanks, Joey. Let me ask you this: After you were injured, how did you find the strength to adapt and overcome?" he asked. "Did you ever want to give up?"

It was a good question, and I told him so. "But before I answer," I told him, "we need to start at the beginning. With why I became an explosive ordnance disposal technician in the first place."

"Makes sense," said Jason. "Why *did* you volunteer to be a bomb tech? Why would you choose to put yourself in those dangerous, uncomfortable situations?"

"When I first joined the Marine Corps, I was stationed in Hawaii, responsible for security at a nuclear submarine station on Pearl Harbor. I loved being a marine, but thought that I had more to offer than standing watch all day. During our training, we would wargame potential threats to the facility. Our senior leaders would plant fake IEDs to test our ability to identify and handle those types of threats. When we found a fake bomb, we would call in the EOD guys to come take care of it. I thought it was amazing how these guys could neutralize the threat with nothing more than their bare hands.

Not only did they remove the threat, but they gave us a sense of security and safety. I wanted to be on the other end of that, to be in control of my own fate. I didn't want to rely on someone else. I wanted to have the knowledge and skills to overcome those challenges—not only for myself, but more importantly, for the marines around me.

But it's a challenging job. You need more than just big balls. Those guys have to know so many things to be good at their jobs: nuclear physics, chemistry, engineering, explosives, all while getting shot at.

That's what first attracted me to the EOD profession.

I compare it to being a snake handler. If you're a snake handler, you have the knowledge and skill set to control that snake, making it less dangerous to you and the people around you. A snake bite is just as deadly to the snake handler as it is to everyone else. You are not immune to the venom; you just have a lesser chance of getting bit because you know how to handle it. By expertly handling the snake, you make sure others don't get bit either."

"True," Jason said, "But you also are less likely to get bit if you don't willingly place yourself around snakes."

"Right, but when they were around, I didn't want to scream and run away from a snake or ask someone else to catch it for me. I wanted to be the guy. That's what being an EOD tech is. Knowing which snakes are the most dangerous, which ones are venomous, and how to make sure they don't bite anyone.

Besides, I figured if I was in the Marine Corps and we were in the middle of war, I was gonna be around these IEDs for the foreseeable future. Somebody had to walk down there. Why shouldn't it be me? I just wasn't comfortable letting someone else risk their life to dismantle a bomb for me. Saving lives was what really made me excited to be an EOD tech.

When I finally deployed to Afghanistan on a two-man EOD team, the place we went to was bonkers. IEDs everywhere. Troops in contact every day. It was every bit of combat a guy could want. And we were doing great, dismantling all these bombs. Then, after about six months, the odds finally caught up with me.

My unit was tasked with clearing an entire village. One group would start on the far southern end of the town and clear a Medevac route through the center, while my group would be the main clearing element. Our goal was to get a big enough perimeter to go back and clear all the buildings. My team was responsible for dealing with the majority of IEDs.

By the fifth day, we had dismantled about forty IEDs and had finally cleared the streets. Then we got a call at 0600 that the engineers found some bomb pieces in one of the buildings.

"Holy shit!" I yelled to no one while gearing up. "Don't these assholes eat breakfast and take a shit before they start saving the world?"

When we got there, one of the marine engineers told us, "There's a bunch of IED components in there and what looks like a giant bomb. You guys need to take care of this."

Then the engineers backed away so I could go in for what we call the "long walk." Whether it's a conventional mortar hung in a launching tube, a grenade downrange that didn't explode, or an IED, an EOD tech has to walk to the area to check it out and take appropriate action.

Usually, my teammate and I approach the marine who identified the bomb, and they direct us to it from a safe distance. He tells us what they think we got. Then one of us will walk up to the bomb to dismantle it. And we always take that long walk alone.

Remember, we have to know how to handle every single type of ordnance that can be found on a battlefield. On top of that, we have to deduce and intuitively prosecute homemade bombs that could function in any number of ways. It takes a lot of wisdom, hard work, and research to succeed at this job. You gotta do your due diligence. You gotta have instincts. You gotta have knowledge. And you have to trust your teammate to make the right decisions as well.

Unfortunately, I couldn't quite trust mine. For most of that deployment, my teammate was lacking in at least a few of those areas. You know how in most organizations the bottom 10 percent should get cut? Well, in this case it didn't happen. I just couldn't trust my teammate. But while you don't always get to pick your teammates, you can choose how your team operates. I chose to lead from the front and ensure that everyone operated to the standard, even when I didn't have the team members I'd have liked. You can still instill a culture that ensures everyone abides by your command. That was what I tried to do, but I was struggling to keep him focused and doing the right stuff.

Anyway, the two of us approached the building with Daniel Greer. Daniel was a marine engineer from Knoxville, Tennessee. I'd met him early in the deployment and had mentored him about the style of IEDs we were seeing in that area so he and the other marines could search for them too. He was planning to get out after this deployment. That day, Daniel joined us to help look for bombs and pull security.

When we entered the building, it was completely dark, so we had to use our helmet lights to see. The floor was covered with dirt and debris, which meant we couldn't tell where the hell we were stepping. For all we knew, this facility was booby-trapped to high heaven.

We got down on our hands and knees and started clearing the debris, looking for wires and bombs. It was hot as balls in there, and I was wearing full gear. The river of sweat dripping down my face and into my eyes made it incredibly difficult to focus on the task at hand.

We finally cleared a large area that revealed RPGs and bomb-making materials. A seven-foot-long rocket flare that we found was especially concerning. These things are normally dropped from planes. The weight of the flare pulls a lanyard and sets a fuse, which winds down until it finally strikes a primer. It becomes a giant flaming candle in the sky, lighting up the battlefield at night. These flares have about an 80 percent success rate. But even the one out of five that doesn't function correctly can arm and go off once it hits the ground. Sometimes they'll just hit the ground and lie there. Then you come by, move one slightly, and set off a giant fireball.

In EOD school, I learned everything you could possibly want to know about different types of bombs. We have information on tens of thousands of pieces of ordnance, so really all you can do is categorize them and learn the names. Unfortunately, you only get to practice on a small percentage.

Well, I was in luck. It just so happened that I had worked on a rocket flare in school, and I knew just what to do. I'd just put a thermal grenade on it and let it burn itself out. But when I looked over, I saw my teammate walking out of the room with the rocket flare on his shoulder.

"What the hell are you doing, man?" I yelled out. "I worked on those in school, and the number-one rule is, you don't move it!"

He set the flare down outside in the back of an alley, next to a little three-foot wall about ten yards from where we were working. I told him to go to the other end of the building and let me take care of it. As he walked away, I leaned over the flare to see if the fusing system had armed. I don't remember what I saw next because as I leaned away from the wall, my right foot stepped on another IED.

I just remember feeling like I was weightless. Everything went tan, like I was in a sandstorm. The sand filled my eyes, my pants—hell, even my mouth. As I opened my eyes, everything had been replaced by a cloud of sand. A tan nothingness. My spirit had left my body, and an empty self-awareness remained.

I landed on my back and was like, "Damn, I know exactly what just happened. I just got blown up. I just stepped on an IED."

Then I thought, "I am a marine EOD technician, and I failed to find an IED, and then I stepped on it. What a dumbass…God damn it."

You know, there are a lot of misconceptions about getting blown up, and you can probably blame Steven Spielberg or Ron Howard for some of that, but you don't always get knocked out. For me, I didn't have the whole "everything slowed down and I could see people talking but not hear them." The reality is, I don't know if I even heard the bomb go off. The severity of it just kind of muted my ears for a second. The blast was so loud that it must have overpowered my ability to comprehend it.

My first instinct was to look down and see how much of my legs were left. I had been around long enough and put enough guys on birds to know what to look for. It wasn't good. Both legs were gone. My left arm was twisted behind my body in a way it wasn't meant to go. The most intense sensation came from my lips. It felt like they had exploded from the inside out, like a cherry bomb had blown up in my mouth.

I started going through the motions of trying to grab a tourniquet. I reached up with my right hand to reach a tourniquet on my body armor. But when I pulled that arm up, my hand stayed in my lap. The bone and muscle had been severed, leaving only the muscle on the top and skin to hold it together. My right forearm was like spaghetti. Every blood vessel and ligament tendon was hanging down.

I stopped moving around too much, thinking I was probably going to bleed out. Another marine was close to me, lying on the ground. It was Daniel.

I started yelling at him to see if he was coherent and could get up and get himself to cover. After an IED goes off, it's usually followed by people shooting at you. Simultaneously, you worry about other IEDs. My thought was to get Daniel out of there.

He was knocked out on the floor and not moving. I didn't see any blood, so I tried to wake him up to start laying down fire in case somebody started shooting at us.

I remember thinking, "Man, I hope some marines get here soon." When they did, I yelled for them to look for my footsteps and follow my path in case there were other IEDs. I directed them to Daniel first.

When the first marine reached my side, I made him recite the Lord's Prayer with me. We only made it through two lines; that was all either of us knew. I was like, "Well, I hope that works."

By that time, they had Daniel on a stretcher and left with him. I kept asking how he was, but no one knew.

I started to go through a whole cycle of "I'm gonna die" and then "I'm not gonna die." I thought, "What do I have left? I can live without legs, but if I lose my legs and an arm, I won't be able to work out. I won't be able to push a wheelchair. It's gonna be tough finding a girlfriend or a wife after this." I was in really good shape and loved to work out, so I figured if I had my arms intact, I'd be OK.

I tried to hide the injuries to my arms. I pulled my arm into my belly as best I could so they couldn't see the damage. I knew there was a mobile trauma bay about two miles away, which is basically a sterile surgeon's box on the back of a truck. I'd seen it too many times before. Because they don't have all the right equipment, they would just cut an arm off to save a guy's life. I was trying to hide how bad my arm injury was, hoping they would send me to a bigger hospital and save my arm.

After what seemed like an eternity, I saw a marine applying tourniquets to what was left of my legs.

"Are they both above?" I asked.

That's a question well anticipated by marines who see their brothers get hit. If you lose a foot, you'll be OK. If you lose a knee, it sucks. If you lose both of your knees…it's not good. He confirmed I had lost both knees.

I asked for morphine, and they finally shot me up. Once the morphine hit, my mind started to wander. I knew I was going into shock. I told the marines working on me, "Hey, guys, I'm going into shock. I need you to calm me down. Talk to me. I need my heart rate to speed up. I can't pass out." I told them my kill number, which is your pertinent information because most of us don't carry dog tags anymore. You don't want that shiny object moving around and making noise.

They got me on a stretcher and loaded me into the Humvee for transport to a desert outpost with a mobile trauma bay. From there they medevaced me to another hospital in Afghanistan, where I had to stay two extra days before being transferred to Germany because I had lost so much blood that they couldn't get enough back in me.

I woke up Germany two days later in a hospital room not unlike what you'd expect—with machines and IVs and the smell of sterile plastic and metal. When I opened my eyes, the first thing I noticed was the strange color of the walls. They were painted a tired shade of sea-foam green, a color especially noticeable to an EOD technician because almost all white phosphorus munitions are painted that shade. My body was wrapped in blankets, each of my limbs, or what was left of them, propped on a bed of pillows. I could see my right arm in what appeared to be a wireframe; I couldn't see my left arm at all. I didn't quite know the extent of my injuries, but I remembered everything from the incident. I knew I didn't have legs, and I knew my life had changed forever.

I was pretty heavily medicated, so I don't remember exactly how much pain I was in, but I'm sure there was some. For the most part I was just trying to figure everything out. They woke me up by taking a breathing tube out of my throat, so for the first few minutes of consciousness I couldn't speak, only beg for water that they couldn't give me. Instead, the nurse would wet my lips with a sponge. It was the most tormenting thirst you could imagine.

As my memory began to clear, my new horrendous reality set in. I realized it wasn't yesterday when I had been hit. I had been out for a few days. I thought back to right before I had lost consciousness. Seeing Daniel's face staring back at me, motionless. It would become a haunting reminder of how lucky I really was. I'd seen people die before, but when Daniel was looking back at me in those moments, it felt like death itself reaching out, laughing at my vulnerability and helplessness. I screamed, begging for him to wake up, to speak, wink, show me that he hadn't left and that it wasn't all my fault.

There was a nurse in the hospital room with me after I came to. She must have been the one who pulled the breathing tube out. I have no idea why, but I remember her with a southern accent. About an hour after waking, I regained the ability to speak. I had only one question. I looked at the nurse for a moment, silent, and then asked "How is Daniel?"

She answered quickly. She told me that when I had stepped on the IED, a piece of the wall that I was leaning over kicked up and hit Daniel in the head, causing catastrophic brain damage. Daniel's family had taken him off life support that same day.

I was devastated. But I realized that I had to drive on.

During that deployment, I had learned that I had a son. An old friend from high school had come over to a Halloween party, and one thing led to another. We had a one-night stand, and I got her pregnant. I am a marine, after all. One shot, one kill, I guess. I knew that Daniel had a wife and a son near the same age. I said to myself, "I owe it to Daniel to get out of this bed and be a good dad because he can't." I decided not to focus on what I didn't have. I decided to focus on what I did have and what I could do with it.

For me, it's all about having emotional strength. It was my ability to compartmentalize things. To put things in a box and set it over there and focus on what's in front of me. To not let whatever is in that box affect my mood, the task at hand, or the moment. I had too many people depending on me to be sad. I didn't have the time or luxury to worry. Whatever I had gone through, I had survived it, and it couldn't control me anymore.

I find myself using the lessons I learned in combat in my daily life now. Like all of us, I've got a hundred things to worry about. All kinds of things bother me. But I make a choice to not let those stressors affect the next thirty minutes of my life. Or hour. Or day. The most important thing for me right now is to enjoy this ball game with my son. I have to push all the other distractions away. Until the end of this baseball game, I'm going to enjoy my time with my son and not have a care in the world. Anything worrying me can be dealt with later."

"Damn. Joey, that's powerful. I'm proud of you, brother. Thank you for digging deep and sharing that with me. I appreciate you exposing your heart. That can't be easy," Jason said quietly.

"I don't share these experiences in that amount of depth too often, but I did for you," I responded. "But why do you bring this up? What does your boss want you to know? I mean, you've only been there a couple days; you couldn't have screwed up that bad yet. Or is it that he wants to know why marines are better than Green Berets?"

"That's it!" Jason affirmed. "Marines—the first in! After SF, Rangers, SEALs, 160th, and AFSOC." We both laughed, and then Jason got serious again.

"Bro, my company commander wants me to understand how certain people in his company go about their business on a day-to-day basis. I gotta tell you, the people I've talked to so far are absolutely incredible. It just got me thinking about the most impressive people I knew in my own life. I consider you one of those people. I wanted to call you and find out how you think and why you are so emotionally strong. Talking with these guys and learning about their experiences is really making me rethink a lot of my preconceived thoughts about leadership."

"Well hell, I'm honored then. When you coming back down to Georgia?"

"Depends. When are you getting us cast as extras on the set of *The Walking Dead*?"

SOF to Science with Dr. Sarah Spradlin,
Chief Emotional Science Officer

As discussed in chapter 4, Nate Last describes the mind as a sniper team where we can be both the spotter and the shooter in order to direct and shift our attention to sensory information on demand. In this chapter, Joey Jones demonstrates an interrelated process that is key to self-regulation, called *compartmentalization*. Compartmentalization is the ability to filter through conflicting values, thoughts, and emotions and focus on one priority task at a time in the performance moment. Getting comfortable with compartmentalization is a skill developed and refined through deliberate practice over time (Selimbašić et al., 2019).

This chapter begins with Captain Van Camp asking Joey, "After you were injured, how did you find the strength to adapt and overcome?" As Joey's inspiring story unfolds, we learn of the explosion, his life-threatening injuries, Daniel's passing, and Joey's grueling recovery. In the end, Joey succinctly answers Captain Van Camp's initial question by explaining that his ability to adapt and overcome is all about emotional strength and the capacity to compartmentalize things in an efficient and effective manner.

Joey's compartmentalization is best described using the analogy of organizing his thoughts and emotions like a filing system. Each thought and emotion represents a file in Joey's mind. He can filter through and prioritize all the available files, use the files he needs, put away the ones he doesn't, and then focus on the most important tasks at hand. Like many veterans who have experienced the violence and trauma of combat, there are some files that stay with you forever. For example, the physical pain of losing his legs and the emotional pain of losing a friend are permanent files that can't be deleted.

Yet as Joey explains, we all have the power to choose how we think and what we want to focus on. On one hand, you can choose to allow those permanent files of what happened and can't be undone to remain at the forefront of your mind. These files are unproductive and not helpful because they can consume you in a negative way. On the other hand, you can choose to focus on the files that are productive and helpful. These files are what allow you to learn and grow despite setbacks and hardship. It's uncomfortable to celebrate losing your legs, but it can be seen as a blessing, knowing damn well you could have lost your life.

So What?

Today's global market is more dynamic and interconnected than ever before. We're constantly exposed to and at times bombarded by external stimuli that demand our attention and energy. The basic human capacity to respond to sensory information is finite, which is supported by research suggesting that multitasking is a myth. Despite being armed with this knowledge, we fallibly take on as much as we can anyway because we think we have more bandwidth than we actually do. This deficit can trigger distress and feelings of being overwhelmed by conflicting tasks and competing responsibilities. Quite simply, we become distracted. When we're distracted and not focusing on the most important things worthy of our attention and energy, our performance suffers.

Fortunately, through compartmentalization, you can leverage a divide-and-conquer approach to productivity, which can significantly improve your self-regard, self-actualization, interpersonal relationships, stress management, and overall emotional well-being.

Compartmentalization can significantly help you:

■ filter through and prioritize tasks to focus on what's important in the moment,

■ stop procrastinating to improve your productivity,

■ effectively manage your emotional energy to increase task performance, and

■ decrease harmful distress to elevate your overall emotional control and well-being.

Now What?

Now that you recognize the value of healthy compartmentalization, you need to redefine how you approach procrastination and goal setting in order to improve your overall productivity, task performance, and emotional well-being.

How can I do it?

Redefine how you think about procrastination.

Nearly 95 percent of the population reports they procrastinate at some point, and research suggests that procrastination has nearly quadrupled over the last three decades. Additionally, 40 percent of people claim to have experienced financial loss due to procrastination (Gura, 2008).

So how do you stop procrastinating? First, you have to reframe how you think about procrastination. Recognize that procrastination is deeper than the simple act of delaying or postponing something.

You have to ask yourself, Why I am delaying or postponing the act? The truth is that the answer to the question actually stems from the emotion that is attached to executing the act, not the act itself. People do not delay or postpone the act itself. Rather, they push away or postpone having to experience negative emotions that are attached to executing the act or task at hand. When you procrastinate, you fail to compartmentalize.

Techniques to Apply:

Intellectualize. Then ask the CIA questions as outlined below (Thompson & Thompson, 2008).

The next time you find yourself procrastinating, intellectualize the task at hand. Intellectualization is a defense mechanism that employs our sense of logic and reasoning to block negative emotions and associated stress. Essentially, intellectualization allows you to emotionally remove yourself from the situation on a temporary basis so you can think logically; compartmentalize your thoughts; and focus on, mindfully engage in, and follow through with the task at hand. Ultimately, healthy intellectualization serves as a precursor to effective compartmentalization. To intellectualize, first ask yourself:

- What are the facts?
- What are the feelings?

Both are equally important, but in order to move forward, you must first separate the two. Consider how the negative feelings and emotions are preventing your ability to focus on, mindfully engage in, and follow through with the task at hand.

Next, consider the negative emotions attached to the task that you identified through intellectualization.

Once you've identified the emotional root of the procrastination problem, ask the CIA:

C—Can I **C**ontrol it?

I— Can I **I**nfluence it?

A—Do I need to **A**ccept it?

Lastly, you need to own it. Decide to control, influence, or accept the negative emotions associated with the task to move forward and reach optimal performance from moment to moment. In this chapter, Joey explains that his ability to adapt and overcome is all about emotional strength and the capacity to compartmentalize things in an effective manner.

No matter how many stressors, conflicting tasks, or competing responsibilities you face every day, the ability to identify and push past the negative thoughts and emotions associated with procrastination can significantly help you learn to compartmentalize. Get comfortable with the uncomfortable skill of filtering through your file system of thoughts and emotions, prioritizing the files that you to attend to the most, and then mindfully engage in and follow through with the task at hand.

Remember

1. Redefine how you think about procrastination.
    1. You do not fear the task itself.
    2. You delay experiencing the negative emotions associated with executing the task.

2. Intellectualize
    1. What are the facts?
    2. What are the feelings?
3. Ask the CIA
    1. Can I Control it?
    2. Can I Influence it?
    3. Do I need to Accept it?
4. Own it
    1. Get comfortable with the uncomfortable and own it.

Practical Application with Jason Van Camp

I keep a plaque by the front door of my house that reads: CYB. It stands for "Check Your Baggage." Every time I come home from work, I check my "baggage" at the front door. This means that I don't come home and vent or complain or talk about work. I check my bags at the door and leave them there. My immediate task is to spend quality time with my family. How do I turn off my work brain and shift focus to my family? It's about mastering the skill of compartmentalization.

The truth is, we are all fighting internal battles that most of us don't even realize. On close-knit Special Forces teams, if those internal battles are affecting you at work, affecting your performance, then it is affecting the whole team. If you aren't focused, your brothers might pay the price. That's why it's so important for the team to have a built-in support system. If you are going through difficult times at home and it is affecting your work performance, *we* need to resolve it. If you are going through a divorce, *we* can help you get through it. If you suspect your wife is cheating on you, I promise you *we* can confirm or deny that in a day. If your kids have special needs or there's a family emergency, *we* can help. There are many things that can be on your mind to distract you from the task at hand, and everybody's lives depend on you getting that task right. That's why it's important to understand what each of us is going through so we can act accordingly. We want to always be in "act" mode instead of "react" mode.

The thing about compartmentalization in the military is this: We deploy. We have our deployed life. When we deploy, we are pretty good at putting a pause on our lives back home. The Special Forces tend to be very good at selecting people to which that comes naturally. The negative side is that guys completely shut off their lives back home, and their relationships start falling apart, or they cheat on their wives while deployed because it's their "deployed" life. Turning it on and off so that you can come back from a mission, call your wife, get caught up on what the kids are doing, make her feel that what she is going through is heard and appreciated, is crucial to succeeding and finding balance both personally and professionally. Not easy, but crucial. Some of us need more attention than others, and that's OK.

That philosophy of healthy compartmentalization can be applied to business or our personal lives. Be present. Be focused on what you are currently engaged in. Check your baggage and move forward.

Dawn Halfaker, West Point graduate, military veteran, and founder and CEO of Halfaker and Associates, is one of the most successful leaders at compartmentalizing I know. In 2004, during combat operations in Baqubah, Iraq, Dawn's platoon was living and working out of an Iraqi police station. During a routine overnight patrol, Dawn rolled out with one of her squads at 0100. After a few hours of patrolling, they came around a corner and drove right into a small-arms fire and rocket-propelled grenade (RPG) ambush. One of those RPGs came through the front of her Humvee, underneath the windshield where there was a soft spot in the armor. The RPG went right through the vehicle and through Dawn's shoulder.

"My arm felt like somebody was like hacking away at it. It hurt worse than childbirth with no drugs. I made eye contact with my driver. He was still coherent and looked back at me. I said, 'Get us the fuck out of here!' The driver eventually got us back to the police station, where we were initially triaged and then medevaced. I was sent to Walter Reed Army Medical Center in Washington, DC, in an induced coma."

When Dawn woke up, she learned that they had amputated her arm.

"I had to figure out how to keep living my life. I didn't want my injury to define me. There were a lot of emotional battles that I went through and still go through on a daily basis. I had a crazy hard time sleeping because I was having nightmares about what had happened and reliving it in my sleep. Then I'd have panic attacks randomly."

What got Dawn through this life-changing experience was being a leader. She invested in her identity as a leader. "I was a platoon leader. That's who I was. I was close with my troops, and I didn't want to let them down. I wanted to be strong—not for myself, but for them. I wanted to stay mentally and physically strong to show them that 'hey, everything is going to be OK.' Although I was suffering, my strength was in my team. I said, 'I'm going to continue to make the best of the situation and be an example to them.'"

Dawn was able to isolate and compartmentalize her injury, which allowed her to focus on what was most important: Leading the greater team. If she had wallowed in misery about losing her arm, giving more credence to what *had* happened than what was *going* to happen next, it could have led to additional misery and angst. But she chose to accept the uncomfortable and focus on moving forward.

Dawn continues: "In the military, I learned that with every adversity, there is opportunity. I knew that the driver and gunner were going to be taking care of me when the bullets started flying. And I wanted to make sure they knew I was taking care of them. In business, leaders forget who's going to be covering for them and who's going to be sticking their neck out when the bullets are flying. Sometimes leaders tend to get into an 'ivory tower,' and it's important to remember that the ivory tower is not what makes the company successful. You just can't sit there and watch everybody else sacrifice and not be out there with them or taking care of them."

Dawn took this adversity and redirected into her business, Halfaker & Associates, which employs hundreds of employees and generates hundreds of millions of dollars in revenue annually.

One of Mission Six Zero's biggest supporters is Ryan Leaf. Ryan was a legendary Washington State quarterback and finalist for the Heisman Trophy. He was drafted second overall, right behind Peyton Manning, in the 1998 NFL draft, and started as a rookie for the San Diego Chargers. But his career didn't go the way he had planned. He soon found himself out of the NFL without a plan or purpose and addicted to painkillers. He went to prison for breaking into homes to steal oxycodone and Vicodin from friends' and strangers' medicine cabinets. Ryan reached rock bottom and started looking up ways to kill himself.

"I tried killing myself with a dull knife," he told me. "There was blood. It was a selfish, selfish thing to do. But I couldn't go through with it. Then I thought about pulling into my parents' garage and letting the engine run so that my parents would find me. That would have been the end-all, be-all."

Only after Ryan reached rock bottom did he find himself. When he finally did, he was able to let go of his past. He freed himself from the oppression of his own mind. Ryan didn't deliberately choose discomfort—discomfort found him, yet he found a way to persevere nonetheless. He found a way to compartmentalize. Here Ryan explains how he did it:

Be Honest

We often suffer more in imagination than in reality. In most cases, it's not as bad as it is in your own head. But perception is reality; if you are suffering, whether it be from PTSD, mental illness, or personal demons, you are one of the toughest people on the planet. I say that because I know how difficult it is. My philosophy is to be honest about your problems, ask for help, and know that no one is ever successful without a team around them. Keep reiterating to yourself: *You are valued. You are loved.*

Be Accountable

Accountability is huge. If I had been able to see my part in the things where I considered myself a victim, it would have given me a much different perspective. I didn't fully understand that until I went to prison, until I was able to look at myself in the mirror and say, "You're here because

232

of what you did and no one else; your decisions got you here." Before prison, I blamed others. I blamed the media, the doctors, the NFL, even my family. I never looked at what my part in all of it was. When I was playing in the NFL, I thought that I was a god. I thought that I was better than everyone because I could play a silly sport. Now I fully understand that I am merely a small part of this universe that we all live in as human beings. Stop being a victim. You are the reason for your problems.

Express your Pain

My behaviors—the way I deal with stuff—have been in my life for almost forty years. Your problems aren't going to go away because you start getting help or, in my case, because I removed the substance. You have to work at it every day. The ability to see clearly and be aware of the problem and then take a healthy mode of action is the difference. No matter what, your past is going to show up. What are you going to do about it? Are you going to be able to recognize it and be aware when it happens and take healthy steps to confront it? When my past issues used to show up, I didn't deal with it in a healthy way. My way was to self-medicate or fall into a depression or take a victim's stance rather than deal with it in a healthy way. I'd react to something impulsively and get angry or do things that I used to do my whole life out of muscle memory. Now I have a team helping me. I have people around me who help me be aware of it and hold me accountable. Instead of getting defensive, they hold a mirror up, and I can take the necessary steps to move forward and address the issues. Suicide won't end the pain. It will just pass the pain on to those who love you.

Ask for Help

There are people out there who get you. They speak your language. Find them. Maybe I can't fully understand what you've gone through, but I can tell you how I walked into the light: by asking for help and showing vulnerability. Vulnerability is not a weakness. This is a human experience, and the things that happened to you would affect anybody.

Seeking professional help is a strength. I know that when I finally asked for help and accepted it, life got better. Asking for help is the strongest thing you'll ever do.

Instead of asking for help, I just retreated into a defensive stance. I had all this money and power. I didn't really have to listen to anyone, and it completely backfired on me. With the media. With teammates. My family and things like that. It came down to a point that I had to be humbled. That happened to be with a drug addiction—through Vicodin, which I was introduced to through all my orthopedic surgeries through playing. It turned out that going to prison because of that drug addiction finally humbled me. Humble yourself, or someone will do it for you.

Stop focusing on yourself and serve others

My roommate in prison was an infantry guy, an army guy, a veteran of Afghanistan and Iraq. One day he just got on me really bad. He was yelling at me that I had my head buried in the sand. He said I didn't understand the value I had for other people—not only the people in there, but also the people when I got out. He said, "You are going to come with me today to the library, and we're going to help guys who don't know how to read learn how." That was probably the first time I was of service in any way. And he was a big part of that transformation for me. All those things that I went through—it was meant to teach me a lesson. The lesson was that I needed to be of service to others.

Forgive yourself

One of the most uncomfortable things you can do is forgive. Oftentimes, it's forgiving yourself. You can only control yourself. You can't control how other people are going react. You can't control the past. This is a day-by-day, minute-by-minute type thing, and I attack it that way.

I think having that epiphany while I was sitting in a prison cell was the most liberating and free moment in my life! It's weird to say this, but since I've walked out of prison, I can't remember feeling anything even relatively close to negativity. The power of choice, knowing that I can choose to be happy or open minded in that moment, has been a huge tool for me. The disease of drug addiction took all choice away. When I was in that obsession driven world, the idea that I could actually gain back control by choosing positivity was so significant. It's so simple. You can choose to be happy in this moment. You can choose to forgive yourself.

Remember:

- Check your baggage.
- Ryan Leaf wisdom:
    - Be honest.
    - Be accountable.
    - Express your pain.
    - Ask for help.
    - Stop focusing on yourself and serve others.
    - Forgive yourself.
- Be kind. Everyone is fighting a battle you know nothing about.

---

11 The Player

with **Nate Boyer**

Nate served nine years in the US Army Special Forces (Green Beret) as a noncommissioned officer. He deployed three times to the Middle East and participated in training missions to Israel, Bulgaria, and Greece. He walked on to the University of Texas football team as a twenty-nine-year old true freshman and eventually became the starting long snapper. He went on to play for the NFL's Seattle Seahawks.

It had been an eye-opening and intense first week at group, and I had yet to visit a good friend from training who had been assigned to another ODA in my battalion. I walked into Nate Boyer's team room, excited to see him and get his perspective on his first Special Forces experiences.

"Spirit Bear! Great to see you, Jason!" Nate greeted me warmly, using the nickname that had been bestowed upon me at Q Course, something about my size and my unbelievably beautiful hairy chest. We slapped hands, and Nate grabbed a Fat Tire out of the team fridge, an old 1970s Hotpoint.

"Sorry, I don't have any salmon for ya, bear."

"All good, man." I laughed.

Nate had been one of my favorite guys at the Q Course, and I was thrilled that we were in the same unit. Nate had kept me awake, on point, and, most importantly, laughing, during late-night patrols and instruction. He was the type of guy you needed to help get you through training, and any Green Beret will tell you that you can't graduate the Q Course without those guys. Nate had arrived at 10th Group a few weeks earlier and in some ways already looked like a seasoned veteran.

"What's up, Nate! Good to see you, man. Where's the rest of your team?" I asked.

"Some guys are at the gym, some at the chow hall, some just hanging around Group."

I was glad we were alone. "Good. I wanted to ask you about Major Petit. What have you heard about him?"

Nate leaned back in a rickety government chair and stared at the ceiling, thinking. He didn't seem surprised that I was asking. He knew that Major Petit liked to have his new team leaders talk with some of the more experienced guys in the unit and assumed I had been given the same task.

"Why, did Major Petit ask you to talk with *me*?" Nate asked.

"No, man. You just got here. You're not a legend...yet."

We both laughed, but I knew even then that Nate would become a legend someday.

"I'll tell you this," Nate said. "The guys love him. He knows what he's doing, and it's clear the major has a plan. I just can't tell you what that plan is."

I raised an eyebrow quizzically. "You can't tell me what his plan is?"

"What I mean is, you're going to have to figure it out on your own. If you're going to truly buy into what he's trying to create, you can't be told what to do. You need to figure it out yourself."

"I think I'm on my way to doing that. What would you say to the major?" I asked.

"The truth."

"About what?"

"Why I joined SF," said Nate.

"I don't think I even know that story. I never really thought to ask you. Why did you?"

Nate took a long chug on his beer before proceeding.

"I was twenty-three years old. I'd been a deck hand on a fishing boat, drove a bike taxi, and made a half-assed, futile attempt at a career as an actor in Hollywood. My friends from high school had all graduated from college and were starting their professional careers. I felt left behind. Lost, in a way.

"I didn't have a purpose, didn't have a mission. I didn't even know what I wanted to do. I felt insignificant, just drifting through life, with no real direction and no inner drive. I didn't feel a real connection to anything or like I made a damn bit of difference in anybody's life. I wasn't even making a difference in my *own*."

I interrupted. "That surprises me. You—not motivated? You mean you were the dude who was still hanging out at the gas station, smoking weed, and partying when everyone came back from college? No way. That doesn't sound like you."

"Ha! Well, no, not exactly. But who I am now is not who I was then. Back then I didn't have a clear vision of what I wanted; I just knew I wanted to do something important. I was fed up with the way things were going and decided that I needed a dramatic change.

While I was searching for a purpose, I happened to read an article about the crisis in Darfur. I decided to fly myself over to the Darfur region of Africa with what little money I had. I landed in Chad, which borders the Sudan. When I got there, the airport was full of reporters and straphangers trying to get to Darfur. I quickly realized that it wouldn't be as easy as I thought to get there. I didn't have proper documentation, I didn't have any connections, I didn't even really have a plan.

I talked my way through security and found myself a stowaway on a United Nations plane heading to the refugee camps. I was eventually caught and questioned.

"Look," I said, "I just want to help out, any way you need me to. I'll dig ditches, put up tents. Hell, I'll just go out and play with the kids or read to them if that's what it takes. I just want to help." Security thought I worked for the CIA. They shook me down, interrogated me, but eventually let me go on to Darfur.

When we arrived, I'd never been to a place like that before, never seen firsthand a third-world developing country. I was in the midst of genocide and just relying on myself to figure things out once I got on the ground. I wasn't allowed to officially join any NGOs (nongovernmental organizations) because I didn't have a college degree. Besides, they said

I didn't have the special skills necessary to be of any assistance to them. My goal was just to help with the relief efforts at the refugee camps any way I could. Helping one person would be enough.

It was frustrating. I knew they were shorthanded, and I had flown myself halfway across the world, yet they still refused my help. I eventually figured out how to get into the camps through the local villagers and started volunteering anyway. That whole experience really opened my eyes to the world. Those people didn't have anything. I mean, all these families were being torn apart. The men were off fighting or killed already, and the Janjaweed militias would sweep through the villages and rape all the women. The people in Darfur just wanted to survive. They wanted food, clean water, and security. That's it.

I understood that these people needed someone to stand up and fight for them more than they needed handouts. I witnessed genocide firsthand in Darfur. The fact that hate and oppression still existed at that level in the world really hurt me. I met countless young Africans who were enamored with America and the opportunities that exist here. Those people would have given anything to experience what I had grown up with, even for just one day.

A few weeks in, I came down with malaria. I was bedridden and lying on a makeshift cot in a mud hut, trying to recover. There was a little radio in the hut, and the only station that came through was the BBC. I listened to the play-by-play account of the Second Battle of Fallujah. The report was live, and it was intense. I just lay there listening to those marines fighting and risking their lives to take back the city of Fallujah for its people. It inspired me to join the military because I realized that if people can't first secure and protect themselves in their homeland, nothing else matters. I was not in the best position to help in Darfur because I couldn't protect the people.

After a few days, I recovered and left Darfur. I left believing that people like the ones I had met were worth fighting for. I wanted to fight for those who were unable to fight for themselves.

But how does someone join the military? I had no idea. I didn't even know there were different branches. I figured out that each branch had its own recruiters, and they all really wanted to sign me up.

When I stepped into the army recruiter's office, I saw the motto De Oppresso Liber and asked him what it meant. He explained that it translated to To Free the Oppressed and that it was the motto of the Green Berets. I was sold. That motto was the reason why I became a Green Beret. I didn't enlist to fight for what we already have here; I did it because I wanted to fight for what the people in Darfur didn't have: freedom.

I joined the Army on an 18 X-Ray contract and was told that there were no guarantees I would make it to Special Forces and that the attrition rate was high. But if I completed all the training, I would become a Green Beret.

When I first arrived at basic training, I wasn't physically prepared. The first week we had our standard army physical fitness test (PT Test): as many push-ups and sit-ups as you could do in two minutes followed by a two-mile timed run. I had one of the lowest scores in my platoon. I only did like twenty-nine push-ups and maybe fifty sit-ups, and ran two miles in over fifteen minutes. My scores made me uncomfortable. I was embarrassed.

I decided to do something about it. I could only control what I could control, and I could control my effort and myself. I decided to simply outwork everyone. Every free second that I could spare, I'd do push-ups or sit-ups or go do a mile of lunges around the track. I would be completely alone, lunging, my legs quivering with each step. Every time I didn't think I could go on, I forced my mind to take another step. I just kept telling myself, "One more step."

That was my mind-set. I did this extra physical fitness work for the entirety of basic training. During our last graded PT session just thirteen weeks later, I did 145 push-ups, 105 sit-ups, and the two-mile run in eleven minutes. It was the highest PT score recorded in our entire basic training battalion. After basic, I was already a better athlete than I had been while playing sports in high school because I finally was working toward a very specific goal.

Captain Dan Quinn and an Afghan national training for an upcoming mission.

Captain Quinn and his team in the traditional Afghan garb.

Captain Quinn training Afghan forces on how to stack on a door.

Captain Quinn and his team high in the mountains of Afghanistan.

Flo Groberg

President Barack Obama awarding Captain Florent Groberg the Medal of Honor.

Captain Groberg saluting the colors.

Captain Groberg conversing with his Afghan counterparts during combat operations.

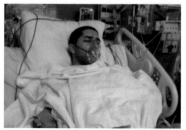

Captain Groberg recovering in his hospital bed after tackling a suicide bomber.

Master Sergeant Leroy Petry saluting the colors.

Master Sergeant Petry at the unveiling of his statue by George Rivera in Santa Fe, New Mexico.

Leroy and his Ranger teammates after rescuing Navy SEAL Marcus Luttrell (Lone Survivor).

Sergeant Higgins and Private First Class Robinson pose with Leroy.

Joey Jones

Joey at home on the couch with his two dogs and prosthetics.

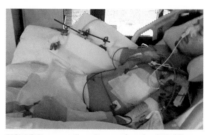

USMC Sergeant Joey Jones after the IED blast that took his legs.

Sergeant Jones taking a break from dismantling IEDs.

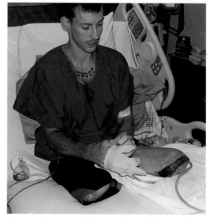

Sergeant Jones conducting physical therapy.

Staff Sergeant Nate Boyer prior to a mission in Iraq.

Staff Sergeant Boyer training an Iraqi soldier on the proper way to hold an AK-47.

Texas Longhorn Nate Boyer running on to the field proudly carrying the Red, White, and Blue.

Nate standing next to Colin Kaepernick during the National Anthem.

Brian Petit

Brian as a young soldier on a mission in the Balkans.

Colonel Petit posing with a Bulgarian BASK Airplane that has seen better days.

Colonel Brian Petit on the tarmac in Afghanistan.

Brian outside his home in Colorado.

Shelley Smith

Michael Gerson

Casey Van Camp

Jason Mitchler

Rebecca Cañate

Mission Six Zero

Nate Boyer provides heavy weapons training to the Minnesota Vikings players and coaches.

Jason Van Camp and Nate Boyer work with the Seattle Mariners.

Mission Six Zero Instructor Dave Hageman playing the role of the Afghan War Chief and making it tough for Santonio Holmes.

Mission Six Zero taking our clients to the next objective on a UH-1 Vietnam-era HUEY Helicopter.

I would think "Small victories" and then set out to do things that I wasn't sure I could do and complete them. That feeling became contagious. I loved pushing myself beyond what I thought my limits might be. I learned that the human body is capable of so much more than we realize. Once you start to feel pain, the mind starts to doubt. I learned that the mind quits long before the body does. Once you push past that weak mind-set, you understand that the body can still operate at a pretty high level under incredible physical stress or neglect. You just have to convince your mind to take the next step. I learned that you are in control of your mind and that making the choice to keep pushing through discomfort is the key to moving beyond your limits.

When I got to Special Forces selection, I was known as a PT stud. It was purely a product of how much extra effort I put forth in basic training. None of that really mattered when the individual PT sessions were over and we had to work together as a team to accomplish our required graded missions. You don't know which guys you can really count on and trust until you sweat and bleed a little together. True leaders are revealed when days are long and you're out of breath and both physically and emotionally drained. When you're put in those situations as a team, you get to know what people are really made of. You get to know who the true badasses are. Through my entire experience from selection to the qualification course, I got my "gos" in training and earned my Green Beret, not because of my individual performance but because of my team. I earned my Green Beret only because of the quality of guys around me.

Hearing Nate tell his story made me realize his why was similar to mine. "Now we get our chance to help the helpless, to free the oppressed," I said.

"Damn straight," Nate agreed.

As I leaned back and we started talking about life since Q Course, I couldn't help but think that Nate's insight was just as valuable as the battle-hardened team guys I'd already talked with.

Over the next few years, Nate and I maintained a close friendship during our time together at 10th Group. One day, after our second deployment together, he came by my house. It was a lazy afternoon, and we were hanging out in the kitchen when he said, "Jason, please don't tell anybody about this, but I wanted to let you to know that I'm getting out of the army."

"Wait. What? Why?" I asked incredulously. "What are you going to do?" This was shocking to me. But if Nate was going to get out of the military, I wanted to make sure he had a plan. I was an officer. The mentality of taking care of my soldiers was ingrained in my psyche.

"I'm going to college," he said.

I could buy that. "If you're getting out of the military, going to college is a great reason to do so. Where are you planning to go?"

"Either USC or Texas."

"Why those two schools?"

"They have the two best college football programs."

I laughed. "Nate, bro, you can't go to a university just because they have a good football team."

"No, J, you don't understand. I'm going to college to *play* football."

This time I didn't laugh, because I knew Nate was serious. "You're going to *play* football?" I repeated.

"Yeah, man."

I resolved to help Nate face the reality of his situation. "Nate. You're thirty years old."

"Well, almost."

"You're five nine."

"I'm five ten."

"You're 170 lbs."

"Actually, closer to 160."

I could tell Nate would not be deterred. "Well, OK. What position did you play in high school?"

"I didn't play high school football."

"You didn't play high school football? What about Pop Warner, when you were a kid?"

"My mother wouldn't let me play football when I was a kid."

I went silent while Nate and I just looked at each other, neither one backing down. I couldn't resist a great adventure.

"Well, Nate, we've got a long road ahead of us. I'll help you out. I think there's a chance we can find you a spot as a slot receiver or strong safety."

"Thanks, Bear."

About thirty seconds passed before Nate spoke up again.

"Hey, Bear, what's a slot receiver?"

Over the next year, I helped Nate as best I could, having him run routes, teaching him different positions, Xs and Os. But truth be told, he didn't need any of my advice or experience. He did it all on his own.

During that time, Nate told me that graduating from college was something he needed to do. He had promised his mother he would and figured, "If I'm going to do it, I'm going to do it in epic fashion."

That spring, Nate got accepted to the University of Texas. The first thing he did after stepping on campus was to walk into the Longhorns' strength and conditioning coach's office. Nate told him that one way or another he was going to walk on to the team during spring practice. The strength coach told Nate that there would be a hundred other walk-ons trying to make the team, but he would see to it that Nate got a shot.

I asked Nate what his mental state was during that time. He told me, "I knew that I could make the team. Anything is possible. I truly believe that. Our training and our time in combat taught me that it's about going as hard as you can at all times, regardless of mental and physical pain. You're tired and hungry. It sucks. But you make it through that, and you know you can't be broken. I know now there is nothing I can't handle. I may not survive it, but I won't quit. I don't know how to."

During one of the last spring practice conditioning drills, head coach Mack Brown stood in the middle of the field with the strength coach. "All right, here's what we're going to do: the entire team—scholarship players and walk-ons—take six laps around the field. You walk-ons trying to make the team better not let any of my players beat you."

The entire team sprinted around the field. Nate lapped them twice.

Nate's dominant performance impressed the coaching staff so much that he was given a spot on the team. He became a twenty-nine-year-old true freshman strong safety and special teams player, redshirting his freshman year. Mainly, he tried to motivate his teammates, playing on the scout team during practice and racing out of the tunnel at home games carrying the American flag.

Nate started to get some special teams action his second year on the team. Around the same time, he signed up for the US Army National Guard in Texas. He would be rejoining the Special Forces community, serving as a staff sergeant in the 19th Special Forces Group.

During his third college football season, Nate was looking for an opportunity to be a starter. He noted that the team's starting long snapper had graduated, so he walked into Mack Brown's office and told him that *he* was going to be his starting long snapper next season.

Coach Brown asked him, "Have you ever long snapped before?"

"Coach, I never played football before I got to Texas."

Coach Brown laughed, then asked, "Aren't you deploying to Afghanistan this summer?"

"Yes, Coach. But I'll bring a football and practice every day."

"Nate?"

"Yes, Coach?"

"Get out." As Nate turned to leave, Coach Brown advised, "Don't get shot now. We need you in one piece."

In Afghanistan, Nate watched YouTube videos on how to long snap. During his off time, he would practice long snapping out in the desert by himself. If he was going to earn an opportunity, he knew he would have to outwork everyone else.

Nate got back to Texas just before August two-a-days began. He went up against several other players vying for that position, and it came down to him and a freshman they had recruited to long snap for the next four years. Nate beat him out to earn the starting job. That season he also was awarded ESPN's Disney Spirit Award for college football's most inspirational player.

When his football career at Texas was over, Coach Brown asked him, "In your entire career, you never had a bad snap. What's the secret?"

"Coach, when you've been through Special Forces training and combat, you come to find that there's good stress and bad stress. The good stress helps you focus and makes you sharper, and at the end of the day when you're in doubt, just *aim small miss small*," he answered.

That wasn't the end of Nate's football career. The NFL's Seattle Seahawks signed him as an undrafted free agent, where he battled it out during the preseason before ultimately being cut after playing in only one career NFL game.

The following preseason, San Francisco 49ers quarterback Colin Kaepernick began sitting on the bench during the nation anthem. It was, he said, a political statement "to protest racial inequality and police brutality." Nate explains what happened next in his own words:

"When I heard that Kaepernick sat down during "The Star-Spangled Banner," I was pretty disappointed. I grew up a big 49ers fan and was pulling for this guy. The *Army Times* approached me to write an article about my thoughts on the Kaepernick situation. At first I declined. But when they asked me again, I figured it might be an opportunity to do some good, so I decided to write an open letter to Colin. I wrote what I felt in my heart. I wanted to understand where he was coming from and what he hoped to accomplish specifically. I wanted to listen. The letter went viral immediately, and I got a call from Kaepernick's publicist. She told me that Colin wanted to meet with me before the 49ers played the Chargers in San Diego the next night. I agreed without hesitation.

The next day Colin sent an Uber to take me from Los Angeles the three hours down I-5 to San Diego. I got dropped off at the team hotel and saw Colin waiting in the lobby for me with his teammate, Eric Reid, who supported Colin in his protest. We all sat down on a couch in the hotel lobby to talk.

I reiterated what I said to Colin in my open letter which was, "Listen, I'll be honest. When I first heard about what you were doing, I was upset.

But right now, I want to listen to what you have to say and why you are demonstrating. The last thing our country needs right now is more hate. Plenty of people are fighting fire with fire, and it's just not helping anyone or anything. I'm going to listen with an open mind. For me to say I can relate to what you've gone through is as ignorant as someone who's never been in a combat zone telling me they understand what it's like to go to war."

Colin spoke, and I listened. In fact, we talked for several hours. (It goes back to what Major Petit said: "The difference between a good Green Beret and a great Green Beret is his ability to listen.")

Earlier that week, Colin publicly stated: "I am not going to stand up to show pride in a flag for a country that oppresses black people and people of color. To me, this is bigger than football, and it would be selfish on my part to look the other way. There are bodies in the street while people are receiving paid leave and getting away with murder."

I told him that I understood his intent but that it was hard for a lot of people to get past what he was doing because the national anthem was a sacred time for them. I explained that sitting on the bench isolated from his team was not inspiring anyone. It just looked as if he didn't care.

Colin asked if there was another way to protest that wouldn't offend people in the military community. I told him that no matter what he does, someone will be upset. There is no perfect form of protest. But I suggested that instead of sitting, he could kneel during the anthem. I explained that in the military, we would kneel to show respect for a fallen comrade. At least that way he could be alongside his teammates instead of isolated and alone.

I told him about how in my one game in the NFL, when I ran out of the tunnel with the American flag and stood on the sideline with my hand over my heart during the anthem, I burst into tears. I thought about how far I'd come and about the men I'd fought alongside who didn't make it back. I thought about the guys still overseas risking their lives that very moment. I selfishly thought about what I had sacrificed to get to where I was. That moment meant even more to me than playing in the game, and to be honest, if I had noticed a teammate sitting on the bench, it would have really hurt me.

Colin listened.

That night, he took a knee during "The Star-Spangled Banner." I stood next to him with my hand over my heart.

I don't agree with a lot of the things Colin has said and done, and Colin knows that. As I also stated in my open letter, while I support Colin's First Amendment right to protest, I look forward to the day Colin is inspired to once again stand during our national anthem. When that day comes, I'll be standing right there next to him.

After I took a stand for what I believed was right, I was attacked from all angles. By everybody: conservatives, liberals—even some of my Special Forces brothers disparaged me. Guys I had gone through the Q Course with told me that I was a disgrace to the Green Beret. I listened to them too and tried to understand what they were saying and why they were angry. I'd tell people, "I didn't tell Colin to do anything. I definitely didn't tell him to protest. What I did was meet with him and make suggestions on different ways to go about it after he was already protesting. I worked with him to find a middle ground."

Everybody says, "Kaepernick is protesting the anthem." I can tell you from firsthand experience that Colin is not protesting the anthem. He's protesting racial inequality and police brutality. I try to tell people that thinking like this is not fair to Colin, it's not fair to me, and it's not good for our country.

SOF to Science with Dr. Jason Mitchler,
Physical Science Officer, and Andy Riise

Jason graduated from the University of Northern Colorado with a degree in kinesiology. He also has a doctorate in physical therapy from Army-Baylor University. He is an orthopedic certified specialist and a certified strength and conditioning specialist. He served as a US Army Special Forces (Green Beret) medic and physical therapist with multiple tours in Afghanistan.

Nate's story represents the remarkable journey of a lost young man without purpose—through his transformation into a Green Beret, combat veteran, and sports icon. While he is celebrated for his achievements, it's important to understand the mundanity of his excellence—the process behind the outcomes. Although his story could encapsulate every chapter of this book, the focus of this chapter is Nate's physical dominance—how he adapted and pushed his body beyond its limits to achieve superhuman feats.

To be clear: Nate is not genetically gifted or a physical freak. There are no hacks, shortcuts, or secrets to his success. What separates Nate from most people is his bias for action. Nate has always lived in the moment and taken action when others may otherwise hesitate, deliberate, or wait to seek more information. From his trip to Darfur, we learn that Nate tends to act first and figure out the details later. He thrives at being adaptable. Most people can't relate to this behavior because it seems crazy or irresponsible. However, goal-setting research suggests that the first steps are considered the most difficult and critical toward achieving high and hard goals. (Latham et al., 1978).

When Nate first walked into the army recruiting station, he had absolutely no idea what he was getting himself into. He showed up anyway. When Nate told Jason he wanted to play college football, he didn't even know the names of different positions, let alone how to play them. He walked onto the field anyway. Nate excels at action. He excels at showing up—an action that each of us can control.

Nate learned early in his army career that physical strength begins with work capacity. Work capacity is the ability to perform purposeful activity in a given period of time. It's no secret that if you want to get physically stronger, you must adequately stress your body to achieve positive adaptation. The Hans Selye's general adaptation syndrome explains that when the human body is exposed to higher levels of physical stress than it is normally accustomed to, it will respond by compensating and becoming stronger (Selye, 1950).

Nate learned how to embrace adaptability. He increased his capacity over time by outworking his peers through additional physical training. When the barracks lights were turned off at night, Nate stayed up and did extra push-ups and sit-ups in the dark. When his peers left post on their day pass, Nate stayed behind and did lunges around the track. It was probably very uncomfortable for Nate to choose work over sleep and extra PT over hard-earned time off, but he did it anyway. He showed up. He put in the work to increase his capacity.

Hard work by itself is not the answer. This flies in the face of conventional wisdom that through hard work, good things will happen. This ideal is woven into the fabric of our nation based on immigrant values, and it is reflected in our modern civilian workforce and military. The reality is that Nate's physical dominance also manifested through an effective energy management strategy and deliberate recovery tactics. The relationship between stress and recovery has significant implications on physical performance over time. As discussed previously, stress can be both productive (eustress) or harmful (distress) (Gutman & Benson, 1971). The relationship between stress (stimulus response or arousal) is explained through the Yerkes-Dodson law: increased stimulus response (called arousal) can help improve performance up to a certain point through eustress. Yet when arousal response becomes excessive, performance diminishes (Yerkes & Dodson, 1908).

This relationship means that humans have to balance physical work and recovery as evenly as possible to build and sustain growth over time. When this relationship in unbalanced, there is a significant increase in the probability of physically underperforming or "crashing" in extreme circumstances. While the level of arousal is task and situation specific, we know that deliberate recovery through rest, sleep, and mobility exercises is critical for many physiological aspects, including physical growth of muscles and neurological connections within the brain. Despite his intense training schedule based on the high physical demands of his missions from the battlefield to the football field, Nate made a point to build recovery into his plan.

So What?

1. Show up

In the military there is an old saying that just showing up is at least 50 percent of winning any battle. If you're in the right uniform, at the right place, at the right time, you're at least halfway to making good things happen. It's simple and it's true. Nate's story personifies this adage because we tend to focus on the waypoints and destinations along his journey because they stand out—yet we gloss over his first steps. Show up by doing more and thinking less. This will get you and your team pointed in the right direction.

2. Work hard

Your physical capacity is nowhere near your perceived limits. Nate proved this time and again over several seemingly impossible points along his journey. Once you show up and start, keep going. Push through the pain and discomfort. You're going to be sore, you're going to get injured, it's going to suck, and you're going to want to quit, but do it anyway. Over time, your body will adapt and increase capacity through a new tolerance and threshold. What was once uncomfortable will then become more comfortable; that's your cue to work harder.

3. Deliberately recover

"Sleep when you're dead" is not only a common quote but a way of life in the military. It's no wonder why West Point's Center for Enhanced Performance has told cadets for over thirty years that "hardcore stress requires hardcore recovery." This quote is as relevant in the military as it is in corporate culture—one could argue that we are experiencing a human energy crisis.

Now What?

- What would you accomplish if failure wasn't an option?
- What's a big goal or dream you've always wanted but you just can't seem to get started?

- What are the barriers holding you back?
- What are the first steps for taking action toward your goal?
- What's your current work capacity to do physically demanding activities?
- What's the upper limit of your ability, and when was the last time you reached that limit?
- What's your energy management strategy right now? How do you see and approach recovery? What are you doing now to help your body recover better?
- How are you tracking or monitoring your recovery progress?
- What resources are you leveraging to learn more?

Practical Application with Jason Van Camp

I went down to see Nate at the University of Texas in Austin during his freshman year in 2010. It was Veterans Day weekend, and the Longhorns were playing the Oklahoma State Cowboys. I was on the field when Nate, wearing number 37, led the team onto the field while carrying the American flag.

I was incredibly proud.

During the pregame introductions, the team brought out Admiral McRaven, the former SEAL Team 6 commander who led the bin Laden raid; Frank Denius, a World War II hero; and Nate Boyer. They all stood in the middle of the field to be recognized for their service. Nate was the last to be introduced and the only one to receive a standing ovation from a crowd of one hundred thousand fans.

Unfortunately, the Longhorns did not perform particularly well that day. A crushing defeat by the Cowboys left them at a disappointing 4–6 win-loss record. After the game, Nate and I sat in the locker room together. As any true friend would, I gave him a hard time about the loss and poor season.

"Damn, Nate. Last year the Longhorns went to the national championship game. Boyer arrives, and you guys lose six games," I joked.

Nate laughed. "Yeah, man, it's crazy. We have virtually the exact same team that we had last year. When you look at our roster, we only really graduated our quarterback and some starting offensive linemen."

"What's the problem, then?" I asked, curious to know what had changed.

"Bear, we have guys who can run 4.3 forty-yard dashes. We have guys who can jump out of the gym. We have guys who can bench press five hundred pounds. The talent is there. The problem is leadership. That's the difference between winning championships and having a losing season. For a guy like me, thirty years old, a Special Forces combat veteran, someone who knows true leadership when I see it, I know that's what the problem is on this team. We don't have any leadership."

"Why don't you stand up and lead then?" I asked.

"I don't play on Saturday. Regardless of my background, I don't think I have the right to lead that locker room unless I'm on the field playing meaningful snaps."

That was the moment of our epiphany. It all comes down to leadership. Leadership in sports, business, and life is the critical component that determines your success. Leadership is the difference between winning and losing.

Nate and I have both frequently thought back to that conversation. In fact, it was the catalyst for Nate and me to create Mission Six Zero. We are passionate about leadership. We know that the difference between winning and losing isn't measured in forty-yard dash times and bench press reps. It's measured in leadership.

Being a leader means being willing and able to adapt. In order to be adaptable, you must be humble while also having the quiet confidence and courage to move out of your comfort zone and try something new. Being adaptable means accepting reality and realizing that you should not continue on your current path just because you're already on it. It's about setting aside your ego and taking action to change.

One of Mission Six Zero's most adaptable clients is Vivint, a private home services provider headquartered in Utah. Vivint was acquired by the Blackstone Group in 2012 for $2 billion and currently boasts 1.4 million customers in the US and Canada. Mission Six Zero helps train their decision makers and employees to become vocal and adaptable leaders. Jeff Mendez, a vice president at Vivint who has been with the company since it was formed, calls this training "learning before earning."

As with any business, Vivint learned some tough lessons along its journey. Jeff explains, "When we first started, we were very focused on the bottom line, and we were very selfish with the investments we made in our employees. We soon realized that we were doomed to fail unless we made some drastic changes. In order to thrive, we needed a different mind-set, a different way of doing things. We decided to take the uncomfortable risk of investing heavily in our people. That's a risky strategy to take in our industry, because there is a high attrition rate. Our leaders were asking, 'What happens if we spend this time and money on these people and then they take what they've learned and leverage it to find a new job?'

"My answer was, 'What happens if we don't invest in them? They're definitely going to leave, and they won't be as valuable while they're here.' So we decided to switch course and start to not only invest in our people, but inspire them to invest in themselves.

"What we decided to do was unique and risky," Jeff explains. "We started asking our employees about their long-term goals and objectives and then doing whatever we could to help them achieve those dreams.

"Our calculated gamble to adapt our system and invest in our people paid off in a big way. We had better-trained, happier employees who stayed with the company longer. The new approach inspired loyalty. We learned that when people are free to leave, that freedom inspires them to stay. We empowered our people to become CEOs of themselves. We stopped trying to make people 'fit' into our company and instead focused on having them 'belong' to our company.

"Now, when a young employee knocks on my door and wants to know how to get started, I tell them, 'Be the best version of you. Be inquisitive. Be willing to learn. Be willing to embrace the suck. Be willing to go create more value than you take away. If you can be a value creator instead of a value taker, then you are going to succeed.'

"I tell them that I'll do everything I can to empower them to be the absolute best and provide whatever information they need to be their own entity. That we're all in this together. And for me, this model puts me in a position where I have to step up my game. I have to get uncomfortable, face fear, learn, and grow. I can't stay still."

Being adaptable is also a focus of Ron Rivera, head coach of the NFL's Carolina Panthers. Mission Six Zero has worked with the Carolina Panthers to achieve adaptability. During our work with the team, Coach Rivera said, "I always tell my guys how hard it is to play defense in the NFL, and the new rules are making it even harder. The only way we can get better as a defense is to accept that level of difficulty and then work at being comfortable when we are uncomfortable. That's something that we weren't doing. As a defensive player, it's hard to split the double team. It's hard to draw a faker and hold the point. It's hard to burst when you have to, but we have to! It doesn't matter how hard it is. It's just the way defense is. Nothing is ever simple for us, so we must accept that, make it a part of who we are, and go out and do it."

As Nate, Jeff, and Ron showed us, adaptability is hard. Nate realized that he was tired of being insignificant, so he decided to do something about it. He was tired of being weak, so he worked to become the strongest soldier in his unit. He was tired of sitting on the bench, so he taught himself how to long snap and became a starter. Nate mastered the art and science of being adaptable. These were conscious decisions and efforts to change.

Jeff Mendez realized that unless he made a change, his business was going to fail, so he took an uncomfortable leap of faith and began to invest in his employees.

Ron Rivera realized that in order to create a culture of winning and accountability, his defensive players needed to make changes. He accepted the rules changes—something he and his team had no control over—and adapted his defense around them. He knew his team needed to deliberately embrace discomfort and accept hard things.

Adaptability starts with a willingness to change. Over the years,

Mission Six Zero has seen some common enemies of adaptability with our clients:

Fear—Don't create a culture of anxious employees who are afraid to take the initiative or trust their judgment. Adaptability encourages daring, bold moves. Remind yourself that everything will be all right in the end. If it's not all right, it's not the end.

Habit—Don't create a culture that eliminates thought. If you hear the answer, "We do it this way because this is the way we've always done it," you know you have created a mindless culture. Adaptability encourages questioning the status quo to discover a more efficient and cost-effective way to do things.

Inflexible systems—Don't create a system that hinders individual autonomy and self-management. When systems become more specialized, opportunities for improvement becomes less possible.

Insufficient experimentation—Don't rush to failure. Don't just copy what someone else is doing. Experimentation will cost time and resources, but it will give you the peace of mind that you nailed the pain and have the best solution.

Uniformity—Don't promote conformity at the expense of divergence. A lack of diversity will restrict your ability to ideate and consider all options fairly. There is no growth if there is no conflict. If everyone is thinking the same, then no one is thinking.

Deliberately choosing discomfort means that we must be willing to put in the work to pivot. We must recognize if we aren't on the correct path, and then have the courage to switch courses. First, you must want to change. Then you must act. As you act, you will understand how to change. Then you put in the work to change.

Remember:

■ Small victories—Aim small, miss small. A simple goal accomplished is better than more missed opportunities.

■ The mind quits long before the body does.

■ Determination will never betray you.

■ Leadership is the difference between winning and losing.

■ Investing in your people inspires loyalty.

12 The Beginning

with Brian Petit

Brian is a retired US Army Special Forces (Green Beret) colonel. He commanded Special Operations units in the Balkans, Iraq, Afghanistan, Southeast Asia, the Philippines, Europe, and Africa. In sum, he served in over thirty-three countries, including more than five years in combat or conflict zones. He has earned the Defense Superior Service Medal (DSSM), the Legion of Merit (LOM), and three Bronze Star Medals.

I could tell he was comfortable. I sat behind my desk watching as Captain Van Camp entered the B-team office with a noticeably more confident posture. It had only been a week since I challenged him to embrace discomfort—to meet new people, ask questions, and be vulnerable. Now he was leaning up against one of the lockers cracking jokes with the sergeant major and a few of the B-team NCOs. I was happy to see the positive transformation. I stopped typing on my laptop and took a moment to quietly celebrate our progress together.

Even though my bandwidth was absolutely maximized with the responsibilities of getting ready for combat, I never close my office door. It's a small manifestation of my commitment to transparent communication. I want my team to know where I am and what I am doing at any given time. Keeping my door open shows my company that although I am the commander, I'm still a contributing member of the team. It provides me the opportunity to see what's going on outside, listen to rumors, and understand the command climate—the pulse of the team.

I couldn't spend too long admiring my work, though. It was time to refocus. I had an incredible amount of work to do. Preparing to deploy is an overwhelmingly daunting responsibility. I put my head down and went back to work, typing away on my computer.

After a few minutes, my sergeant major poked his head in my door.

"Hey, sir. I know you are incredibly busy, but your new captain wanted to know when he should come back to speak with you."

"Captain Van Camp?" I asked.

"Roger, sir."

"Tell him to come in," I quickly responded.

I was neck deep in paperwork for my boss, but I owed my leaders my full attention. The greatest gift I can give as a commander is my full attention. It's a habit that I had to spend considerable time developing: pulling my attention away from something that was urgent to me to focus on something that was important to someone else. I had learned to turn off my phone and email and prevent my mind from wandering. It's a difficult skill to master when you have people who want things, you're late on deadlines, your boss is unhappy, and your emails are stacking up, but it's necessary to being a good leader.

I took a deep breath. I reminded myself that there was a guy coming in who needed a moment of leadership attention, and if I did that right, it would be massively beneficial to me and the company. If I ignored this opportunity to develop a leader, in the long run, it would come back and bite me in the ass.

Taking the time to develop subordinate leaders is paramount to unit success. It takes a commitment to be in the moment, connecting and developing. I purposely choose to set aside all the stuff that is on my plate, fully knowing that it's not going away, and focus on this leader. In our business, our culture, there is a higher expectation to take time away to develop leaders, and I have always sacrificed to carve out that time and space. This is what **focused communication** is all about.

Captain Van Camp stood outside my door, holding a green log book, waiting for me to motion him inside. I stood up and walked to the doorway.

"Jason, come on in. How has your first week been?"

"Fine, sir. Just fine. It's been quite an experience. I've never really met a group of what I'd legitimately call heroes all in one spot," he answered.

"Well, I would be careful about calling them that," I said, pulling my chair closer to Jason. We both sat down.

"I know they don't like to be called heroes, but the thing is, heroes don't get a vote, sir. With guys like that in the company, in the unit, serving our country, how could I—we—possibly fail?"

"Interesting takeaway," I said. "Expand on that."

"My mother always used to say to me, 'Show me your friends, and I'll show you your future.' By surrounding myself with those leaders and knowing what they've gone through, I have the blueprint for successfully leading my team in combat. They were so forthcoming, I'm not only privy to *what* they were thinking, but *how* they were thinking."

"Jason, I'm glad you're excited, but I need you to understand that it's not going to be that easy. You're going to go through a lot more failure and disappointment before you can thrive in uncertainty," I cautioned.

"I am ready to embrace that process," he said.

"And I will give you every opportunity to do so," I responded. "Jason, I tasked you to speak with some of the leaders in our company. These leaders are what I consider to be the backbone of our unit. I tasked you to meet with them, ask them questions, and find out what makes them tick."

"Yes, sir. I spent the past week doing exactly what you told me to do. These guys inspired me so much that I went out on my own and spoke with several other friends and leaders I admire and respect. Some of these other leaders I've known for a few years; I just never asked them how they were able to do the things that they did. In this process, I became fascinated with learning about how these individuals think."

"What did you learn?" I asked.

Jason pulled out his green logbook from under the chair, opened it, and handed it to me.

"Sir, the first person you asked me to speak with was Steve Mueller. When Steve and I spoke, we discussed—"

I quickly interrupted.

"Jason, I'm going to stop you right there. This isn't a test. This isn't a check on learning. This is me actionably building trust with you and developing you as a leader. I am not looking for a book report or a full summary of your interactions. I want to know what you learned for yourself."

I handed his logbook back to him. Jason sat in his chair and went silent for a moment. Thinking. I could tell it didn't bother him to show me that he was thinking.

"Sir, there's so much that I've learned this week. It's been unbelievable. I would say that there are three lessons that had the most significant impact on me: First, this is a learning organization. We are willing to take risks and fail in order to achieve success. Second, this company values trust. Trust goes both ways and is measured with actionable tasks. Third, there is something profound about making a decision to voluntarily, deliberately choose discomfort. Each leader I spoke with achieved success because they internalized and lived this mind-set of getting comfortable being uncomfortable, embracing the suck, and believing that the difficult times will eventually lead to the good times. This last lesson was the most powerful for me."

I smiled.

"I'm proud of you, Jason. It's important you embrace those lessons as you develop as a leader. I encourage you to consistently refer back to those notes in your logbook, because as you lead, you're going to reread the same notes. You'll find that based on circumstances and your situation, different lessons will pop out at you, become more relevant, and stand out as the most important lessons in that period of your development."

"Sir, I guess that's what I need help with. I've got a logbook full of notes. I have a lot of information here. Some of the stuff I heard I agreed with, and some stuff I didn't. How do I take all this information, process it, and internalize it? Where do I even begin? How do I avoid getting paralyzed by all this information?"

"Jason, only you can answer that. This is all just information. It's not informing your actions; it's informing your judgment. No one but you is going to know what's right or wrong in the hundred decisions you make each day. For this company to succeed, you must go forward and apply the best judgment in every situation. These decisions and subsequent actions are yours, not mine. I am asking you to take this information and turn it into something that matters. I have the trust and confidence that you will. To show you that, I am giving you command of our company's mountain team."

I took a moment to let that sink it. Jason tried to hide his excitement but found it difficult to hold back a smile.

"Congratulations, Captain," I told him. "But this isn't going to be easy. This mountain team hasn't had a team leader in a while. There were some issues with the last captain, but I want to caution you: don't talk negatively about their former team leaders. As you continue to move forward in your career, don't focus on the negative. There will always be guys who are loyal to the last commander. Don't go in there and say, 'The previous commander was jacked up. I'm going to make things better. I'm going to fix everything.' Because you weren't there. You don't know the circumstances. You don't know the situation. There is absolutely zero value in impugning anybody who came before you. It shows insecurity and it's poor form. I say this because on my first team, I replaced a team leader who was fired."

"What did you say to your team, sir?" Jason asked.

"I took over a detachment that had a reputation of being a super undisciplined team. The team leader had just been fired. The team sergeant should have been fired too. Everyone was telling me how screwed up they were. I came in right off the bat and said, 'Hey, listen, I'm the new commander. I know people use first names here, but I'm Captain Petit, and you call me "sir" until we establish ourselves on a professional footing of trust.'

"That was my first decision. I did that to reset the command climate. I was not going to tolerate an undisciplined team or have the reputation of one. I did that to separate myself as an officer and a leader. I drew that line because I couldn't come in there and be buddies with these guys right off the bat. I made a judgment call based on what I felt the team needed at the time. I felt it needed a command climate reset to focus on discipline."

He nodded respectfully.

"Jason, I need you to understand what I am asking you to do. You are going to lead men into combat. You are going to be at the tip of the spear. Your decisions and actions are paramount to the security of our country, not to mention the lives of the soldiers you are leading."

"I understand, sir," Jason said confidently.

"Good. C'mon, let me introduce you to your team."

We both stood and began slowly walking out of the B-team room and down the company hallway. I continued my leader development as we walked.

"Jason, what's the first thing you're going to do when you walk through those doors?"

"I'll have plenty of time to assert my leadership over the team; the first thing I'm going to do is listen," Jason said.

"Spot on," I said, slapping him on the back. "I don't know what's right in that team room. You will. I am trusting you to report the ground truth, to help me make the best decisions for this company. Remember, make an evaluation of your twelve guys. Find out where they want to go. Find out what they are bringing. Look underneath the hood before you kick the tires."

He nodded again as we approached the double doors to the mountain team room—solid and painted gray with a cipher lock.

"OK, ready?" I asked.

"Definitely," Jason replied.

I punched in the code on the cipher lock and twisted the door handle.

"Oh yeah, one last thing," I said before pushing the doors open. "I'm going to tell you what my boss told me when he gave me command of this company: you're in command now. Do something with it."

SOF to Science with Dr. Rebecca Cañate, Professional Science Officer

Rebecca earned her bachelor's degree from Princeton University and both her MBA and PhD in philosophy and psychology from Brigham Young University. As a psychology PhD, she specializes in providing development opportunities to strategically close the gap between where employees are today and where they need to be.

Humans think they want infinite choices, but give us that bounty and we freeze. What we actually need are cultivated options—usually no more than three—to feel in control of our future and continue to move forward.

We live in a world where **Information Overload** is a given. This means we are at the mercy of overexposure, excessive consumption, and wildly abundant information and data. Quiet has become a luxury among the alerts on our smartphones, twenty-four-hour news channels, and Wi-Fi everywhere. Slack and thinking time are the new competitive advantage.

The rise of technology has been the primary driver of information overload on multiple fronts: quantity produced, ease of dissemination, and number of people reached. Our brains are wired to categorize and group information to make decisions possible in a world with complex variables. However, if constantly introduced new factors undermine our categories, then everything has to be individually considered and weighed, and we usually fail. Those in leadership positions today think they are required to make perfect decisions because it seems as if all the information we need is readily available. We end up overwhelmed and defeated—looking for someone else to tell us how to make the call. Our quality of decisions is reduced (if we make a decision at all) by paralysis. We call this **Analysis Paralysis**. This situation occurs when the overthinking and overanalyzing of a situation causes decision-making and forward progress to come to a halt.

Analysis paralysis occurs when you are:

- overloaded with information and/or advice (sometimes contradictory);
- overwhelmed by the available options;
- overcomplicating the decision when you already know the answer;
- compelled by someone or something to pick the "perfect" choice; or
- deeply concerned and afraid of making a wrong move, a bad decision, or the wrong choice.

During this latest interaction with Major Petit in chapter 12, Jason struggles with taking all the information he gathered from the people he met with and making sense of it.

Major Petit's response underscored the importance of not removing Jason from the equation. He says, "This is all just information. It's not informing your actions; it's informing your judgment. No one but you is going to know what's right or wrong in the hundred decisions you make in a day."

So What?

How do you take all this information, process it, and internalize it? Where do you even begin? Let's consider the following steps to making information work for you and defeating analysis paralysis:

1. Decide to stop being a perfectionist

"Perfect" is a moving target. You will never complete a task if the standard is perfection. Reid Hoffman, venture capitalist, author, and cocreator of LinkedIn, encapsulates this theory as it pertains to launching a business.

"If you're not embarrassed by the first version of your product, you've launched too late" (Hoffman, 2017). (Notice that he did not say that you should be deeply ashamed by your first version.) Hoffman encourages his followers to "move fast, break things, and fail fast." For self-admitted perfectionists, this advice is hard to swallow. They will argue that perfection should be our goal in everything. That's the wrong mind-set to have. Every option has pros and cons. Every option has its own set of considerations. Consider your context, take the best information and advice you can find, and then make your best guess. Every military unit knows: no plan survives first contact with the enemy. In other words, you might have a perfect plan, but the enemy (and life) gets a vote. Agility, not perfection, is your advantage.

2. Curb your emotional investment

Decision-making works best with a mix of rational vs. emotional and convergent vs. divergent thinking. Reid Hoffman continues: "Even in our new world, many entrepreneurs still identify so closely with their products or services they cannot bring themselves to adopt a mindset that prioritizes iteration and learning over perfection. You believe that you are going to be judged on your product—or even equated with it— so you want everything to be exactly right upon the initial unveiling. In reality, you should be moving faster than that. If you're willing to be embarrassed, you gain speed and flexibility. You get to market faster when you're not trying to anticipate and design every feature and potential use case. That means you also start collecting feedback from users faster and learn about what happens in instances you didn't or couldn't anticipate" (Hoffman, 2017).

Maintain a healthy emotional investment and be aware of situations in which your personal feelings have a high probability of getting in the way. If it's impossible to remove yourself from a highly charged emotional situation, find (or hire) someone to work with you. An example of that is found in our judicial system, as defendants who are trained lawyers have long accepted the conventional wisdom that representing oneself in court is a bad idea. The saying goes that "a person who represents himself in court has a fool for a client."

3. Identify your objectives

Ultimately, what do you want to accomplish? Having a clear goal can simplify your actions for any project. You should identify one clear and simple goal as your end state. Write it down. Post it boldly, in large print, on a wall. Take it from Southwest Airlines. Herb Kelleher, cofounder and their longest-serving CEO, once told someone, "I can teach you the secret to running this airline in thirty seconds. This is it: We are THE low-cost airline. Once you understand that fact, you can make any decision about this company's future as well as I can" (Strack, 2014).

Whenever their leadership has options, they get weighed against that goal. Are we moving closer to being the low-cost airline or farther away? As you iterate through your options, you will identify pros and cons for each. Without understanding your end goal, you'll forever be debating the relative pros and cons of each choice without a meaningful conclusion.

4. Trust yourself and commit

As we learned from Joe Serna in chapter 5, successful people are rooted in their true identity; they know who they are and what they can do. While outside information can inform their actions, it does not influence their confidence or knowledge of themselves. Once we know that we can manage through any situation, perfectionism becomes much less attractive. We want to get started and commit to our paths. Be accountable and realistic in what you will be able to accomplish in the amount of time that you have given yourself, and then start. That alone guarantees you more success than most.

Now What?

1. Think of a time when you were overwhelmed with information. Imagine there was a video camera filming that moment and it could capture you both on the inside and outside. Write down all the words that describe what that experience looked and felt like.

2. Was the moment described above more aligned with information overload or analysis paralysis? Assign a percentage to both (not exceeding 100 percent). How did you bring skills in before and after the event? How

did you let your skills out in the moment(s) during the event?

3. Like Brian Petit did for Jason, think of a relationship or team you were on that was really good at cutting through the noise and tackling the hard questions. Write down the common attitudes and behaviors that helped to make quality decisions in a timely fashion.

4. Think of a time when you were able to overcome your fear and paralysis. What was the situation? Why was it initially so difficult? What did you do to overcome the challenge?

Practical Application with Jason Van Camp

One of Mission Six Zero's Major League Baseball clients is the Seattle Mariners. Recently, I was provided a unique opportunity to observe their process when evaluating and ranking players for the Major League Baseball first-year player draft. I sat in a room with player personnel executives, scouts, and the analytics department and watched them debate and rank high school, junior college, and collegiate prospects for hours. Each member of the twenty-five-man staff was afforded an opportunity to provide their unique insight into each player. After everyone had their say, the player was stacked against a similar player and the staff was required to vote on which player should be ranked higher. They would continue to stack that player against other players until he landed in a certain "slot" or draft position. It was fascinating to watch the scouts and the analytics department argue and debate a player's potential future impact.

The Seattle Mariners dedicated countless time, money, and resources into making sure they did everything they could to "get it right" and select the best player available. During the process, Jerry DiPoto, general manager of the Seattle Mariners, asked me, "Jason, how did it work in the Special Forces? Who did you go with? Did you go with the information coming in from the Pentagon or from the guys on the ground? Essentially, I'm asking, Who do you think is right? Is it my analytics guys or my scouts?"

The twenty-five-man staff all looked at me as I stood up to address them. "I can only speak to my experiences in the Special Forces and training with our clients," I said. "For me, it comes down to trust. Who has earned my trust? Who has a proven track record? When it's all said and done, both the scouts and the analytics department's recommendations are subjective. The scouts are using decades of personal experience to help them make an informed recommendation. Their recommendations are completely subjective. You may not realize it, but the analytics department is also providing recommendations based on subjectivity. As they developed their algorithms and processes, they were forced to make decisions—decisions based on their personal biases and emotions. These decisions form the results of their mathematical testing.

"You want to know how to make the best decision possible with all of this information at your disposal. In both combat and business, I listened to all the information presented to me without argument or interruption. I weighed the content of the information with their proven track record and the trust established between us. Next, I asked for opinions of my team, and finally, I trusted my gut."

Major Petit states, "No one but you is going to know what's right or wrong in the hundred decisions that you make in a day. For this company to succeed, you must go forward and apply the best judgment in every situation. These decisions and subsequent actions are yours, not mine." Major Petit highlights listening as a critical tool to success, but he also implies that listening is not only external, but internal as well. For example, a hunter sometimes uses a noise or call to attract specific animals. Animals listen to the calls. When a hunter uses a call device to attract an animal, the animal debates internally whether to trust the call. In the beginning, the animal is skittish because deep down, it knows something is not right. Those animals that are unable to listen to that internal voice saying "Something is wrong here" die. The animals that listen to and trust that internal voice are the ones that survive. In combat, the commanders who have their radar attenuated to both external and inner noise are the ones who seem to always make the right decisions. In other words, commanders use a combination of their heart and their head to process internal and external information to make sound and timely decisions. Finally, they trust their gut.

Jay Long, the chief operating officer at Mission Six Zero, explains: "Big data's expansion into everything from draft picks to training routines requires leaders to see past the binary options of trusting their people or trusting models by combining the strengths of both tools. As your data scientists develop their models, it is vital that they get feedback from experienced leaders within your organization, or they risk solving for the wrong outcomes and integrating dangerous assumptions. Likewise, your analysts should challenge the underlying decision-making rules and strategies of your experienced leaders to avoid dangerous assumptions or cognitive biases that can lead to suboptimal outcomes."

As a leader, you must understand how to leverage rational thinking and subconscious pattern identification in an experimentally driven learning environment (Kahneman, n.d.). This approach prioritizes creativity and adaptation based on empirical feedback rather than demeaning the validity of either approach. This complementary style can create algorithms that refine human decision-making, optimizing speed and precision to create dominant competitive advantages (Dalio, n.d.). The first step toward achieving this outcome is shattering artificial barriers between these groups and encouraging collaboration through rapid and iterative experiments.

Analytics vs. Experience—Who wins?
- Create and develop trust with both groups.
- Enforce transparent information sharing—empower your "scouts" to provide recommendations as the basis for your algorithms.
- Listen to all sides of the argument.
- Ask questions and opinions.
- Trust your gut and make a decision (when you are ready).

Who wins when you do this? You do. When you are in command, you don't have the luxury of sitting back and letting someone else make the tough choices. That's on you. If you don't make those choices, no one else will. I get it: it's difficult. You are afraid of making a bad decision. You are afraid that people won't like you anymore. Being a commander means that you are willing to make those tough, unpopular choices. It's about pulling the trigger, right or wrong, because you believe in the outcome. It's about deliberately, voluntarily, courageously choosing discomfort.

Remember:

- As a commander, the greatest gift that you can give someone is your full attention.
- Defeat analysis paralysis:
  - Decide to stop being a perfectionist.
  - Curb your emotional investment.
  - Identify your objectives.
  - Trust yourself and commit.
- Don't let perfection get in the way of progress.
- Never throw anyone under the bus. When you throw someone under the bus, your audience imagines a future meeting where they are on the business end of those tires.
- Choose the path of most resistance.

Conclusion

When Major Petit opened the doors to my team room for the first time, I walked in alone. All eyes were on me. The room was silent. No one spoke. I immediately felt uncomfortable. My natural human response was fear.

But fear of what? If I'd learned anything, it was that I no longer had to be afraid of the unknown. I needed to identify what it was that I feared and overcome it.

I realized I was afraid of being disliked or disrespected by my new team. I was afraid of saying or doing the wrong thing. I was afraid of starting off on the wrong foot. In this moment of discomfort, I stopped and laughed to myself. I remembered what I had learned. Instead of fearing this discomfort, I embraced it. I realized that discomfort will never go away. It will always be there. I can't control it, and I shouldn't try. What I can control is how I choose to view and manage that discomfort when it manifests itself in my life. I can choose to be proactive and deliberately embrace discomfort.

With that realization, I lifted my head and looked up. I no longer saw disapproving, judgmental eyes from my new teammates, the men I would lead. I saw eyes that wanted to welcome me in and win together. I told myself, "I'm in command. Do something with it."

REFERENCES

Chapter 1

Lund, G. (1995). Elder Henry B. Eyring: Molded by "defining influences." https://www.churchofjesuschrist.org/study/ensign/1995/09/elder-henry-b-eyring-molded-by-defining-influences?lang=eng

Rotella, R. J. (1995). *Golf is not a game of perfect.* New York, NY: Simon and Schuster.

Csikszentmihalyi, M. (1997). *Finding flow: The psychology of engagement with everyday life.* New York, NY: Basic Books.

Bandura, A. (1977). Self-efficacy: Toward a unifying theory of behavioral change. *Psychological Review, 84,* 191–215. doi: 10.1037/0033-295X.84.2.191Zak, P. J. (2018). The neuroscience of high-trust organizations. *Consulting Psychology Journal: Practice and Research, 70*(1), 45–58.

Army Doctrine Publication (ADP) 6-0, Mission Command. U.S. Army. May, 2012. Headquarters, Department of the Army. Washington, DC.

Wine, S. (2012). Jets' Holmes benched after squabble with teammates. NFL.com. http://www.nfl.com/news/story/09000d5d8259d36b/article/jets-holmes-benched-after-squabble-with-teammates

Chapter 2

Ryan, R. M., & Deci, E. L. (2000). Self-determination theory and the facilitation of intrinsic motivation, social development, and well-being. *American Psychologist, 55*(1), 68–78. doi:10.1037110003-066X.55.1.68

Slemp, G. R., Kern, M. L., Patrick, K. J., & Ryan, R. M. (2018). Leader autonomy support in the workplace: A meta-analytic review. *Motivation and Emotion, 42,* 706–724. doi:https://doi.org/10.1007/s11031-018-9698-y

Gagne, M. (2003). The role of autonomy support and autonomy orientation in prosocial behavior engagement. *Motivation and Emotion, 27*(3), 199–223.

SDT Theory Overview. (n.d.). Retrieved from Center for Self-Determination Theory: https://selfdeterminationtheory.org/theory/

Gagne, M., & Deci, E. L. (2005). Self-determination theory and work motivation. *Journal of Organizational Behavior, 26,* 331–362. doi:10.1002/job.322

Deci, E. L., Koestner, R., & Ryan, R. M. (2001). Extrinsic rewards and intrinsic motivation in education: reconsidered once again. *Review of Educational Research, 71*(1), 1–27.

Chapter 3

Csikszentmihalyi, M. (1997). *Finding flow: The psychology of engagement with everyday life.* New York, NY: Basic Books.

Kotler, S. (2014). *The rise of superman: Decoding the science of ultimate human performance.* Boston: Houghton Mifflin Harcourt.

Nakamura, J., and Csikszentmihalyi, M. (2014). The concept of flow. In Csikszentmihalyi, M., *Flow and the foundations of positive psychology.* Dordrecht: Springer (pp 239–263).

Maslow, A. H. (1943). A theory of human motivation. *Psychological Review, 50*(4), 370.

Creswell, J. D., et al. (2005). Affirmation of personal values buffers neuroendocrine and psychological stress responses. *Psychological Science, 16*(11), 846–851.

Sherman, D. K., et al. (2009). Psychological vulnerability and stress: The effects of self-affirmation on sympathetic nervous system responses to naturalistic stressors. *Health Psychology, 28*(5), 554.

Devloo, T., Anseel, F., De Beuckelaer, A., & Salanova, M. (2015). "Keep the fire burning: Reciprocal gains of basic need satisfaction, intrinsic motivation and innovative work behavior." *European Journal of Work and Organizational Psychology, 24*(4), 491–504.

Chapter 4

Tolle, E., & OverDrive Inc. (2010). *The power of now: A guide to spiritual enlightenment.* Novato, CA: New World Library.

Chapter 5

Lefcourt, H. M. (2014). *Locus of control: Current trends in theory & research.* New York, NY: Psychology Press.

Mentalhelp.net (2019). Personal responsibility and locus of control. Retrieved from https://www.mentalhelp.net/addiction/personal-responsibility-and-locus-of-control/

Kiener, R. (n..d.). A Judge Sentenced a Fellow Vet to Jail—Then Joined Him in His Cell for the Night. Reader's Digest. https://www.rd.com/true-stories/inspiring/an-army-of-two/

Chapter 6

Greenberg, M. (2017). *The stress-proof brain*. Berkeley, CA: New Harbinger.

Uvnas, K. (2003). *The oxytocin factor: Tapping the hormone of calm, love, and healing*. Boston: Da Capo Press.

Frankl, V. (1962). *Man's search for meaning; an introduction to logotherapy*. Boston: Beacon Press.

Chapter 7

None.

Chapter 8

Army Doctrine Publication ADP 6-22 Army Leadership and the Profession July 2019

Peterson, C., & Seligman, M. E. P. (2004). *Character strengths and virtues: A handbook of classification*. Washington, DC, APA Press and Oxford University Press.

Paradis, K. & Martin, L. (2012). Team building sport: Linking theory and research to practical application. *Journal of Sport Psychology in Action*, 3, 159–170.

Midura, D. W., & Glover, D. R. (2005). *Essentials of team building principles and practices*. Champaign, IL: Human Kinetics.

Weinberg, R. S., & Gould, D. (2011). *Foundations of sport and exercise psychology*. Champaign, IL: Human Kinetics.

Zak, P. J. (2017). *Trust factor: The science of creating high-performance companies*. New York, NY: American Management Association.

Chapter 9

Benson, H. (1975). *The relaxation response*, New York, NY: HarperCollins.

Herman, J. P, Figuerierdo, H., Mueller, N. K., Ulrich-Lai, Y., Ostrander, M. M., Choi, D. C., et al. (2003). Central mechanisms of stress integration: Hierarchical circuitry controlling hypothalamo-pituitary-adrenocortical responsiveness.

Kotler, S. (2014). *The rise of superman*. New York, NY: Houghton Mifflin Harcourt.

Shpancer, N. (2010, September 20). Overcoming fear: The only way out is through. *Psychology Today*. https://www.psychologytoday.com/us/blog/insight-therapy/201009/overcoming-fear-the-only-way-out-is-through

Chapter 10

Selimbašić, Z., Kurtić, A., Selimbašić, M., Brkić, M., Hrvić, D. (2019). Psychological characteristics of war veterans after the war in Bosnia and Herzegovina, *Medicinski Glasnik, 16*(2).

Gura, T. (2008). Procrastinating again? How to kick the habit. *Scientific American,* Retrieved from https://www.scientificamerican.com/article/procrastinating-again/

Thompson, S., & Thompson, N. (2008). *The critically reflective practitioner.* New York: Palgrave Macmillan.

Chapter 11

Selye, H. (1950). Stress and the general adaptation syndrome. *British Medical Journal. 1*(4667), 1383–1392.

Latham, G. P., Mitchell, T. R., & Dossett, D. L. (1978). The importance of participative goal setting and anticipated rewards on goal difficulty and job performance. *Journal of Applied Psychology*, 63, 163–171.

Mary C. Gutmann and Herbert Benson, (1971). "Interaction of Environmental Factors and Systemic Arterial Blood Pressure: A Review."

Yerkes, R. M. & Dodson, J. D. (1908). The Relation of Strength of Stimulus to Rapidity of Habit-Formation. *Journal of Comparative Neurology and Psychology,* 18, 459-482.

Chapter 12

Hoffman, R. https://www.linkedin.com/pulse/arent-any-typos-essay-we-launched-too-late-reid-hoffman/

Strack, D. https://seekingalpha.com/article/2555555-southwest-airlines-the-low-cost-airline

Kahneman, D. (2011). *Thinking, Fast and Slow.* New York: Farrar, Straus and Giroux.

Explanation of United States Special Operations Forces

What are Special Forces?

In the United States military, "Special Forces" refers exclusively to the United States Army Special Forces, also known as the Green Berets. Oftentimes, the media misapplies the term to Navy SEALs or Rangers or to other members of the US Special Operations Forces. There is only one US Special Forces—the Green Berets.

Green Beret teams are composed of highly trained soldiers who conduct missions in hostile areas and harsh environments. Before graduating from the Qualification "Q" Course, soldiers will learn an operational specialty, such as communications, engineering, combat medicine, weapons training, and/or intelligence. All Special Forces operators must pass a foreign language test and receive training in that culture's specific language. The Special Forces Qualification Course takes a year and a half to two years to complete. Only then can the graduate don the Green Beret.

Green Berets operate in A-Teams (Operational Detachment Alpha or ODA). A typical ODA contains twelve to fourteen team members, with each member specializing in one of the following categories:

Special Forces Detachment Commander (18A)

A Special Forces captain is the team leader. The officer organizes the mission, outfits the team, and debriefs them on the mission objective. The officer is the strategic planner and takes responsibility for everything the team does or fails to do.

Special Forces Team Sergeant (18Z)

The Special Forces team sergeant is the most experienced team member. Usually a master sergeant in rank, the team sergeant is responsible for the day-to-day operations of the ODA. The team sergeant and team leader must coexist cohesively to ensure mission success.

Special Forces Warrant Officer (180A)

The Special Forces warrant officer is the assistant team leader. Nobody really knows what they do.

Special Forces Weapons Sergeant (18B)

The Special Forces weapons sergeant is the expert on anything and everything to do with weapons. They are capable of operating and maintaining US, allied, and other foreign weaponry. They usually work out a lot and love to talk about guns in their spare time.

Special Forces Engineering Sergeant (18C)

The Special Forces engineer sergeant is an expert in demolitions, construction, and topographic survey techniques. They are usually the most fun guys to be around.

Special Forces Medical Sergeant (18D)

The Special Forces medical sergeant is considered to be the finest first responder in the world. Primarily trained with an emphasis in trauma medicine, they also have a working knowledge of dentistry, veterinary care, public sanitation, water quality, and optometry. You treat them with a high degree of respect because they will save your life one day.

Special Forces Communications Sergeant (18E)

The Special Forces communication sergeant can operate every kind of communications gear, from encrypted satellite communications systems to old-style high-frequency Morse key systems. They are experts in sending and receiving critical communications to command-and-control elements. They are arguably the most important men on the battlefield.

Special Forces Intelligence Sergeant (18F)

The Special Forces intelligence sergeant is trained in advanced Special Operations techniques, including intelligence collection and processing target analysis. If the intelligence sergeant is lazy or incompetent, the ODA will not have targets to execute.

Every member of the A-Team is specially trained in their area of expertise and is required to cross-train every other member in their discipline. In order for the A-Team to succeed, each member must provide blunt feedback to improve the quality of the person, the team, and the organization. This facilitates redundancy in training, immediate candid communication, and mentoring between senior team members and junior team members. A-Teams work closely and rely on one another under isolated circumstances for long periods of time, both during combat deployments and in training.

Who are the other Special Operations Forces?

US Navy SEALs (Sea, Air, and Land) teams operate in a small platoon-sized element (around thirteen operators) and conduct counterterrorism, counterinsurgency, high-value target missions, foreign internal defense missions, reconnaissance and intelligence gathering, and direct-action missions. Training to wear the coveted SEAL Trident can take anywhere from 1.5 to 2 years. BUD/S (Basic Underwater Demolition training) is a six-month-long grind that leaves most trainees battered both emotionally and physically, with a failure rate that hovers around 80 percent.

SEAL Team 6—Known as "DEVGRU," the United States Naval Special Warfare Development Group—consists of intensively trained SEALs who perform highly classified missions in the most dangerous areas in the world.

US Army First Special Forces Operational Detachment—Delta (First SFOD-D), known as "Delta Force." The name of this organization has changed often over the last several years. Members of this organization are the Tier 1 operators in the US Army's Special Operations community. These soldiers go through a very secretive, thorough selection program and conduct missions that most Americans will know nothing about. Many of the members of this group are former Rangers or Green Berets and conduct some of the most demanding, politically sensitive and dangerous missions assigned to the US military.

US Army Rangers—Platoon-sized elements trained in airfield seizures and counterterrorism/counterinsurgency missions, experts in aggressive maneuvers such as raids and ambushes. Rangers eventually become overall masters of basic infantry tactics. Rangers are known for being incredibly disciplined, well-conditioned, highly respected, and elite soldiers in the US Army. The Ranger tab signifies a graduate of one of the toughest military courses in the world, the three-month-long US Army Ranger School.

US Marine MARSOC (Marine Special Operations Command)— Known as Marine RAIDERS, MARSOC is a relatively new organization, organized in 2006 to augment the overall mission of US Special Operations Command. It takes over four years to create a Marine Raider, as the applicant must have three years' prior service as a marine before applying for the course. With a training timeline similar to the US Army's Special Forces Qualification Course, the Marine Raider aspires to be a "critical skills operator." Trainees must complete a lengthy course of language school, advanced weapons training, self-defense, SERE training, and counterinsurgency/counterterrorism training before calling themselves Marine Special Operators.

US Air Force Pararescue—Air Force Pararescue conduct human-itarian missions, rescue or recover downed pilots, provide medical care and evacuation for wounded soldiers/sailors/marines, all of which occur in hostile territory. They provide light infantry support if needed. Also known as "PJs" their training protocol lasts two years, with a failure rate also around 80 percent. A Pararescue man will receive training in military free-fall school, Combat Diver School, military combat medicine, and

Survival School (SERE), as well as training in weapons and patrol tactics. The air force also has special tactics officers, air liaison officers, combat controllers, Special Operations weather technicians, and tactical air controllers, all of whom conduct or support Special Operations missions. These personnel go through one to two years of training and will work directly with navy, marine, and army Special Operations units.

160th Special Operations Aviation Regiment (SOAR)—Known as the Night Stalkers, the helicopter pilots in this US Army unit are considered the best in the world. Outside of their intensive flight instruction, these aviators receive training in land navigation, combative skills, weapons, small-unit tactics, and combat medicine. Pilots and crewmen/women from the 160th train with and conduct missions moving SEALS, Rangers, Green Berets, and other Special Operators to and from targets.

LIST OF VALUES

Abundance
Acceptance
Accountability
Accomplishment
Accuracy
Achievement
Acknowledgment
Adaptability
Adventure
Affection
Aggressiveness
Agility
Alertness
Ambition
Anticipation
Appreciation
Assertiveness
Attentiveness
Audacity
Awareness
Balance
Beauty
Belonging
Blissfulness
Boldness
Bravery
Brilliance
Calm
Candor
Carefulness
Caring
Certainty
Challenge
Change

Charity
Cheerfulness
Clarity
Cleanliness
Collaboration
Comfort
Commitment
Communication
Community
Compassion
Competence
Competition
Concentration
Confidence
Connection
Consciousness
Consistency
Contentment
Content over fluff
Continuity
Continuous
Improvement
Contribution
Control
Conviction
Convincing
Cooperation
Courage
Courtesy
Creativity
Curiosity
Daring
Decisiveness
Delight

Dependability
Desire
Determination
Devotion
Dignity
Diligence
Discipline
Discovery
Discretion
Diversity
Drive
Duty
Eagerness
Education
Effectiveness
Efficiency
Elation
Elegance
Empathy
Encouragement
Endurance
Energy
Enjoyment
Enthusiasm
Equality
Excellence
Excitement
Experience
Expertise
Exploration
Expressiveness
Fairness
Faith
Fame

Family
Fidelity
Flexibility
Focus
Forgiveness
Fortitude
Freedom
Friendship
Frugality
Fun
Generosity
Giving
Goodness
Grace
Gratitude
Happiness
Harmony
Hard work
Health
Helpfulness
Heroism
Holiness
Honesty
Honor
Hopefulness
Hospitality
Humility
Humor
Imagination
Independence
Influence
Ingenuity
Inner peace
Innovation
Insightfulness
Inspiration

Integrity
Intelligence
Intensity
Intimacy
Intuitiveness
Inventiveness
Joy
Justice
Kindness
Leadership
Learning
Liberty
Logic
Longevity
Love
Loyalty
Love
Making a difference
Mastery
Maturity
Merit
Mindfulness
Motivation
Opportunity
Optimism
Organization
Originality
Outcome
Outstanding service
Passion
Peace
Perceptiveness
Perseverance
Persistence
Poise
Positive attitude

Power
Practicality
Precision
Preparedness
Presence
Preservation
Privacy
Proactivity
Progress
Punctuality
Quiet
Rationality
Recognition
Relationships
Reliability
Resourcefulness
Respect
Responsibility
Risk-taking
Safety
Security
Selflessness
Service
Simplicity
Sincerity
Stability
Teamwork
Timeliness
Tolerance
Tradition
Tranquility
Trust
Truth
Wisdom

THOSE WHO CHOSE DISCOMFORT

Too often we enjoy the comfort of opinion without the discomfort of thought.
—John F. Kennedy

I like being uncomfortable. I like getting comfortable being uncomfortable—where I'm pressing the limits & the buttons on the people that were before me that didn't want to do it.
—LeBron James

The ultimate measure of a man is not where he stands in moments of comfort and convenience, but where he stands at times of challenge and controversy.
—Martin Luther King Jr.

The world offers you comfort. But you were not made for comfort. You were made for greatness.
—Pope Benedict XVI

We find comfort among those who agree with us—growth among those who don't.
—Frank A. Clark

If you look for truth, you may find comfort in the end; if you look for comfort you will not get either comfort or truth.
—C. S. Lewis

This is no time for ease and comfort. It is time to dare and endure.
—Winston Churchill

Comfort is a powerful sedative.
—Samantha Garman

Anything that disturbs your comfort factor is good for you.
—Tony La Russa

Comfort and prosperity have never enriched the world as much as adversity has.
—Billy Graham

People need to rediscover the ability to find comfort amid discomfort. It is only while enduring discomfort that we find solutions.
—Hanno Langenhoven

God does not comfort us to make us comfortable, but to make us comforters.
—John Henry Jowett

Move out of your comfort zone. You can only grow if you are willing to feel awkward and uncomfortable when you try something new.
—Brian Tracy

Getting to a place of comfort can be uncomfortable.
—Marcus Samuelsson

Your comfort zone is not a place that you want to remain in. Dare, discover, be all that you can be.
—Catherine Pulsifer

Nobody ever died of discomfort, yet living in the name of comfort has killed more ideas, more opportunities, more action, and more growth than everything else combined. Comfort kills.
—T. Harv Eker

We cannot become what we want to be by remaining what we are.
—Max Depree

Comfort the afflicted, and afflict the comfortable.
—Finley Peter Dunne

Growth and comfort do not coexist.
—Ginni Rometty

In no direction that we turn do we find ease or comfort. If we are honest and if we have the will to win we find only danger, hard work and iron resolution.
—Wendell Wilkie

Life begins at the end of your comfort zone. So if you're feeling uncomfortable right now, know that the change taking place in your life is a beginning, not an ending.
—Neale Donald Walsch